MATHEMA

Maths
at Work

Appreciating the uses of mathematics

Edited by
Geoffrey Howson
and
Ron McLone

 Heinemann Educational Books

Heinemann Educational Books Ltd
22 Bedford Square, London WC1B 3HH
LONDON   EDINBURGH   MELBOURNE   AUCKLAND
HONG KONG   SINGAPORE   KUALA LUMPUR   NEW DELHI
IBADAN   NAIROBI   JOHANNESBURG
EXETER (NH)   KINGSTON   PORT OF SPAIN

ISBN 0 435 52567 0

© G. Howson and R. McLone, 1983
First published 1983

British Library Cataloguing in Publication Data

Howson, Geoffrey
  Maths at work
  1. Mathematics
  I. Title   II. McLone, Ron
  510   QA36

  ISBN 0-435-52567-0

Filmset by Mid-County Press, London SW15
and printed in Great Britain by
Biddles of Guildford

Contents

Foreword by Sir James Lighthill, F.R.S. v

Introduction 1
Dr A. G. Howson and Dr R. R. McLone, Faculty of Mathematical Studies, University of Southampton

1 **How safe is it?** (an example from the chemical industry) 5
Professor T. A. Kletz, Visiting Professor, University of Loughborough, formerly Petrochemicals Division, Imperial Chemical Industries Ltd

2 **Nursing mathematics** 15
Susan Pirie, Shell Centre for Mathematical Education, University of Nottingham

3 **Mathematics in store** (an example from the retail trade) 29
A. S. Noble, Joint Managing Director, Debenhams Ltd

4 **The mathematics of mimicry** (an example from biology) 41
Dr Deborah Charlesworth, School of Biological Sciences, University of Sussex

5 **Increasing the shipping capacity of the Suez Canal** 51
Dr J. D. Griffiths, Department of Mathematics, University of Wales, Institute for Science and Technology

6 **Runs and sums: the application of mathematics to the analysis of running records** 65
Dr B. B. Lloyd, Chairman, The Health Education Council

7 **Traffic flow in roundabouts** 79
G. Maycock, Head of Traffic Systems Division, Transport and Road Research Laboratory

iv Contents

8 Sound mathematics: measuring noise annoyance — 93
Dr I. H. Flindell, National Aeronautics and Space Administration, Langley Research Centre, Virginia, U.S.A.

9 Disentangling data (an example from archaeology) — 109
Dr S. Shennan, Department of Archaeology, University of Southampton

10 Spreading the risk (an example from insurance) — 127
Professor R. E. Beard, Visiting Professor of Industrial Economics, University of Nottingham, formerly General Manager, Pearl Assurance Co. Ltd

11 Borrowing and lending — 135
T. J. Critchley and J. R. Nation, Business Research Section, Barclays Bank Ltd

12 The design and analysis of a consumer preference test — 147
Dr P. Prescott, Faculty of Mathematical Studies, University of Southampton

13 Modelling in hot water (exploiting geothermal energy) — 161
Dr J. G. Andrews, Head of Engineering Mathematics, Marchwood Engineering Laboratories, Central Electricity Generating Board

14 Probably guilty: the evidence against a parking meter offender — 173
B. J. R. Bailey, Faculty of Mathematics, The Open University

15 Thunderstorms (an example from meteorology) — 183
Dr D. A. Bennetts, Meteorological Office

Do it yourself (some problems and ideas for project work) — 197

Sir James Lighthill

Foreword

Recently, mathematics has been used more and more to help with many of the things that really matter to us. We care about the air we breathe, its freshness and the climate that it brings us. We care about the water that quenches our thirst, cleans us and irrigates our crops. We care about the earth, as a source of food and raw materials. We depend upon fuel for warmth and mobility. We want health and the conditions of life that promote it, and we want to see a balanced and healthy wildlife around us. All these things are included when people talk about the environment. In the fight to improve it, mathematics is much used.

Again, we care about jobs. This means that we need our industries to be competitive and to avoid wasteful use of resources. Prosperity for all of us depends upon work being organised economically. We need to communicate with each other, so we want good telephone systems and good transport systems. Indeed, we want networks distributing to our homes and factories these essential services and many others, such as power. There is a direct benefit to standards of living from efficiency in all of these areas. In the fight to improve it, mathematics is much used.

We depend also upon trade. We all want shops where we can find what we need, and money which shopkeepers will accept for goods we want to buy and which people will pay us for services we can give. We care about our industries earning enough from the goods they sell to be able to pay their employees, buy their raw materials and pay for re-equipment. So we expect them to concentrate on marketing: making goods available that customers really want, and letting customers know about them. We need money set aside for our pensions. We want to be protected from various possible disasters by insuring against them. Money saved, or put aside for insurance or pensions, must be invested where benefits will be high. In commerce and industry, then, and indeed also on the national scale, where of course (because of sheer size) the problems are hardest, we need sound finance and planning. In the fight to improve these, mathematics is much used.

The present excellent book gives examples of mathematics at work in all these newer areas of application of the subject. The editors are to be congratulated on covering in one slim volume such a wide range of generally less familiar examples of mathematics 'at work'. Admittedly, many good practical uses of mathematics (for example, in engineering) are already quite widely appreciated. By contrast, the equally important, but much less well known uses which are set out so readably in this book, must be expected to arouse the keenest interest in its readers.

If their interest is so aroused the readers can be recommended by the, admittedly not quite impartial, author of this foreword to pursue their interest further through the medium of at least one other book devoted to a generally similar objective. This is *Newer Uses of Mathematics* (edited by James Lighthill) published by Penguin Books Ltd. Much more generally, the interested readers of the pages that follow can be recommended to use every opportunity to become conscious of as many examples as possible from those unexpectedly vast areas of life today where, with great effectiveness, mathematics is being put to work.

Geoffrey Howson and Ron McLone

Introduction

This book had its origins in a workshop held in 1978 to raise questions about the interactions between 'mathematics' and 'the real world' (*see* Booss, B. and Niss, M. H. (ed.) 1979, *Mathematics and the Real World*, Birkhäuser). At this workshop one of us contributed a paper in which he considered the view of mathematics that future teachers were likely to have as a result of their own education, and how they might better be helped to appreciate the role of mathematics in society. A further impetus to consider this problem followed the establishment of the BACOMET (Basic Components in the Mathematics Education of Teachers) project — a small international group of mathematics educators, to which the two of us belong. It was decided that we, as part of our contribution to that group's work, would look in greater depth at such concepts as 'appreciation' and 'awareness'.

Originally, then, our thoughts were directed at teachers-to-be; only later did our aims widen as we sought to produce a book which would interest and inform a much wider audience. As a result of a generous grant from the Education Support Committee of the British Petroleum Company, we were able to mount, as preparatory work for this book, a series of lectures in a number of venues. These lectures were attended, and apparently enjoyed, by sixth-form students, student teachers, serving schoolteachers, teachers from institutes of higher education, and industrial mathematicians. It is our hope that this book, based on a selection of the lectures given, will have an even greater appeal. We still hope that the book will have some role to play in pre- and in-service training courses for teachers, and to help facilitate this we have included at the end of the book a short section containing exercises and suggestions for project work. These are not meant to 'test' understanding of the material in the book in any conventional sense, but rather to indicate to tutors how questions can be set relating to the book's contents. Some of the questions examine techniques described in the book; others being of a more open nature, can be used to develop the students' abilities to construct mathematical models. The mathematical demands have been especially tempered to lie within the range of senior sixth-formers (with some knowledge of statistics and probability), first year undergraduates in mathematics, science, and engineering faculties, and B.Ed. students specialising in mathematics. Those students not planning to become teachers will, we hope, find the book useful in indicating how they might be called upon to use mathematics in a variety of different careers. However, it must be remembered that what is presented here is but a sample taken from a vast range of applications; moreover, it is a sample limited by the level of mathematics used.

As the reader will observe, the chapters are not homogeneous in nature, some describe a variety of 'bread and butter' applications of mathematics, others concentrate on how mathematics has been employed to solve one particular problem. This variety is deliberate, for it would be as wrong to imagine that mathematics is always used in a routine fashion, as to think that its use is restricted to one-off moments of inspiration.

Our general aims when preparing the book can be gauged from our original instructions to authors:

> The intention is to show how, for example, from an initial discussion with other interested parties, a practical situation is seen to be amenable to mathematical treatment and a 'problem' is thus formulated from which a mathematical model may be developed. In addition to illustrating how mathematics is used in a large variety of 'real-world' situations, the purpose of the book is to:

(i) show how practical problems become 'mathematical';
(ii) discuss the value of a mathematical approach and solution (compared with alternative – say, *ad hoc* – solutions);
(iii) indicate how insight into a problem can be obtained from the use of mathematics;
(iv) examine the nature of a mathematical solution, i.e. the acknowledgement that a 'solution' has been reached and the interpretation of this solution in terms of the initial problem;
(v) demonstrate the use of mathematics in a day-to-day context as well as its value in 'flashes of inspiration'.

Contributors were, however, reassured that we did not expect all these purposes to be covered in any particular contribution! Nevertheless we hope that, overall, the published collection achieves these original goals, and also serves to illustrate how even comparatively low-level mathematics can prove effective in solving practical problems in many different areas of application.

Considerable freedom, then, was given to contributors in determining the nature of their chapters. In a similar way we did not try to impose a 'mathematical' structure on the book by seeking coverage of specific topics, for example by providing examples of how calculus, linear algebra, probability, statistics, etc. might be applied. No attempt was made to achieve a distribution of contributions which covered any particular school examination syllabus. We hoped rather that the range of mathematics used by the contributors and the frequency with which they employed individual topics might be used to provide some evidence on which to evaluate existing curricula.

In fact, as the reader will no doubt observe, a perhaps surprisingly high proportion of topics to be found in A-level mathematics syllabuses have been used somewhere or other by our contributors. In assessing mathematical balance or possible omissions, there are a few possible inferences to be drawn. As will be seen from the number of graphs and diagrams in the following pages, considerable importance is attached to graphical representation and interpretation. This makes one wonder if sufficient emphasis is placed on such work at school level (particularly on interpretation); for instance, ought nomograms to find a more secure place in the main school curriculum for *all* pupils? Again, these studies suggest that a strong case could be made for giving all senior mathematics students at least some experience of computer simulation. On the other hand, the constraint that the contribution should be capable of being understood by senior school students has resulted in relatively few physical examples being included. It is apparent that applications using mechanics, for example, demand a relatively high level of mathematical competence and also a substantial knowledge of physical principles, and it is probable that the applications described here under-represent this area of mathematical expertise.

These, though, are very specific points arising from the book. More generally, we hope the ensuing chapters will help readers to gain an increased understanding of the way mathematics is used in some everyday problems. The ability to construct, develop, and evaluate valid mathematical models has always been an eminently desirable and much-sought-after talent but one which was generally regarded as being in very short supply and which was seen almost as 'a gift' belonging to a select few involved with high-level, 'difficult' mathematics. In consequence, the range and manner of the applications of mathematics was thought to be considerably circumscribed. It is apparent in these contributions that this need not be so; the range of applications is considerable and the level at which the mathematics is used often surprisingly simple. However, perhaps the most important observation is of the many different ways in which mathematical models are used.

The chapter on biology illustrates that it is often possible to use essentially *qualitative* models to draw valuable inferences about likely behaviour – in this case of the populations of various species. Other examples are more quantitative, but in a very 'robust' sense. For instance, there are so many factors that will influence whether or not a particular type of dress will sell well, that it would be ridiculous to try to refine the accuracy of a model beyond a certain level. Here something rough and ready will serve the purpose adequately and still be a better guide than would a non-mathematical approach. On the other hand, one does want a comparatively precise estimate for traffic flows in a roundabout. Yet here we can readily check theoretical models against practical experience. The mathematician forecasting the benefits to be extracted from geothermal power is not so fortunate. Only when it might prove too late (and very expensive) will it be possible for him or her to check the validity of the model. Mathematical models, then, take a variety of forms according to the needs of the problem-solver and we ask the reader to bear this in mind and to try to distinguish the characteristics of particular models as (s)he reads on.

As a help to the reader we have tried to arrange the chapters in approximately increasing order of mathematical difficulty. However, the range of mathematics used is considerable and so it may well be that the reader will find a later, technically more demanding, chapter easier to grasp than an earlier one, simply because the mathematics on which it is based is more familiar. We hope that readers will pick and choose amongst the chapters, and will also persevere. The final chapter may be the most challenging mathematically, but it would be a great pity to miss the insights it provides into the art of modelling!

We also hope that teachers will find examples in this book which they can use with their classes and which will add new interest to lessons on distance–time graphs, the Poisson distribution, etc, and that those who use mathematics professionally may obtain some new ideas. Most importantly, we hope that the book will foster an appreciation of the widely differing contributions which mathematics makes to our society and that, as a result, those engaged in mathematics education will make decisions from a more informed position.

Finally, we should like to acknowledge our gratitude to all who participated in the project either by lecturing or by mounting the individual talks, to Sir James Lighthill for writing the foreword, to the typists in the Faculty of Mathematical Studies, Southampton University, to Heinemann Educational Books, and to the British Petroleum Company Ltd.

Trevor A. Kletz

1 How safe is it?

I am an enthusiast for the quantification of the unquantifiable, for the use of numerical methods whenever possible as an aid to decision-making. I agree with Lord Kelvin that 'When you can measure what you are speaking about and express it in numbers, you know something about it', and with Leonardo da Vinci that 'No human investigation can really be called science if it cannot be demonstrated mathematically'.

Early in my career I took over responsibility for my first chemical plant while it was shut down for a change of catalyst. The day I took over, the engineer in charge of the catalyst change reported that three catalyst tubes were choked and could not be emptied. The tubes would have to be replaced; this would extend the shut-down for a day. Alternatively, the tubes could be blanked off and changed at the next shut-down in six months time, when time would be available. As I was new to the job, I asked my boss what we should do. In reply he asked me, 'Which will lose the most production, losing the whole plant for one day or three tubes for six months?'

Soon after I was married, my wife, to show how economical she was, went to a particular shop for sugar as it was cheaper there than elsewhere. I pointed out that the cost of driving there exceeded the saving on sugar. (You can imagine how popular this made me!)

These simple examples show how simple arithmetic, simple numerical comparisons, can help us make better decisions. The problems were fairly simple because the objectives were clear, to maximise output in one case, to minimise total cost in the other.

Quantifying safety

When I tried to extend my enthusiasm for quantification to safety, the problems were more difficult because there is no single agreed scale for measuring safety. Some people measure fatal accidents, others injuries causing absence from work; some people measure damage to plant, others lost production.

6   Maths at Work

Fig. 1.1 A photograph of the Flixborough disaster: what the industrial safety officer must strive to prevent. *Keystone Press Agency*

I decided to use the probability that someone might be killed as the main measure of safety – for several reasons. Most injuries are trivial compared with fatal accidents and, as Heinrich pointed out many years ago, if we halve fatal accidents from a particular cause such as explosions, we also halve injuries, damage, and lost production.

The next step was to find out the present fatal accident rate in the chemical industry and, for interest, to compare it with other industries. The fatal accident rate (FAR) is usually expressed as the number of deaths in a workforce of 1 000 in a working lifetime, a total of 10^8 hours. Table 1.1 gives some values for FAR and, for comparison, the risk of staying at home in case you consider work too risky. (It should be pointed out that the figure for air crew is not as bad as it seems, as they work fewer hours per week than the others on the list.) You will see that the chemical industry is no more hazardous than British industry as a whole, although most of the materials handled are flammable, toxic, or corrosive, and sometimes possess all these properties.

The figures in the table are, of course, average figures. Some jobs in the chemical industry involve more risk, some less. If we can measure the risk attached to each job, we can give top priority to reducing the risks that are

Table 1.1 Some fatal accident rates

Occupation	Number of accidents
All premises covered by Factories Act	4
Clothing and footwear	0.2
Chemical industry	4
Metal manufacture	6.5
Mining and quarrying	10
Railway shunters	45
Construction erectors	67
Air crew	250
Staying at home (men 16–65)	1

above average. However, we cannot measure the risks of each job by counting the number of people killed, because in most cases no-one has been killed. Instead we have to use synthetic methods, which I will illustrate later. Similarly, we should make sure that the risks on a new plant are not above the average, and the average will then gradually fall.

Often we cannot quantify all the risks to which a person is exposed, and then we say that each major risk should not exceed, say, one-tenth of the average (0.4). It would be wrong to spend resources on reducing such a low risk when bigger risks are waiting to be dealt with. We should deal with our biggest problems first.

An example

I would now like to describe an example of the ways in which these ideas have been applied.

A common chemical process is oxidation. Hydrocarbons are oxidised with air or oxygen to form other compounds. Oxidation is used, for example, in the manufacture of the raw materials required for nylon, polyester, and antifreeze. The oxidation is carried out in a controlled way so that the hydrocarbon is not burnt completely (it is partly oxidised). If too much air or oxygen is added, the hydrocarbon will burn completely and may even explode. The concentration of oxygen in the plant is therefore measured continuously by instruments which shut off the air or oxygen supply automatically if the oxygen concentration approaches the danger level; this system is known as a trip.

It might be thought that this would prevent an explosion ever occurring, but this is not the case, as the measuring instrument, or the valve in the air or oxygen line, or the 'black box' in between is sometimes out of order. We test them regularly to see if they are working and if they are not we repair them, but there is a period of time – the 'dead time' – between the equipment going wrong and the discovery of this by testing. Let us see if we can work out the length of this dead time.

Experience shows that the equipment (that is, oxygen measuring device, black box, and air (or oxygen) valve) develops a dangerous fault on average once in every two years. Suppose we test it once a week. Once every two years it is expected to fail between tests; it could fail at any time but on average will fail half-way between tests. Thus for $3\frac{1}{2}$ days every two years the safety equipment is dead. The fraction of the time for which the equipment is dead is therefore:

$$\frac{3.5}{365 \times 2} = 0.0048 \text{ or } 0.48\%.$$

If you employed a watchman, would you be happy if he was asleep for 0.5 per cent of the time, that is for nearly two days per year on average? This depends on how often someone tries to steal the goods he is guarding. If a thief tries once a year, then, on average, you will have to wait 200 years before the goods are stolen. More precisely, there is a chance of one in 200 per year that the goods will be stolen. If you employ 200 similar watchmen to watch 200 similar buildings you may expect one theft every year. On the other hand, if someone tries to steal the goods ten times per year, the number of thefts will be higher. We can say

hazard rate	= *fractional dead time*			× *demand rate**	
(number of thefts per year)				(number of attempted thefts per year)	
e.g. $\frac{1}{200}$	=	0.005	×	1	
or $\frac{1}{20}$	=	0.005	×	10	

The same equation can be applied to our 'oxygen watchman'. If we know from experience that the oxygen concentration will approach the danger level once every year, then it will actually exceed the danger level once in 200 years. For an explosion we need a source of ignition, but experience shows that one may be present and we assume that it is.

As an explosion in an oxidation plant could kill the operator, once in 200 years is far too often. We need a more reliable watchman. By duplicating the protective equipment we can, in theory, reduce the fractional dead time from 0.005 to $(0.005)^2 = 2.5 \times 10^{-5}$. In practice the reduction is not as great because the two protective systems are never truly independent. They may both depend on the same electricity or compressed air supply, or both be

---

* The word 'demand' is used in the French sense (*demander* = to ask). The demand rate is the frequency with which the watchman is asked to turn away a thief or the high oxygen trip to shut off the air or oxygen supply.

maintained by the same person who makes the same mistake while repairing them. These are known as common mode failures.

Fortunately, however, a rise in oxygen concentration is usually accompanied by a rise in temperature and pressure, and by measuring these, and perhaps other properties as well, we can get the fractional dead time down to 10^{-4} or even 10^{-5}. This is very good; a fractional dead time of 10^{-5} means that our watchman is asleep for only five minutes per year.

If the oxygen concentration approaches the danger level three times per year, the hazard rate or explosion rate is:

$$\text{fractional dead time} \times \text{demand rate}$$
$$= 10^{-5} \times 3$$
$$= 3 \times 10^{-5} \text{ per year or once in } 30\,000 \text{ years}$$
$$\text{or once in } 2.6 \times 10^8 \text{ hours.}$$

If every explosion causes a fatality, there will be one in 2.6×10^8 hours or 0.4 in 10^8 hours, that is, the FAR is 0.4. This is the level of safety we said earlier on we should aim for.

Some questions answered

Why not just make the plant as safe as possible?
We can never make the plant 100 per cent safe. By adding more and more protective equipment we can make the fractional dead time less and less, but never zero. Zero is approached asymptotically (see page 12 for another example on the same theme).

How do we know where to stop? — only by setting a target for safety and by adding on protective devices until the target is met. The target is set, as explained above, by deciding to concentrate our resources on our biggest problems. If your windows are broken you repair the biggest holes first.

Why not just rely on a human operator to isolate the air (or oxygen) supply?
There are several reasons for not just relying on a human operator.
(a) The operator cannot see that the concentration of oxygen is too high. Instruments must be used to measure this and they have a dead time.
(b) A human operator cannot act quickly enough. Action is needed in seconds.
(c) People also have a fractional dead time. It can be as high as 0.1 if they are busy or under stress, 0.01 is quite common in day to day working; 0.001 is about the best you can hope for.

Who watches the watchman?

The calculations above assume that the protective equipment is tested regularly and properly maintained. If this is not done, explosions will be more frequent. It is necessary to have a management system to make sure that the testing and maintenance are done. Results should be recorded, and regular and spot checks should be made.

All calculations are based on certain assumptions. Often they are taken for granted and not written down. However, if the assumptions are not true, the results are not true – garbage in, garbage out. In our case we have assumed that the protective equipment is tested regularly, repaired promptly if found faulty, and put back properly after test or repair. It helps if we make our assumptions clear.

Note also that by using automatic equipment we have not removed our dependence on people. We have merely transferred it from one person to another. Instead of depending on the operator we are depending on those who design, install, test, and maintain the automatic equipment. It is right to do this because the people who do these jobs work under conditions of less strain than the operator, but let us not kid ourselves that we have removed our dependence on the operator.

Belts and braces

Let us now consider a further, simple example of the application of numerical methods to safety problems, showing that a hazard can be reduced to any desired level but not eliminated completely.

The accident we wish to prevent is a man's trousers falling down and injuring his self-esteem. Since braces are liable to break, the protection they give is not adequate. We assume that breakage through wear and tear is prevented by regular inspection and replacement, and that we are concerned only with failure due to faults in manufacture which cannot be detected beforehand and which are random events. Experience shows that, on average, each pair of braces breaks after ten years' service. Experience also shows that belts fail in the same way and as frequently as braces. The collapse of a man's trousers once in ten years is not considered acceptable.

How often will the belt and braces fail together? If one of the two fails, this will not be detected until the belt or braces are removed at the end of the day. Assuming they are worn for 16 hours per day, then, on average, every man is wearing a broken belt for eight hours every ten years and broken braces for eight hours every ten years. The fractional dead time (FDT) of the braces is

$$\tfrac{8}{16} \times \tfrac{1}{10} \times \tfrac{1}{365} = 0.000\,137.$$

The FDT of the belt is the same.

How safe is it? 11

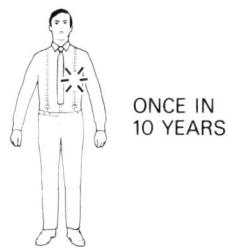

ONCE IN
10 YEARS

Fig. 1.2

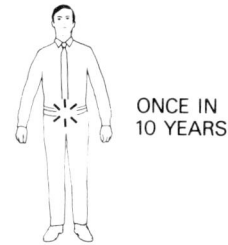

ONCE IN
10 YEARS

Fig. 1.3

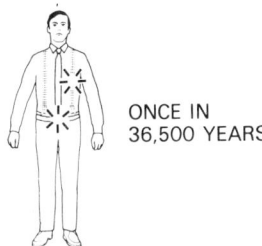

ONCE IN
36,500 YEARS

Fig. 1.4

ONCE IN 36,500
YEARS PER MAN
MEANS 685
MEN/YEAR IN
BRITAIN

Fig. 1.5

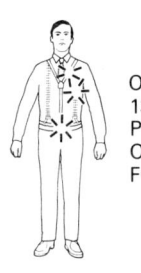

ONCE IN
133,000,000 YEARS
PER MAN OR
ONCE IN 5 YEARS
FOR BRITAIN

Fig. 1.6

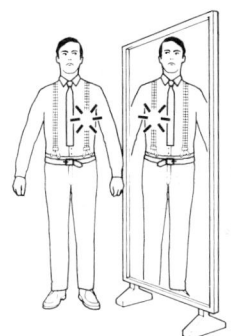

IF WE INSPECT
EVERY 2 HOURS,
DOUBLE FAILURE
OCCURS ONCE IN
292,000 YEARS
OR 85 TIMES/
YEAR IN BRITAIN

Fig. 1.7

The chance of the second protective device failing while the first one is 'dead' is:

$$\text{hazard rate} = \text{demand rate} \times \text{FDT}$$
$$= 2 \times \tfrac{1}{10} \times 0.000\,137 = 2.74 \times 10^{-5}/\text{year}$$

or once in 36 500 years.

Failure of belt and braces together, therefore, occurs once in 36 500 years. At the individual level this risk is acceptable. However, there are about

12 Maths at Work

25 000 000 men in Great Britain, so that, even if every man wears belt *and* braces, 685 men will lose their trousers every year. At the national level it is considered unacceptable that so many men should be embarrassed in this way.

To reduce the risk further, every man could wear a third protective device, a second pair of braces. This would reduce the failure rate for the individual man to once in 133 000 000 years* and for the country as a whole to once in five years. A third protective device, however, involves considerable extra capital expenditure and makes the system so complicated that men will fail to use it. An alternative is to get every man to inspect his belt and braces every two hours to see if either has broken. This will reduce the failure rate for the individual to once in $36\,500 \times 8 = 292\,000$ years and for the country as a whole to $685/8 = 85$ men/year. This may be considered acceptable, but is it possible to persuade men to inspect their 'protective system' with the necessary regularity, and what would it cost in education to persuade them to do so?

This example illustrates the following general points:

(i) The risk can be reduced to any desired level by duplication of protective equipment but it cannot be completely eliminated. Some slight risk always remains. Even with three protective devices it could happen that coincident failure occurs not after 133 000 000 years, but next year.

(ii) The *method* used above is sound but the result is only as good as the *input data*. If the failure rate for belt or braces is not once in ten years but once in five or twenty years, then the conclusion will be in error, not by a factor of two, but by a factor of four for two protective devices and by a factor of eight for three protective devices.

---

* Coincident failure of belt and two pairs of braces can occur in three ways, namely: (a) belt fails when both pairs of braces have already failed (b) braces 1 fail when belt and braces 2 have already failed (c) braces 2 fail when belt and braces 1 have already failed. The FDT for the coincident failure of three devices is $(1/3)f^2T^2$ where f=failure rate (0.1/year) and T=test interval (1/365 year). For each failure mode the hazard rate

$$= \text{demand rate} \times \text{FDT}$$
$$= 0.1 \times f^2T^2/3$$

Hence total hazard rate

$$= 3 \times 0.1 \times \frac{f^2T^2}{3}$$
$$= 0.1\left(\frac{0.1}{365}\right)^2$$
$$= 7.5 \times 10^{-9}/\text{year}$$

or once in 133 000 000 years.

(iii) The event which we wish to prevent is not collapse of the man's trousers but injury to his self-esteem. Half, say, of the collapses will occur when he is alone or at home and will not matter, and this introduces an extra factor of two. (It is not explosions we wish to prevent but the damage and injury they cause; explosions which produce neither are acceptable.)

(iv) A risk which is acceptable to an individual may not be acceptable to the community as a whole.

(v) It is easier to devise protective equipment or systems than to persuade people to use them. More accidents result from a failure to use equipment properly than from faults in the equipment. The high number of unwanted pregnancies, for example, is not due to failure of the 'protective equipment' but to the failure of the 'operators', through ignorance, unpreparedness, or deliberate choice, to use the equipment and methods available.

Suggested Reading

1 Kletz, T. A. (1976) 'The application of hazard analysis to risks to the public at large' in W. T. Koetsier (ed.), *Chemical Engineering in a Changing World*, Elsevier, Amsterdam, p. 397
2 Leach, G. H. (1972) *The Biocrats*, Penguin Books, chapter 11
3 Mooney, G. H. (1977) *The Value of Life*, MacMillan, London
4 Various official lists of statistics such as the *Annual Abstract of Statistics*

2 Susan Pirie
Nursing mathematics

The word 'mathematics' has various effects on people: to some it represents a challenge which can provide intellectual stimulation and enjoyment, to others it means failure and drudgery. To nurses the word may well create a feeling of apprehension, for, however confident a nurse is, there must always be the realisation that a mathematical slip may be disastrous. An accountant who miscalculates may waste time and money; a nurse who miscalculates may kill someone!

Do nurses really do any mathematics? The answer is a categoric 'Yes'. Much of it is dependent on basic arithmetical skills and graph work, but modern technology and drugs make for constantly changing mathematical demands.

In this chapter we shall not consider one particular mathematical problem arising in nursing — in this respect the chapter differs from most of the others — but rather will look at the mathematics a nurse needs to be able to handle, the associated problems of practicality and interpretation, and the areas in which the nurse's mathematical role is changing.

The nursing profession is atypical of the majority of employments open to the school leaver. Although an aspiring nurse may satisfy the entrance requirements when 16 years old, training cannot usually be commenced before 18 years of age. This age restriction is imposed because within six weeks of beginning training the learner is likely to be on a ward where a mature attitude towards patients and pain is essential. The two year delay, however, can cause a loss in mathematical skills, and the learner may well also have lost the habit of academic learning. Another relevant factor is that 40 per cent of Britain's nursing force is in training. This fact, coupled with the cyclical nature of a nurse's training — two or three months on a ward, two or three weeks back in the school of nursing, two or three months on a ward, etc. — means that the mathematics of the training course and the mathematics of the job should be identical. Of course, one could ask that the mathematics stipulated in the entry requirements should exceed, or at least equal, the necessary mathematical knowledge. Surprisingly, however, only six out of approximately 200 schools of nursing demand O-level mathematics from their entrants, and, more worryingly, in one large hospital, over 70 per cent of

16 Maths at Work

Table 2.1 Some mathematical topics required by nurses

Topic	Example
(a) Addition of whole numbers	$254 + 329$
(b) Subtraction of whole numbers	$360 - 177$
(c) Addition of fractions	$\frac{3}{5} + \frac{3}{20}$
(d) Multiplication of fractions	$\frac{2}{5} \times \frac{2}{7}$
(e) Changing fractions to decimals	$\frac{5}{8} = ?$ (0.625)
(f) Changing decimals to fractions	$1.25 = ?$ ($1\frac{1}{4}$)
(g) Meaning of decimal places	Which is larger, 0.07 or 0.1?
(h) Multiplication of whole numbers	262×13
(i) Division of whole numbers	$294 \div 70$
(j) Addition of decimals	$0.26 + 3.15$
(k) Subtraction of decimals	$0.25 - 0.06$
(l) Multiplication of decimals	0.725×132
(m) Division of decimals	$26.43 \div 30$
(n) Division by decimals	$4.9 \div 0.8$
(o) Simple percentage	What is 20% of 800?
(p) Ratio problems	Problems involving 'solution strength 1 in 80' or 'solution made up in ratio 1 to 4'
(q) Use of metric and SI units	Convert 6.2 grams to milligrams
(r) Use of tables	Metric/imperial conversion charts
(s) Using formulae	If quantity of feed $= (150 \times$ body weight$)/$(number of feeds), how much does a baby weighing 3.15 kilograms need if (s)he is being fed five times a day?
(t) Meaning of indices	$5 \times 10^3 = ?$
(u) Making tables	Fluid intake and output
(v) Graphs: plotting values	Body temperatures
(w) Reading and understanding graphs	Knowing when a patient's temperature has made an important change

Nursing mathematics

Paediatric Fluid Balance Chart
EACH CHART COMMENCES 0800 HOURS
ALL ENTRIES IN MILLILITRES
ALL INTRAVENOUS RECORDINGS IN RED

CHART No. 2   WARD F.21   WEIGHT ...... kg

DATE 27.3.80	INTAKE						OUTPUT				
	Intravenous Route				Oral/Other Route	Cumulative Total In	N/G Aspirate/Vomit and Comments	S/P Urine	Ureteric Tube/Drain	Stools and Comments	Cumulative Total Out
TIME	Type/Fluid and Hourly Rate of Flow	Burette Reading	mls in last hr	Drug Vol	Type/Amount of Feed	IVI / Other					
0800		0/60	50			50 mls	10 mls Aspirate green fluid				10 mls
0900		15/60	45			95 mls	15 mls Aspirate green fluid N/G tube removed	10			25 mls
1000	500 ml 0.18% Saline 4% Dextrose 50 mls hrly	10/60	50		10 mls H₂O	145 ml 10					
1100		20/60	40		10 mls H₂O	185 20					
11·30								110 m 65 mls			200 mls
1200		15/60	45		10 mls H₂O	230 30					
1300		15/60	45		10 mls H₂O	275 40					
1400	·45	20/60	40		10 mls H₂O 50 mls orange	310 50 100					
1500		10/60	50		100 mls orange	360 200		10 ml			210 ml
1600											

Fig. 2.1 Fluid balance chart

nurses who gained entry through having the requisite number of O-levels (in non-stipulated subjects) failed the simple mathematical test set by the General Nursing Council to those lacking O-level mathematics.

Let us now look more closely at the mathematics which nurses will require in their work. Table 2.1 lists the mathematical topics which a nurse needs to be able to handle, together with some of the more difficult examples one might meet. Thus, for example, a nurse will never meet any decimal division as difficult as $172.698 \div 0.0129$.

These topics arise in practice in a variety of ways. For example, Figure 2.1 shows a fluid balance chart, and demonstrates the kind of 'totting up' with which a nurse is regularly involved. This is an hourly chart for a child who is being fed intravenously and, later, also by mouth. The nurse needs to record the quantity left in the drip bag at the end of each hour, put up a new 60 millilitre bag (column 3) and record the fluid taken by the patient (column 4). A running total of fluid intake is kept in columns 7 and 8 and an output tally is kept in column 13. (Have you spotted the nurse's error?)

Fractions and decimals

Fraction handling has been simplified since the SI system replaced apothecary units. Since we are now dealing with drugs dispensed as x mg per y ml, where normally x and y are whole numbers less than or equal to 5, it is now hard to justify uses of fractions other than $\frac{1}{2}, \frac{1}{4}, \frac{1}{5}$. What a nurse must be able to do, however, is simple cancelling. Consider a patient on an intravenous drip. The doctor prescribes 80 ml, I.V. per hour. There are 15 drops per millilitre. The drip rate to be set up is given by $\frac{80}{60} \times 15$ drops per minute. The result, 20 drops per minute, is obtained by cancelling, without the need to handle recurring decimals and rounding up.

The nurse must, however, also have a clear understanding that a/b means $a \div b$, since the result of using a medical formula is frequently a fraction such as $\frac{0.264}{1.5}$, which must be resolved to give a decimal answer. This problem occurs regularly when dealing with diabetics. Insulin is prescribed as x units, y times a day, but is dispensed for injection in three strengths – 20 units per millilitre, 40 units per millilitre and 80 units per millilitre. The choice of which strength is used often depends on what is in the stock cupboard. A patient prescribed 30 units of insulin would need $1\frac{1}{2}$ millilitres of 20 strength, $\frac{3}{4}$ millilitres of 40 strength or $\frac{3}{8}$ millilitres of 80 strength. The syringe, however, is graded in 0.01 millilitre so a conversion to a decimal dose is necessary.

Converting from decimals to fractions is rare and always simple. A calculation using a drug dose formula could give 2.5 pills as an answer, i.e. two and one-half pills is the dose needed.

Since accuracy is of prime importance in nursing, it is essential that a nurse be able to look at a calculation and know whether the result is plausible. Some of this skill, for example, knowing the normal dose for common drugs, can only come with medical experience but mathematical knowledge can help too. If 0.05 milligrams is the adult dose, then 0.1 milligram is unlikely to be the dose for a child!

Many Health Authority areas have a policy that before any drug dose is given it must always be checked by another nurse. Recently, a student and a staff nurse were alone on a ward at night when a patient had to be given an intravenous injection. The student did her calculations on paper. The staff nurse checked the paper and agreed the result. Had the drug been prescribed orally the student would have given the calculated dose. Fortunately, it is also policy in that area that intravenous injections be given only by a qualified member of staff. Not until she went for a large enough syringe did the senior nurse suspect that some error had occurred in the calculation. In fact, the student had multiplied by five instead of dividing by five, thus producing an answer 25 times too large. The stock bottle contained 5 milligram pure drug per 1 millilitre solution but this became inverted to 1 milligram per 5 millilitre when the student substituted in the formula she was using. The staff nurse had checked the working on the paper but not the original formula.

As drugs become more powerful, as diagnostic processes become more precise, as intricate technology comes to the aid of the medical world, so too must accuracy of calculation and measurement be constantly refined. In the paediatric field especially, precision in the administration of the highly effective modern drugs is crucial for the safety of babies and young children. The cytotoxic drugs used in leukemia and other cancer treatments, and digoxin used in heart disease are common examples of drugs with a therapeutic level very close to their toxic levels. Even a small overdose may be fatal.

On the other hand, modern chemistry has considerably reduced the work involving percentage calculations a nurse needs to do. The term 'per cent' is still in frequent use, but merely as a label. To test for sugar in a diabetic's urine, for example, the nurse merely adds a reagent tablet to the urine and checks the resultant colour with a chart supplied by the manufacturer. Nurses still refer to 'two per cent sugar', but already 'orange reaction' is slipping into the jargon. As with fractions, the necessary calculating ability is small, but an understanding that $30\% < 40\%$ whatever quantities or units are being used is important.

Ratio is a simple-sounding concept which is, in fact, hard to understand and which is complicated by varying symbols and usages, for example, x in y, x to y, $x:y$, $\frac{x}{y}$. Yet nurses are frequently called upon to use ratios, and the various forms are used randomly and with gay abandon. Conventionally, 'x in y' is meant, but danger arises when someone who understands traditional mathematical language attempts to make up a solution. In the range of 1 in 80, the consequences may be slight, but there is a marked difference between 1 in 4 and 1 to 4!

SI units

The switch within the health service to SI units was dramatic, final, and very confusing.

A baby born at 23.55 on April 30, 1977 was described as weighing 7 pounds

6 ounces with a head circumference of 13.5 inches. A child, born to a mother in the next bed, six minutes later, had to be recorded as 3.25 kilograms, head circumference 34.5 centimetres. Hospitals were not, however, all equipped with metric scales etc., so nurses had very quickly to become adept at using conversion charts, graphs, and tables. The problem still remains years later. Although the hospitals are by now equipped to cope with metrication, the general public still, on the whole, thinks and works in imperial units, so nurses still need their conversion charts to be able to communicate with their patients.

With the advent of SI units came the 5 millilitre medicine spoon to replace the teaspoon and the tablespoon. An unexpected snag became evident. While a patient was content to take 'two tablespoons in water', he or she was less inclined to accept, or measure carefully, 'six medicine spoons'. This has led to some drugs being dispensed in a more concentrated form in order to reduce the quantity of medicine the patient has to take. The attendant risk, of course, is higher in the event of a miscalculation.

The SI problem is, however, greater than this. Tutors, especially non-clinical tutors who do not work with SI units on the wards, do not yet think instinctively in metric terms. Their learners have probably been taught to cope with 'centi' and 'milli' at school, but not 'micro' or 'mega'. There is a widespread belief among learners that since there are 100 centimetres in one metre, there are 100 micrograms in one milligram. They have never heard of the basic concept behind SI units, which is that all measurements used are in steps of 1000 units. From time to time, a disaster will hit the headlines:

TRAGIC ERROR KILLS BABY
A heartbroken nurse was on sick leave today after her tragic mistake had killed a baby girl. The nurse gave little Sarah one milligram of Digoxin — ten times the correct dose.

How could this happen? Quite easily. The doctor prescribed 100 micrograms of Digoxin. The stock preparation was dispensed in milligrams and the nurse 'knew' there were 100 micrograms in a milligram.

This danger is compounded by those doctors who write 'mg' for microgram – mg means milligram – or who write, correctly, μg in such a way that μ can be mistaken for m. There are others who never use micrograms in an attempt to lessen the risk of error but who appear to write 01 mg, leaving the nurse to interpret this as 0.1 or 0.01. There are yet other doctors who are aware of the danger and introduce notations of their own which merely confuse the situation further, such as mlg, mcg, mog, etc. There is pressure from many who work in the Health Service to have all drugs prescribed and dispensed in terms of micro units, thus eliminating decimals and mg from the scene. The comment of one staff nurse on this idea was, 'If we can't get them to give up apothecary units, we haven't a hope of persuading them to abandon the decimal point!'

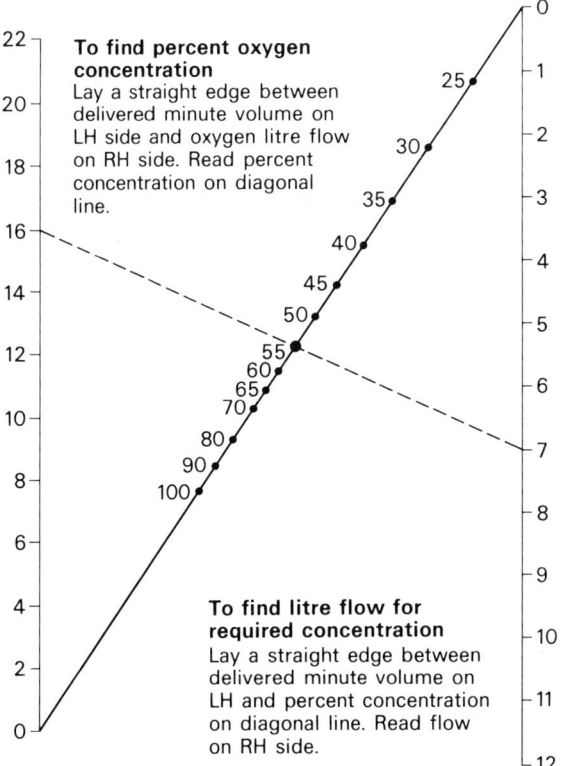

Fig. 2.2 The blood–oxygen calculator

In addition to the conversion aids referred to earlier, nurses may encounter two less familiar charts: the blood-oxygen calculator and the height, weight, surface area nomogram (see Figures 2.2 and 2.3). Notice how percentage is used in the blood-oxygen calculation – merely as a label, with no calculation involved.

The use of the nomogram became widespread when it became apparent that the therapeutic and toxic doses of many drugs were proportional, not to the height, age, or weight of the patient, but rather to the 2/3 power of body weight. This proportionality also applies to many physiological properties such as plasma volume, oxygen consumption, and calorie requirements. Body surface area (BSA) is also roughly proportional to (weight)$^{2/3}$, so the connection between BSA and drug doses was hypothesised. The formula

$$\text{BSA in cm}^2 = (\text{weight in kg})^{0.425} \times (\text{height in cm})^{0.725} \times 71.84.$$

has, in fact been used to calculate the BSA values in this nomogram.

Maths at Work

Body Surface Area of Adults

Nomogram for determination of body surface area from height

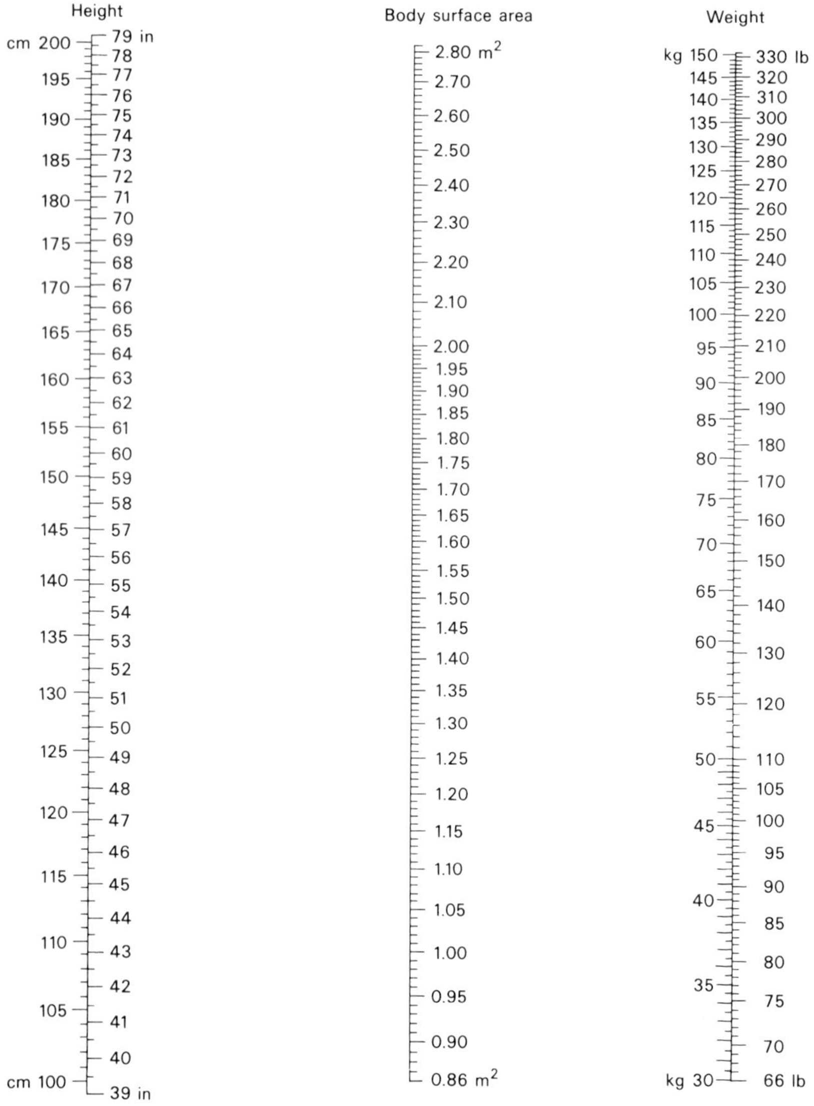

Height	Body surface area	Weight
cm 200 — 79 in — 78 195 — 77 — 76 190 — 75 — 74 185 — 73 — 72 180 — 71 — 70 175 — 69 — 68 170 — 67 — 66 165 — 65 — 64 160 — 63 — 62 155 — 61 — 60 150 — 59 — 58 145 — 57 — 56 140 — 55 — 54 135 — 53 — 52 130 — 51 — 50 125 — 49 — 48 120 — 47 — 46 115 — 45 — 44 110 — 43 — 42 105 — 41 — 40 cm 100 — 39 in	2.80 m^2 2.70 2.60 2.50 2.40 2.30 2.20 2.10 2.00 1.95 1.90 1.85 1.80 1.75 1.70 1.65 1.60 1.55 1.50 1.45 1.40 1.35 1.30 1.25 1.20 1.15 1.10 1.05 1.00 0.95 0.90 0.86 m^2	kg 150 — 330 lb 145 — 320 140 — 310 135 — 300 130 — 290 125 — 280 120 — 270 115 — 260 110 — 250 105 — 240 100 — 230 95 — 220 90 — 210 85 — 200 80 — 190 75 — 180 70 — 170 65 — 160 60 — 150 55 — 140 50 — 130 45 — 120 40 — 110 35 — 100 — 95 — 90 — 85 — 80 — 75 — 70 kg 30 — 66 lb

From the formula of Du Bois and Du Bois, *Arch. intern. Med.*, **17**, 863 (1916): $S = W^{0.425} \times H^{0.725} \times 71.84$, or $\log S = \log W \times 0.425 + \log H \times 0.725 + 1.8564$ (S = body surface in cm^2, W = weight in kg, H = height in cm)

Fig. 2.3 Surface area nomogram (*adapted from J. R. Geigy, S.A. data, reproduced by courtesy of Ciba-Geigy Limited*)

Use of formulae

Formulae have been mentioned, *en passant*, several times in this chapter. They do in fact play a substantial part in the nurse's work. Algebraic expressions, it is true, are rarely encountered. ($C = \dfrac{(F-32)}{9} \times 5$ occasionally appears, but a nurse is much more likely to use a Fahrenheit/Centigrade conversion chart than resort to use of the formula.) A nurse must, however, be able to work with 'word-formulae', ranging from simple statements like:

$$\text{quantity given at each feed} = \frac{\text{recommended daily intake}}{\text{number of feeds}}$$

to the more complicated:

baby's energy requirement =

500 × [birth weight in kg + (age − 2) in weeks

× normal weight gain in kg/week] kJ

Ostensibly, the only skill needed is the ability to substitute the right numbers in the right places. Perversely, it is not the involved formulae, such as that for the energy requirement, which tend to cause problems for nurses. A nurse would almost certainly look up such a formula and so incidentally be guided in the units to be used for the substitutions. In fact, it is the very simple formulae which give trouble. A learner quickly picks up an expression like 'Baby's daily feed = 150 × body weight'. Does this mean that a three kilogram baby needs 450 kilograms of food a day? No, but neither does it mean that the baby needs 450 grams. Actually, the baby needs 450 *millilitres* of fluid feed per day. However, most mothers still think in terms of pounds and pints. Can the nurse give them this simple formula for calculating the milk a baby needs? Does a seven pound baby need 1050 pints per day, or even 1050 fluid ounces?

The most common formula used by all nurses, no matter what area of nursing they are in, is also the most abused and, frighteningly, also potentially the most lethal. It is the formula used by the nurse to convert the prescription left by the doctor into an actual dose to administer to the patient. If the doctor were able to prescribe 'two tablets of Pensprin' or 'three spoonfuls of Liquithol' (the brand names are fictitious) life would be simple. In reality all drugs are marketed and dispensed in a variety of forms and strengths and the doctor will therefore prescribe '30 g of Drugthyl', leaving the nurse to calculate the actual dose to be given from the stock available in the ward drug cupboard. Let us look at a real example.

Prescription: 62.5 μg of Digoxin available as 0.1 mg per 8 ml elixir.
How many spoonfuls should the nurse give?

The most common version of the formula to use here is:

$$\frac{\text{strength you want}}{\text{strength you have}} = \text{amount you give}.$$

Easy to remember — until you try to substitute the numbers! 'Strength' in the numerator has the meaning 'quantity by weight', i.e. x milligrams. 'Strength' in the denominator, however, means 'solution strength', i.e. y milligrams per millilitre. The formula, then, will give the amount in millilitres not spoonfuls. Note that the weight units used in the denominator and the numerator must be the same.

So, for this example we have:

$$\text{number of spoonfuls the nurse must give} =$$
$$\left(\frac{62.5 \div 1000}{0.1 \div 8}\right) \div 5.$$

Not a calculation most people would like to do mentally under the pressures of urgency yet accuracy.

An attempt is being made by drug companies to eliminate the danger attached to a nurse misusing this formula. Companies are now packaging many of their drugs in unit doses so that no dilution or measuring is needed. America is ahead of Britain in this field, and has been packaging drugs in this way for some years now. However, some doctors find the single dose packages lack flexibility and are now prescribing drugs as '$\frac{5}{6}$ unit dose'!

Although responsibility for diagnosis and treatment lies with the doctor, the nurse may frequently be the first to see the reports from the pathology department. These path lab reports bear figures such as $4.85 \times 10^{12}/\text{l}$ (which is red blood cell count per litre) and a nurse needs, therefore, to understand standard form. She (or he) must realise that if $a > b$ then $a \times 10^n > b \times 10^n$ and also that if $p > q$ then $x \times 10^p > x \times 10^q$. With this knowledge she (or he) can inform the doctor of any important fluctuations in the condition of the patient as revealed by the laboratory reports.

Charts and graphs

Graphs have two main purposes in medicine. Firstly, they are drawn as a means of recording symptoms. Secondly, they can be used to look at fluctuations in a patient's condition and to predict possible future changes. Nurses regularly chart pulse rates, temperatures, and blood pressures, and so, as with the lab reports, the nurse is the first to see a change in the pattern of, say, temperature readings, and the responsibility of alerting the doctor is hers (or his).

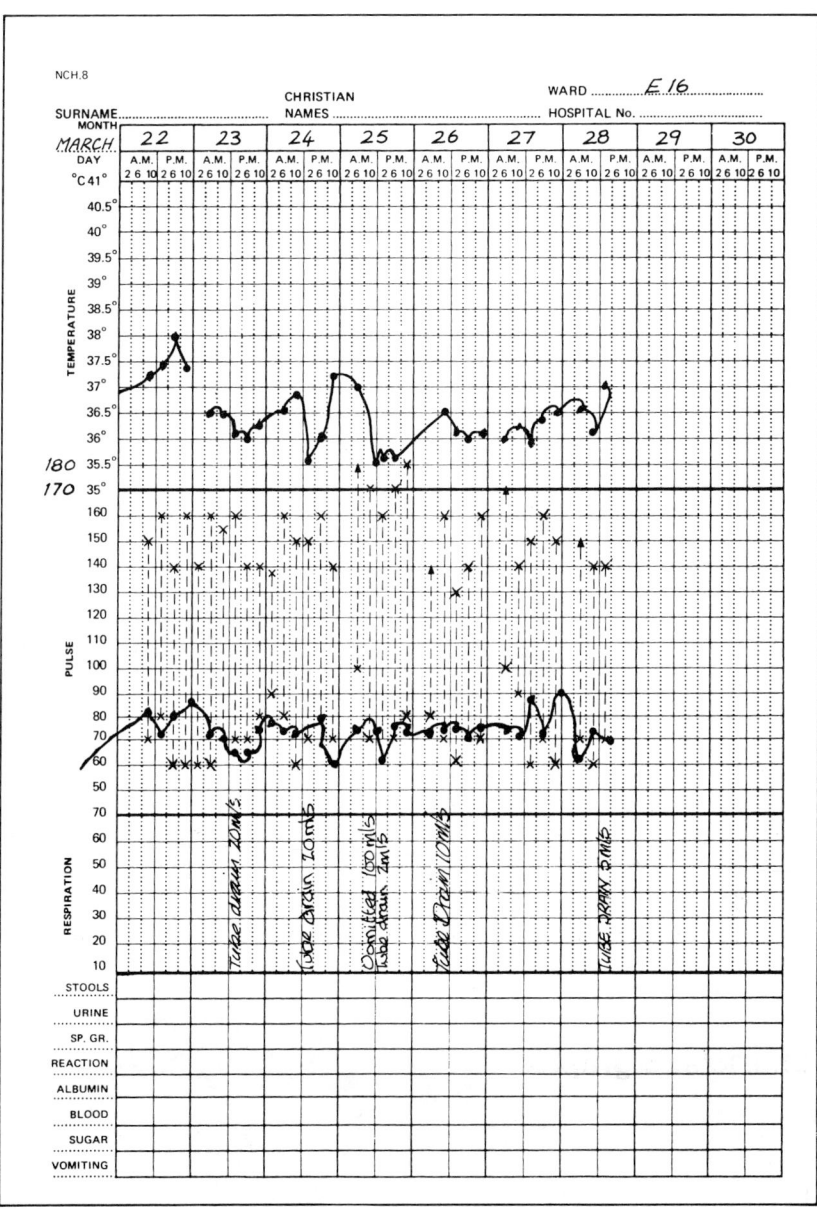

Fig. 2.4 A combined temperature, pulse, and respiration chart

26 Maths at Work

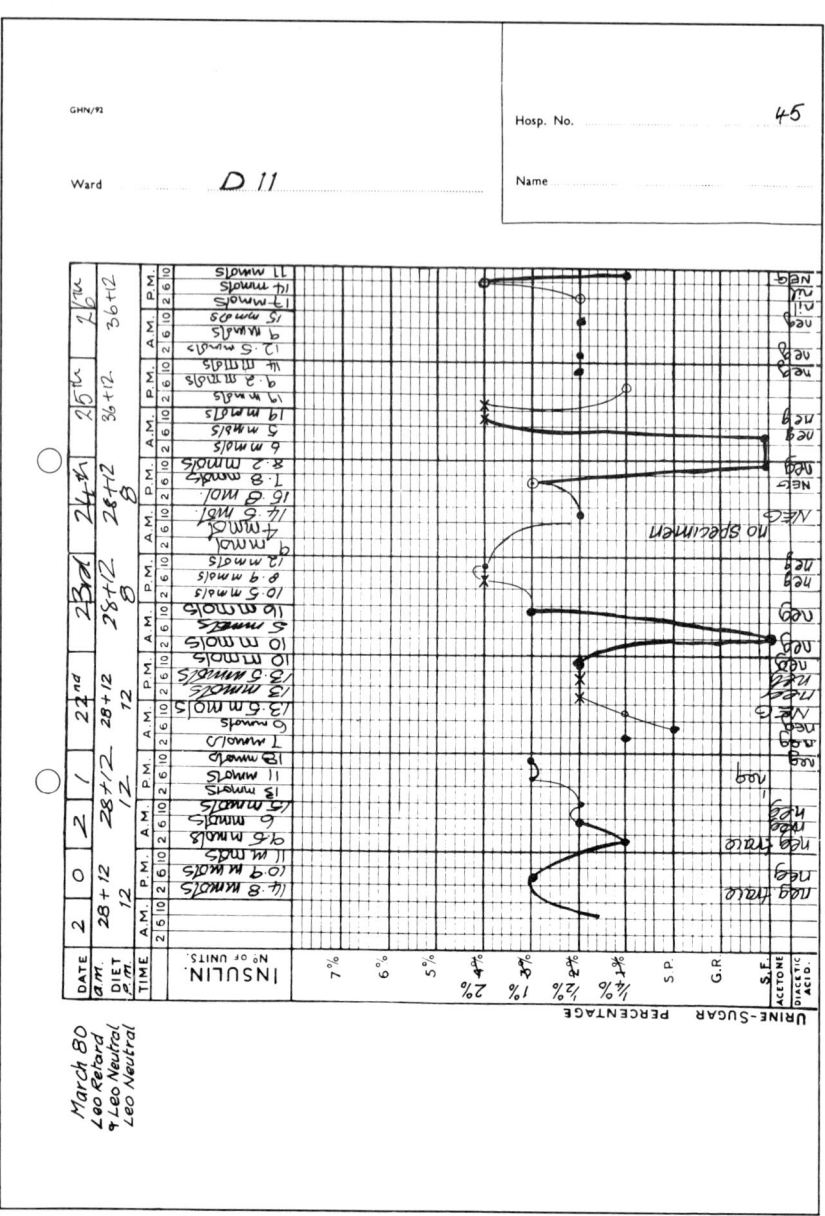

Fig. 2.5 A diabetic's chart

In many hospitals the three charts for recording pulse, blood pressure, and temperature have been amalgamated into one (see Figure 2.4). Admittedly paper is saved by this method, but one wonders just how easy such multi-charting is to interpret. Little is clear from a glance at the overwritten pulse and blood pressure readings. The nurse even found it necessary to extend the blood pressure scale into the area of the temperature graph!

There is no agreement, even among the experts, as to the best way of plotting and indicating trends. The diabetic's chart shown in Figure 2.5, which is used to record a patient's insulin tolerance, has been filled in by a series of different nurses and contains almost the whole range of conventional charting methods: ×, ⊙ and · loops, straight lines, and no joins! In this chart it has been necessary once again to extend the printed scale. Also, something much more alarming has happened. The scale has been altered so that five small gradations on the graph represent simultaneously: $\frac{1}{4}\%$, $\frac{1}{2}\%$, 1%, and 3% sugar in urine! The visual impression of change is, of course, totally distorted by this method of recording.

One of the greatest technological advances in medicine has occurred in the cardiac unit of a hospital. It is possible for one nurse to keep a constant watch on the heart functions of six or eight patients by means of cardiograms and monitor screens. To cope with this advance in equipment the nurse needs the ability to watch a number of independent, changing wave patterns, i.e. continuously created graphs, to interpret these and to be constantly alert to significant variations which would indicate the deterioration of a patient's condition.

One modern mathematical area, which has not so far been mentioned, is the use of calculators. A nursing research interest group, meeting at one of the large teaching hospitals recently, engaged in a fairly heated discussion of the pros and cons of calculators. The senior tutors and management levels of staff were almost unanimously against nurses being allowed to use them. Surprisingly, their reasons were not the very real danger of calculators producing erroneous results which go undetected, but the rather more emotive thinking on the lines of 'Arithmetic is good for them', 'I always do my additions on a piece of paper', 'Patients might lose confidence in the nurses'. Those present who were nearer the young nurses in both age and work content were convinced that the General Nursing Council would have to move with the times: 'Calculators are a fact of life'. They did, nevertheless, also express disquiet at the inability of so many learners to estimate the correct answer.

The final word, however, must be given to the director of a large, prestigious school of nursing, who drew herself up to her full, dominant, matronly proportions and pronounced: 'But, Mrs Pirie, calculators will NEVER be allowed on the wards – you cannot sterilise them!'

Andrew S. Noble

3 Mathematics in store

'Practical Arithmetick is the Soul of Merchandize' claimed Cocker when advertising his *Arithmetic* to merchants and shopkeepers in the seventeenth century. Arithmetical ability is still essential for the successful shopkeeper, but nowadays greater mathematical knowledge is desirable. This is particularly true in the world of department and chain stores where decisions have to be made involving huge sums of money. Here mathematics has an important role in the decision-making processes. In this chapter we shall illustrate the way in which mathematics can be used in retailing and also indicate how it might be employed in future. As elsewhere in this book we shall see how apparently trivial mathematics can yield quite powerful results. One's appreciation of the value of mathematics in solving problems should not, however, be diminished because of the simplicity of the mathematics used.

The competent professional retailer is actually quite a good mathematician although he or she does not know it. The retailer deals mentally with complicated algebraic relationships with amazing alacrity and applies percentage calculations at every turn. In that connection it is disturbing to read in various reports about the apparent state of mathematical (or perhaps you prefer arithmetical) knowledge among school leavers. I had first hand experience of this at a recent course for young recruits to retailing drawn from many different companies. I visited the group on the day on which they were asked to carry out a budgeting exercise. This requires the calculation of many figures involving percentages, such as sales growth next year, gross margin, expense ratio, etc. It was not at all comforting to find that in a syndicate of twelve young adults of between 18 and 21, only one knew how to calculate a percentage correctly, let alone apply a percentage increase.

The importance of being able to carry out such simple calculations correctly is seen as soon as one begins to consider those twin gods of retailing, sales and gross margin (i.e. the proportion of income which contributes towards overhead costs and profit). The simple relationship is:

$$\text{sales} \times \text{gross margin} = \text{gross contribution}$$

where sales and gross contribution are expressed in pounds sterling and gross margin is a proportion or percentage. Thus if sales are £1000 and the margin 30 per cent, the gross contribution is £300. What happens if, in an attempt to boost sales, the shopkeeper reduces his gross margin?

If the margin is reduced by one percentage point, from 30 to 29 per cent (i.e. effectively by $3\frac{1}{3}$ per cent) and sales rise by £100 (10 per cent) then the contribution becomes £1100 × 0.29 = £319, a rise of $6\frac{1}{3}$ per cent.

If, however, the margin is reduced by three percentage points (i.e. effectively by 10 per cent) and sales rise by £100 (10 per cent) then the contribution becomes £1100 × 0.27 = £297 — a fall of one per cent. Indeed, as the reader is invited to check, for the contribution to remain constant, a fall in margin of p per cent requires an offsetting percentage rise in sales of $100p/(100-p)$. Figure 3.1 shows the relationship.

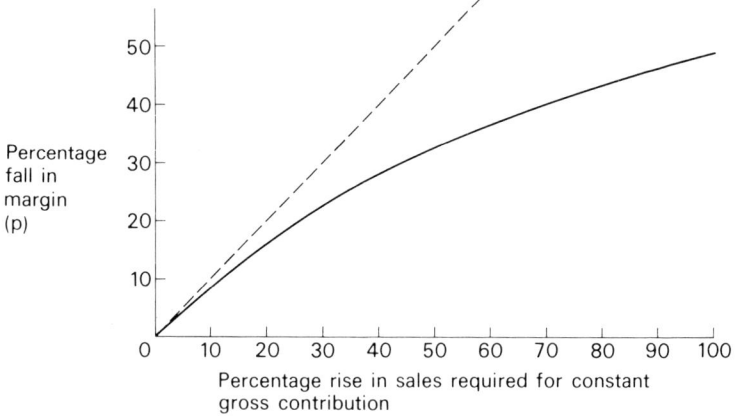

Fig. 3.1 Percentage fall in margin against percentage rise in sales

The trap in this simple relationship is that for small percentages the fall in margin and the offsetting rise in sales are about equal, but after 10 per cent the curve diverges rapidly from the line of symmetry so that a halving of the margin requires a doubling of the sales. Many people are quite unaware of the great rapidity of this divergence. Yet it is very important because the retailer is often temporarily reducing margin in order to increase sales. We shall see the various reasons for this shortly.

Mathematical training is also frequently helpful because it may suggest ways of displaying large amounts of complicated information simply and clearly. Here are two examples.

In any business one of the most important criteria of success is the return

Mathematics in store 31

on capital employed, which may be expressed as:

$$\text{ROCE} = \frac{\text{profit before deducting interest}}{\text{gross working capital} + \text{gross fixed capital}}.$$

Two crude components of this are the gross margin return on stock investment and the contribution per square foot (or square metre for those who insist that we are completely metricated!) — the store's site and building being an important fixed capital investment. The gross margin return on stock invested, which we denote by m, is defined by

$$m = \frac{\text{sales} \times \text{gross margin}}{\text{stock (valued at selling prices)}} \quad \text{or} \quad \frac{SM}{Q}$$

p, the profit per square foot, is given by

$$p = \frac{\text{sales} \times \text{gross margin}}{\text{selling area}} \quad \text{or} \quad \frac{SM}{A}.$$

Each of these equations may be regarded as representing a rectangular hyperbola:

$$m = \frac{S}{Q} \times M = TM, \text{ where } T \text{ is the stock turn}$$

$$p = \frac{S}{M} \times M = dM, \text{ where } d \text{ is the sales density.}$$

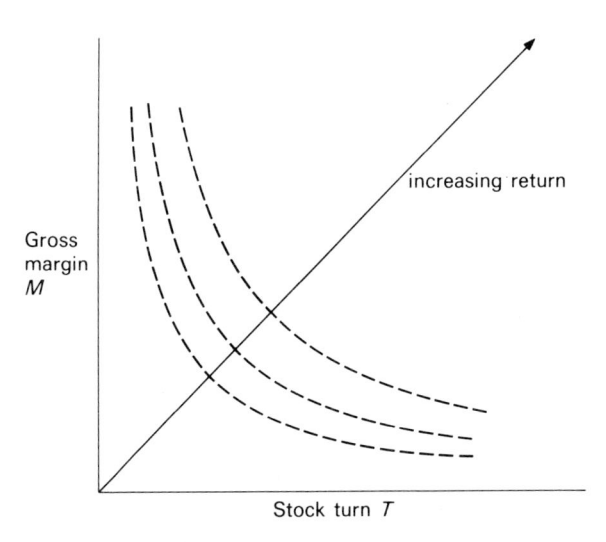

Fig. 3.2 Gross margin against stock turn

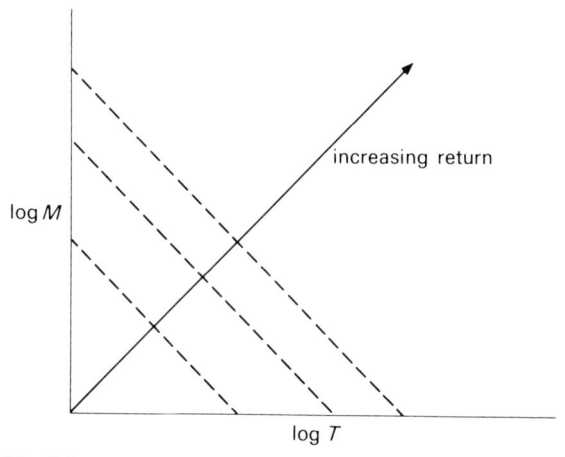

Fig. 3.3

If in the first equation m is given a series of fixed values and T is plotted against M, a family of rectangular hyperbolae results representing curves of constant gross margin return on stock investment, as shown in Fig. 3.2. By adopting logarithmic scales on each of the axes, the curves corresponding to fixed values of m become straight lines (see Fig. 3.3). This gives a powerful method of representing on a single graph the performance of many merchandise departments within a single store or of one merchandise department across many stores.

Since we have started to talk about stock, let me go on a little further. We have seen that stock turn, $T = S/Q$, is an important management ratio for the retailer. He or she is, therefore, often interested in increasing the stock turn even at the expense of some of the gross margin. This is especially true for seasonal or fashion goods where items unsold at the end of the season may either have to be kept until the following season, incurring warehousing and financing costs, or have to be cleared at very low prices. The retailer calls a reduction in price from the original margin a mark down (most often expressed as a percentage of selling price as in Fig. 3.4).

It is not possible here to deal exhaustively with the theory and practice of mark downs. Nevertheless a small example may give the flavour.

A retailer's original plan was to sell the whole of his stock in a given time period at selling price S and margin M. When a proportion P of the stock has been sold, it becomes clear that it will not be possible to sell the rest of the stock at the planned margin in the remaining time. It is estimated that in the whole time period only a fraction K will be sold, i.e. the sterling contribution will be MKS and $(1-K)S$ of the stock will remain. The simple question (rather more complicated in practice) is what mark down D (expressed as a reduction in margin) can the retailer afford, in order to clear the stock within

Mathematics in store

Fig. 3.4 Examples of mark down pricing in a retail store

the time period while still achieving the anticipated sterling contribution MKS? It is left to the reader to check that

$$D = \frac{1-K}{1-P} M.$$

As an example, if half the stock has been sold to date and it is clear that only three-quarters will be sold in the whole time period, then

$$D = \frac{1-\frac{3}{4}}{1-\frac{1}{2}} M = \frac{M}{2}.$$

Thus the original percentage margin may be halved in an attempt to clear the remaining stock. Note that this simple analysis gives no guarantee that the calculated mark down will do anything to increase the rate of sale.

Questions of price versus quantity, the customer's elasticity of price demand, and the complex part-economic, part-psychological characteristics of the retailer's art would lead us far beyond the scope of this paper.

By now you will certainly have got the message that stock is very important to the retailer. I want to turn next to the question of how much stock to buy. The approach is different depending upon whether we are dealing in fashion/seasonal merchandise or in staple, regular stock items. My example is chosen from the first category.

A fashion buyer is considering how many dresses of a particular style to buy in a colour which she thinks will be in great demand this season but which will be unsaleable in the following season at anything approaching normal prices. The dress will sell for £25 and costs £17. Any that are left over will have to be sold at less than half price, say £12. The buyer estimates that the season's sales will certainly exceed 20 000, but are most unlikely to exceed 35 000. How many dresses should she order?

This is, of course, an exercise in probability. Let us assume that the normal distribution is a suitable model for describing sales. Then Fig. 3.5 shows an estimated cumulative probability distribution of dress sales in the season. It is, of course, rather crude because very little information is available, but it is, nonetheless, adequate for our purposes.

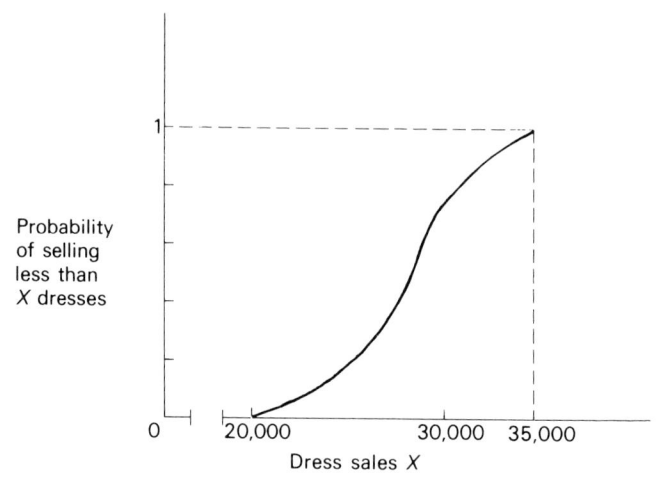

Fig. 3.5

Now it is easy to see that it pays to order more than 20 000 dresses, for the probability that a further dress will be sold (and a profit of £8 made) is almost 1. On the other hand, we are very unlikely to sell the 35 000th dress, which would result in a loss of £5. Where does the changeover point come? Let us suppose that the probability of selling another dress is p. Then the expected profit from that dress is £$8p$ and the expected loss £$5(1-p)$. The balance point occurs when $8p = 5(1-p)$, i.e. $p = 5/(5+8)$. This probability occurs when the cumulative probability (which is 0 when $p=1$) reaches $1-p$, i.e. $1-5/(5+8)=8/(5+8)=0.615$. From Fig. 3.5 we see that this probability corresponds to about 30 000 dresses. This is the approximate number of dresses which ought to be ordered, and is, we note, in excess of the figure obtained by averaging the 'best' and 'worst' estimates.

It would be most satisfying to be able to tell you that this is a widely-used approach in retailing. Unfortunately it is not; mainly, I think, because people are often so uncomfortable in the use of probabilities. Betting on a horse is one thing; applying odds to business decisions is apparently quite another.

So far I have been discussing what might be called 'operational' mathematics, i.e. the mathematics which can assist in the day-to-day operations of a retail business. In a moment I want to turn to 'strategic' mathematics. Before I do that, however, let us look at an equation which binds together much of what has been described already and also introduces the essentially 'strategic' idea of return on capital employed. I call this equation the fundamental retail equation and it is as follows:

return on capital employed % =

[(gross margin %) − (mark-downs %) − (stock losses %) − (expenses %)]

$$\div \left[\frac{1}{(\text{stock turn at cost})} + \frac{1}{(\text{the ratio of sales to fixed capital})} \right].$$

This assumes that the other elements of working capital (debtors, creditors) are in balance and, less realistically, that expenses may be represented as a fixed percentage of sales. A more complicated equation could, of course, be used.

We can also see that if the numerator and denominator of the fraction on the right hand side of the equation are both multiplied by sales value, the relationship is simply a definition:

$$\text{ROCE} = \frac{\text{trading profit}}{\text{stock} + \text{fixed capital}}$$

If we write

ROCE %	= R	expenses %	= E
gross margin %	= M	stock turn (at selling)	= T
mark down %	= D	sales/fixed capital	= K
stock losses %	= L		

then the relationship reduces to

$$R = \frac{M - D - L - E}{\left[\dfrac{1 - M/100}{T} + \dfrac{1}{K} \right]}$$

Let us see what this tells us about making small changes to the various parameters. Now

$$T = \frac{\text{sales}}{\text{stock (at selling)}} = \frac{S}{Q},$$

and so

$$\Delta T = \frac{Q\Delta S - S\Delta Q}{Q^2},$$

where the symbol Δ signifies a small change in the variable. Similarly,

$$K = \frac{\text{sales}}{\text{fixed capital}} = \frac{S}{F},$$

and, since F may be assumed constant in the short term,

$$\Delta K = \frac{\Delta S}{F}.$$

If R (the required return), M, E, and L are assumed to be constant also, then

$$R\Delta\left[\frac{1 - M/100}{T} + \frac{1}{K}\right] = -\Delta D,$$

i.e.

$$\frac{R(1 - M/100)}{T^2}\Delta T + \frac{R}{K^2}\Delta K = \Delta D.$$

Substitution for T, ΔT, K, ΔK gives

$$\frac{R}{S^2}[(1 - M/100)Q + F]\Delta S - \frac{R(1 - M/100)}{S}\Delta Q = \Delta D,$$

which is an equation showing (for a fixed ROCE) the relationship between additional mark downs (mark ups) and changes in sales value and stock (at selling). Clearly this kind of analysis can be carried much further but perhaps the above is sufficient to give an indication of the approach.

When we consider *strategic* planning requirements we are looking for mathematical approaches which will assist in the forecasting and analysis of successive profit and loss accounts and balance sheets over a period of years (at least five), together with the associated cash flows. This is where the computer is now widely used to simulate the financial consequences of various assumptions. Such financial simulation models are common nowadays throughout industry and commerce.

A similar approach may be used to study the cash flows arising from a new capital project. Frequently calculations are made of the discounted cash flow rate of return or the net present values for a range of discount (interest) rates of the stream of cash flows. This may be done at current (inflated) or constant prices.

Increasingly all these types of model are constructed and used by the analyst working directly on the computer, employing a 'user-friendly', 'English' modelling language.

For large investment decisions it may be important to try to assess the risk and uncertainty involved. This is usually done by some kind of Monte-Carlo simulation where the variables in the model are assumed to have known probability distributions and a random selection is made of a value for each variable for each simulation run. After a large number of runs (say 100) the probability distribution of, for example, the net present worth of the project may be estimated. Figure 3.6 shows distributions for three hypothetical projects.

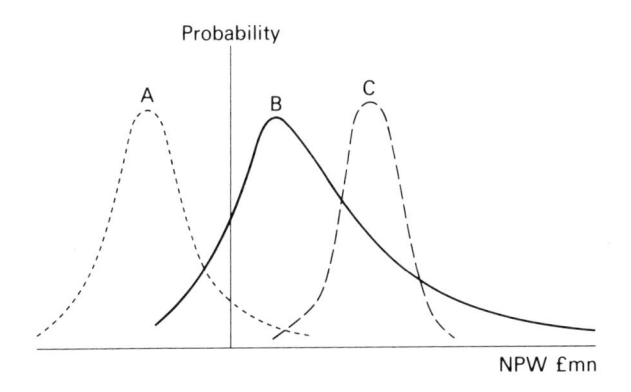

Fig. 3.6

Project A has little chance of showing a positive return. Project B is most likely to show a low positive return but there is a significant chance that it could show a very high return or it might be negative. Project C shows a moderate positive return with little chance of being high or negative. It is easy to reject Project A, but the choice between B and C may be very difficult and depends on one's view of risk. On the whole, as I remarked at the beginning of the paper, although business is supposed to be about risk-taking, everyone begins to feel very uncomfortable when attempts are made to quantify the risk. Most people seem to prefer to bet on completely unknown odds, which is a strange state of affairs.

In most new department store projects only a few of the variables are of great importance and hence only these need be treated as stochastic variables. They are: time for construction of building shell; time for fit-out to complete store; cost of construction (partly time-dependent); cost of fit-out (partly time-dependent); time to reach 'mature' sales density; and actual sales.

Some of these variables are subject not only to the usual type of probability distribution but also to a sharply discontinuous uncertainty function. For example, the construction time may be assumed, not unreasonably, to be normal, with a mean of eighteen months and a standard deviation of two months. However, should the site become the target (for whatever reason) of major industrial action, then a delay of as much as two years might occur with possibly catastrophic effects. The golden rule for projects, irrespective of any risk and uncertainty analysis, is that no company should ever undertake a project which is so large in relation to the financial strength of the company that its going wrong would seriously embarrass the company financially. You may think that this is obvious, but it is so often forgotten.

Lastly, I want to describe to you a key problem which does not yield easily to analytical solution, namely the problem of allocating selling space within a department store to the various merchandise categories or 'departments'. The ideal department store may be thought of as consisting of two or three rectangular floors of the same dimensions. Communication between these is by escalator and lift. The general problem of optimum allocation of space within this rectangular prism seems well beyond feasible analytical methods. However, it may be possible to solve the constrained problem of allocating space to a given number of specified departments on a particular floor. The sales density (sales per square foot or square metre) for a given merchandise category varies in the way shown in Fig. 3.7.

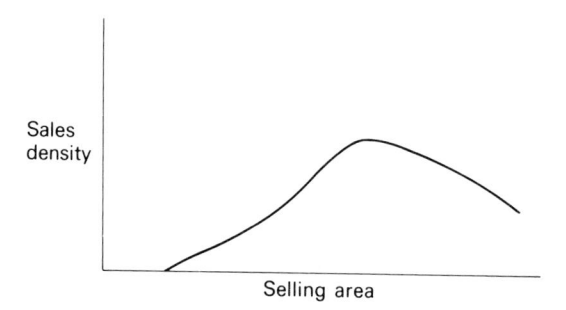

Fig. 3.7

There is a family of these curves with a relationship to floor position which could be defined in a reasonably simple mathematical way. Each merchandise category may be assumed to show a given gross margin and require a given level of selling staff input, so we may derive a family of curves relating net contribution per unit area to selling area. These will have the same general shape as previously. The problem of space allocation to obtain maximum net contribution is then one of mathematical programming, although it may yield more easily to a heuristic approach. As far as I am aware the problem has not been solved, perhaps because it has never been posed until recently, but more likely because of the large amount of initial data required. Also the retailer has tended to be reasonably satisfied with his trial and error solution until the last few years when the pressures to increase space and people productivity have mounted rapidly.

Perhaps I have now said enough for you to see that uses of mathematics are quite widespread in retailing and that there is enormous potential for further applications. When next you visit a Debenhams store (and I hope that will be very soon) think about sales, margin, stock turn, and mark down, and buy as much as you can.

Deborah Charlesworth

4
The mathematics of mimicry

Biologists nowadays use mathematics a great deal, in a variety of ways. Some of these ways are essentially different from those commonly employed by other types of scientists. In this chapter, we shall illustrate this by considering one particular problem. At the end of the chapter, some other types of mathematical work in biology will be briefly reviewed, to give an idea of the diversity of mathematical ideas that biologists may encounter.

Mimicry

Most people have probably been deceived at some time by a hover-fly. These flies are striped in yellow and black, and look remarkably like a bee or wasp. Only when one looks carefully does one notice that the insect is only a fly, and that one is in no danger of being stung. Animals such as toads that might be inclined to eat a fly, will be deceived in the same way that we are, and will avoid hover-flies because they have learnt from previous unpleasant experiences that bees and wasps are not good to eat. Thus the defenceless fly, which cannot sting, gains protection against its enemies by its resemblance to a stinging insect. This is called 'mimicry'. Other instances of mimicry involve defenceless species of butterfly that resemble, often to an amazing degree, other species that have an unpleasant taste. A bird that eats the unpleasant tasting butterflies soon learns not to touch the unpleasant species (called the 'model') and will then avoid the mimic species too, because the difference in appearance is not readily detectable. Mimicry was first discovered by the naturalist Bates, on his expedition to Amazonia in the 1860s. Bates himself was often deceived by the mimicry, and sometimes could distinguish the mimic from the model species only by close examination.

Fig. 4.1 An illustration of mimicry in a particular species of butterfly, *Papilio glaucus*, found in the USA. The mimetic females (left) are black, while the non-mimetic ones, and the males of the species, are yellow with black markings (right). The black females are mimicking *Battus philenor*, another black butterfly.

A mathematical model of mimicry

A biologist will be interested in such questions as the effectiveness of the disguise in warning off predators, the numbers of the mimetic type within the mimic species (that is, the proportion of members of the mimic species which look like the model), and the sizes of the populations of the mimic and the model species. These kinds of questions are studied by the techniques of population genetics. This is one of the oldest-established areas of mathematical biology. It dates from the early years of the present century when the laws of inheritance were first clearly understood, though parts of the field of study have roots going back to the nineteenth-century studies of the degree of resemblance between parents and offspring (or grandparents and grandchildren) with respect to some measurable characteristics. Population geneticists have developed a large body of theory, since these early studies. The model of mimicry which is described below illustrates the way in which a simple model of a complex system can be constructed using elementary probability theory, and shows how a model can be used to make predictions about what would be expected in a real-life situation. Testing the predictions against field observations and laboratory experiments should lead to detection of false assumptions in the model (which itself is based on experience of how animals behave). This in turn will lead not only to a refined model, but also to a clearer understanding of the biological system being studied. Most studies of such models by population geneticists would go much further than this, by taking into account the inheritance of the character under study, and using this knowledge together with the model system to predict the future evolution of the system. Great complexity is often

Fig. 4.2 The two photographs show different species of grasshopper, each in its natural habitat. They show how each species mimics its environment so that it can remain invisible.

generated in such studies. The study described below gives little idea of this, because essentially we shall be confining our attention to just a part of what a population genetics study of a problem normally involves.

To make a simple mathematical model of mimicry we first have to identify what we see as key factors affecting predation. Clearly, one important factor is whether or not the prey is seen by the predator. It is well known that many animals avoid being eaten by their predators because they are hard to see. This is called 'cryptic coloration'. An example is provided by stick insects that look just like a stalk of the plant they feed on. Another example is the sole, a flat fish which can assume a coloration that makes it practically invisible on a sandy sea-bottom. The second factor that affects the predation rate is the probability that a prey animal that has been spotted by the predator will actually be attacked and eaten. This probability will depend on how the predator judges the prey as a food item. A fly, if seen, is probably judged as a tasty morsel by a toad, while a hover-fly is judged as a stinging insect, and will not be attacked by an experienced toad, though a young and inexperienced animal will readily try to eat a bee or wasp and will be stung, thus learning to be more cautious in future. In making a model of the predation process, we use the fact that the two events, being seen by the predator, and being eaten, given that the prey has been seen, are independent events. A flow diagram illustrating the various possibilities is shown in Fig. 4.3.

Here, we have indicated the probability that a predator will see an individual of the prey species during a defined interval of time by C, a measure of *conspicuousness*. Thus

$$\Pr\{\text{prey seen}\} = C$$

It follows, of course, that the probability that the prey will not be seen is $1 - C$.

44 Maths at Work

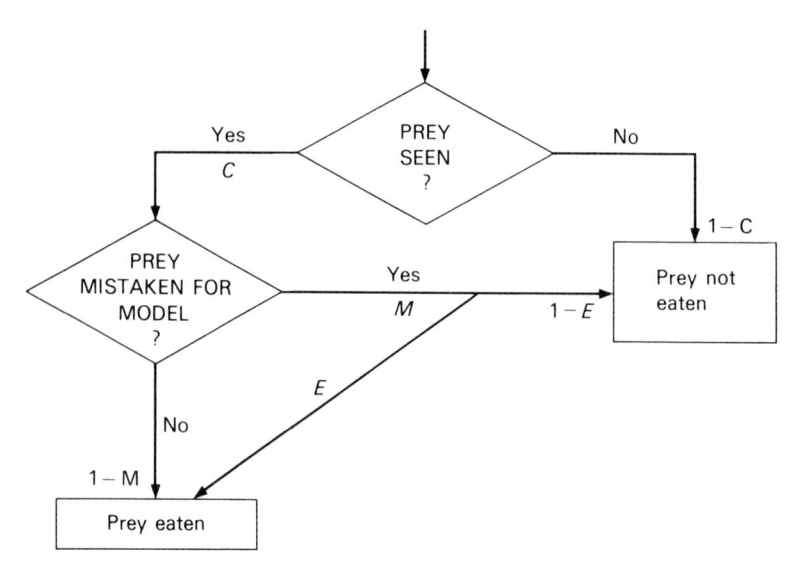

```
              ┌──────────┐
              │ PREY     │
       Yes   ╱│ SEEN    │╲  No
      ┌─────╱ │   ?     │ ╲─────┐
      │   C  ╲│         │╱      │
      │       └──────────┘      │ 1 − C
      ▼                         ▼
┌──────────┐                ┌─────────┐
│  PREY    │                │         │
│ MISTAKEN │  Yes           │Prey not │
│ FOR      │───M──── 1 − E ─│ eaten   │
│ MODEL    │                │         │
│    ?     │                └─────────┘
└──────────┘      E
   │  No
   │ 1 − M
   ▼
┌──────────┐
│Prey eaten│
└──────────┘
```

Prob (prey eaten) = Prob (prey seen) × Prob (prey eaten/seen) = $C(M \times E + 1 - M)$

Fig. 4.3 Factors determining the predation rate

Once the prey is seen, a number of possibilities arise. First, the predator may mistake the prey for the model — let us denote the probability of its doing that by M, i.e.

$$\Pr\{\text{predator mistaken}\} = M.$$

M, then, will be a measure of the mimetic resemblance to the model.

Of course, if the predator is not fooled, then the prey is eaten. There is a probability of $1 - M$ of that happening.

If the predator does mistake the mimic for the model there is still a probability that the prey will be eaten. Some predators will eat the model species. We denote the probability that the predator will eat what it thinks to be the model by E, i.e.

$$E = \Pr\{\text{model eaten}|\text{seen}\}$$

(the probability that having been seen the model is eaten).

Since we can assume that being seen by the predator and being eaten, given that the prey has been seen, are independent events, we get the equation

$$\Pr\{\text{prey eaten}\} = \Pr\{\text{prey seen}\} \times \Pr\{\text{prey eaten}|\text{seen}\} \qquad (1).$$

Now, $\Pr\{\text{prey eaten}|\text{seen}\}$ is obtained by adding two probabilities: the probability that the predator is not fooled $(1 - M)$ and the probability that the predator is fooled but still (and independently) decides to eat the prey

$(M \times E)$. Thus

$$\Pr\{\text{prey eaten}|\text{seen}\} = (1 - M) + ME$$

and, from (1),

$$\Pr\{\text{prey eaten}\} = C[1 - M + ME]$$
$$= C[1 - M(1 - E)] \qquad (2).$$

The equation (2) gives us the predation rate for the mimic – the probability of an individual being eaten in the defined interval of time.

We can use this very simple model to study the conditions that must be satisfied if mimicry is to evolve. Assume that the defenceless species is initially not mimetic, but that a mutation has arisen, producing a new form of the species which has some degree of similarity to a distasteful model species. To ask whether mimicry will evolve is equivalent to asking whether the new mutant form will have a lower predation rate (that is, a higher survival rate) than the original non-mimetic form of the species. Only if this is the case will the mimicry mutation spread in the population. The predation rates on the two forms are found by using equation (2) for each form. For the non-mimetic form, M is, of course, zero, this form is not mistaken for the model. We therefore have as a necessary condition for the mimetic form to be favoured in an evolutionary sense:

$$C_{\text{non-mimic}} > C_{\text{mimic}}[1 - M(1 - E)]$$

or

$$M > \frac{1}{1 - E}\left(1 - \frac{C_{\text{non-mimic}}}{C_{\text{mimic}}}\right) \qquad (3).$$

This inequality shows how good a mimetic resemblance must be achieved for the mutation to increase in the population. If one substitutes plausible values of the C and E parameters into inequality (3), one finds that rather high M values are likely to be required. As expected, the resemblance measured by M need not be so good for a highly distasteful model (low E) as for a model with only a moderately unpleasant effect on the predator. These predictions can be tested by giving predators such as birds prey items, and observing their behaviour. This has been done, using several different models and their mimics, and the mimicry has in all cases been found to be highly effective. Indeed birds seem often to be so inclined to caution that in a measurable proportion of tests even slight resemblance to a highly distasteful model is enough to deter them from attacking.

The next thing to notice is that in inequality (3) C_{mimic} will be larger than $C_{\text{non-mimic}}$, because the models are brightly coloured, conspicuous species, with warning coloration advertising their harmfulness or distastefulness to the predators. If a mimic is to resemble the model it too must become rather conspicuous. It therefore follows from inequality (3) that if the non-mimetic form is well camouflaged (or very cryptic), that is if $C_{\text{non-mimic}}$ is small, then M would have to be very large if the mimic species were to be at an advantage. But it is unlikely that a mutation to mimicry could result in such a good mimetic resemblance to the model. So our model leads us to the conclusion that for the mimicry to evolve $C_{\text{non-mimic}}$ must not be too low. Now this is a testable prediction: mimicry will be unlikely to evolve from a highly cryptic (camouflaged) pattern, but is more likely to evolve when the mimetic species was initially moderately conspicuous. The prediction is borne out in reality.

Let us see what other predictions we can make from our model.

Suppose, for example that $C_{\text{non-mimic}}$ is sufficiently high for the mimic to be at an advantage compared to the non-mimetic type. Then mimics will increase in frequency among the mimetic species. To take this into account, the simple model that has been used up to now must be extended. With an increased frequency of mimics among the prey encountered, the conditional probability of attack (E) increases, because there will be a higher frequency of young predators who have not yet experienced the unpleasant consequences of attacking a model individual (or who have forgotten such an experience because it has been followed by a number of satisfactory instances of mimics eaten). To take this into account in the model, we must treat E as a function of the proportion R of mimics amongst the total of mimics plus models.

Figure 4.4 shows a possible graph of $E(R)$ plotted against R. The least value of $E(R)$ will be when $R=0$, that is, when there are no mimics. However, as the proportion of mimics increases, the chances of a random 'eating' being unpleasant will decrease and so $E(R)$ will increase. In Fig. 4.4 we have assumed that the relationship is linear, but of course, in reality, a curve is more likely. Some data exist which suggest a particular curve, but our model will allow us to make certain predictions even though we do not have details of the exact shape of the curve (or, what is equivalent, of the exact nature of the relationship).

The fact that E is a function of the frequency of mimics among mimics plus models, has an interesting consequence. It is perfectly possible, and indeed quite likely, that mimics may have an advantage over the non-mimetic form of their species only when they are rare. The predation rate on the non-mimetic form does not depend on the number of mimics around; as mentioned above, this form has a predation rate of $C_{\text{non-mimic}}$. If we look again at equation (2), this time using our variable $E(R)$, we see that as $E(R)$ increases, $M(1-E(R))$ decreases, and the predation rate $C[1-M(1-E(R))]$ increases. It is easy to see that if E becomes sufficiently large, the two predation rates could become equal:

$$C_{\text{non-mimic}} = C_{\text{mimic}}\{1 - M[1 - E(R)]\}.$$

The mathematics of mimicry 47

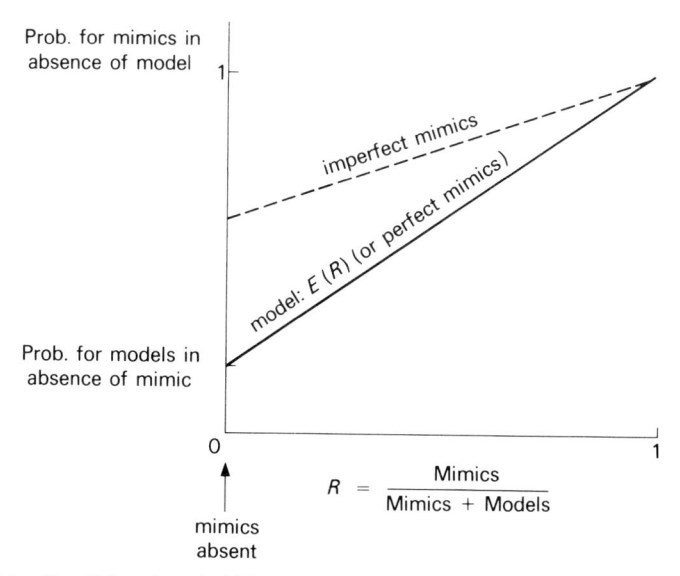

Fig. 4.4 Conditional probability that prey is eaten given that it has been seen

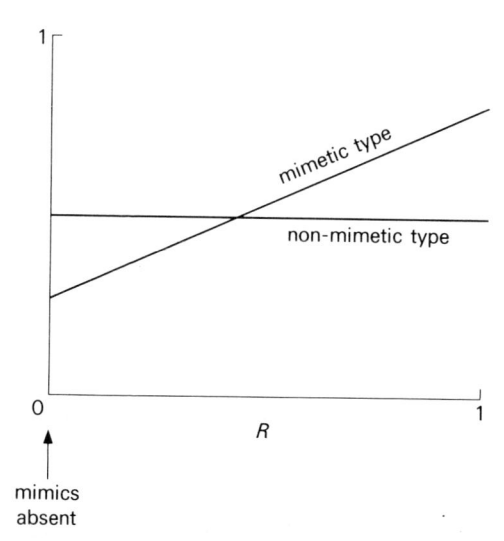

Fig. 4.5 Predation rates on the two types in the mimetic species

Figure 4.5 shows this graphically. Clearly this is not possible if the two types are equally conspicuous ($C_{\text{non-mimic}} = C_{\text{mimic}}$), since in that case the two predation rates would be equal only if $E(R) = 1$, that is, if the models have the same probability of being attacked as the non-mimetic form. However, this would never happen unless mimics were overwhelmingly common compared with models.

In biological terms, this result means that it would be possible for a mimetic form to spread in a population until it reached some level of frequency (i.e. formed such a proportion of the mimic + model population) at which its predation rate was equal to that of the non-mimics. The mimetic mutant would then be at no advantage and so there would be no further changes in frequency. The two types would just suffer the same rate of predation, and the population would be in an equilibrium state. This equilibrium is stable. If mimics became rarer for some reason, they would again have an advantage compared with the non-mimetic type. Similarly, if the non-mimetic type became rarer, the mimics would have an increased probability of being eaten once they had been seen, compared with the value for the equilibrium state; also, the mimics are more conspicuous than the non-mimics and these two factors combine to give mimics the higher predation rate, so the population would tend to return to the equilibrium. So the model predicts that sometimes mimics should co-exist with the non-mimetic type, in the same population, and this is found in many mimetic species that have been studied. It is not always to be expected, however. Sometimes the value of R that would equalise the predation rates on mimics and non-mimics would not be reached even if every individual of the mimetic population were a mimic. In that case, non-mimics would be eliminated, and all the mimetic species would look like the model. However, in either of the two cases just mentioned, if the model species is absent, mimicry will have no advantage (R will equal 1). So we can predict that populations of the mimetic species that live in areas where the model species does not occur, will not contain mimetic individuals. This has often been found to be true.

So we see that even though we do not know the exact form of $E(R)$, we have been able to make certain 'qualitative' predictions from our model. In a similar fashion we were able to make deductions from formulae involving measures of conspicuousness, C, even though in practice it would be difficult if not impossible to assign an exact numerical value to C. Perhaps, at best we could design laboratory or field experiments which allowed us to say of two species, A and B, that $C_A < C_B$. Our model, then, has been of a qualitative nature — in a sense independent of exact numerical values — which contrasts with many of the models described elsewhere in this book. It is not much use to know that there are sufficiently high flows of traffic which will cause a roundabout to be saturated; in that instance we want to know more about the actual size of flows – it is a 'quantitative' model. However, it is often the case in biology, and in other kinds of studies, that we can learn much from models in which we are not able to give precise numerical values to the parameters.

So far no mention has been made of how mimicry is inherited within the mimetic species. All the results described, and the predictions drawn from them, are valid for most likely modes of inheritance, provided that there are only two types, mimics and non-mimics, in the species (i.e. no third type, such as an intermediate form), and also that no other differences are associated with the presence or absence of the mimetic pattern (for example, no difference in palatability to the predator, or in ability to escape from the predator). In those species where the genetics of mimicry has been studied, the mode of inheritance has proved to be very simple. It can easily be combined with the mathematical model described here to develop a computer program that enables one to study the dynamics of the evolution of mimicry, as well as problems such as whether modifier genes which improve the mimicry will be favoured by natural selection. However, these problems are too complex to be dealt with here. I hope that the relatively simple results that have been described are sufficient to show how a simple mathematical model can help one get testable qualitative predictions that are not obvious without such a model.

Mathematical models in biology

As mentioned earlier, the mathematical model of mimicry is just one very simple example of the use of mathematics in biology. I should like to end this chapter by mentioning briefly some other examples. I will do this by showing how they fit into a rough, arbitrary classification scheme of some of the different ways in which biologists find themselves having to use mathematics. I shall probably omit important types of mathematical work, because nobody today can possibly be aware of developments in all areas of the vast and heterogeneous science that biology has become. Some idea of the range can be gained by glancing at the contents pages of such journals as the *Journal of Theoretical Biology*. The kinds of biological research in which mathematics is used, and the kinds of mathematics that are used, are quite surprising.

The first category of mathematical work in biology might be termed 'analysis of data', and includes statistics. All biologists have sometimes to use statistical techniques, and this is so well known as to need no further comment. Such familiar statistical techniques as analysis of variance, and correlation and regression were first developed to deal with problems that arise in the analysis of biological data. Another type of problem that is closely related to statistics is how to measure the degree of similarity between sets of biological data. The data might consist of characters found in a set of different fossils which one wants to classify, or sequences of amino acids in a protein taken from a set of animal or plant species, which one wishes to use to deduce the relationships between the species. This type of problem has received a good deal of study in recent years, because sequence data from proteins or DNA has become available at an ever accelerating rate. The problems of constructing 'phylogenetic trees' incorporating the information about relationships, involves complex techniques in probability theory, and also topological methods.

The second category covers a large range of different kinds of mathematical models in biology. Sometimes these models are purely descriptive. For example, models with quite small numbers of parameters can exhibit many of the features observed in the daily cycles of sleep and waking of animals, including man. Another class of models of this type includes systems of equations to represent certain developmental processes in animal embryos, or models representing the branching patterns of plants in terms of a few fundamental parameters. The laws of genetic inheritance provide a simple example of this type of model. Mendel's 'laws' were formulated to explain the observed results of crosses between strains of peas. They were soon shown to fit well with the inheritance patterns of many characters in a wide range of plants and animals, and later Mendel's proposed factors (now called genes) were shown to have a material basis which is now understood in extreme physico-chemical detail: we know that genes are made of the chemical DNA, and we understand how the structure of DNA gives rise to the laws of inheritance.

In contrast to this type of model is the kind in which the basis of the model is the known mechanism of some process, and the aim is to make predictions about how the process will behave. Frequently, this type of model describes a population process. A theory of population growth based on knowledge of how organisms reproduce, is an example. Such models range from simple ones to show the exponential growth of populations of bacteria which double in the presence of an unlimited supply of nutrients, to those for the future of the human population which take into account the age-structure of the populations and the birth rates to females of different ages, to models of animal communities consisting of several different species. Another example, which might perhaps be more appropriate in the previous category, is the study of the kinetics of enzyme reactions, based on some knowledge of the properties of enzymes. The mathematical study of multi-enzyme systems is based on knowledge of the properties of systems of single enzymes with their substrates and products. These problems involve the techniques of analysis of differential equations. A totally different example of the mathematical exploration of a system with some known properties is the study of the topological properties of circular DNA molecules. These properties result from the fact that DNA itself has a double helix structure.

These examples should serve to illustrate the importance of model-building in biology. Making a mathematical model of a biological system often helps to uncover implicit assumptions that may frequently be rather unclear. These assumptions, once clearly formulated, can be tested, either directly or via predictions derived from a model incorporating them. There are thus two gains from making mathematical models: uncovering the assumptions behind a theory, and generating predictions that may lead to tests of the assumptions and may also provide explanations of known biological phenomena.

5

Jeffrey Griffiths

Increasing the shipping capacity of the Suez Canal

For centuries mathematicians have been concerned with optimisation – finding the 'best' solutions to particular problems. If one is dealing with a function of a single variable then elementary calculus can be used to find maxima and minima, and similar methods have been developed for functions of several variables. A further development concerns cases where some of the variables are subject to constraints. We shall consider such a problem in this chapter.

During recent years optimisation techniques have been increasingly applied to problems from business, commerce, and industry, where the task may be to improve the performance of a piece of machinery or to upgrade efficiency. In many cases the most difficult part of the problem has been to formulate the mathematical equations and constraints used to model the real-life situation. To do this well it is usually necessary for the mathematician to acquire an intimate knowledge of the overall background from which the problem stems. In this chapter we cannot deal with all aspects of a case-study, but we shall attempt to describe the essential features of a problem tackled by the author when engaged as consultant to a large civil engineering company. The study was concerned with improving the efficiency of shipping operations in the Suez Canal. We shall see that the solution of the problem involved the use of mathematical techniques, but also in some instances just common sense.

Background information

The Suez Canal lies on the shortest navigable route between the Eastern and Western Worlds; typical savings in transport costs compared with using the Cape route are 35–50 per cent.

The length of the Canal is 160.3 kilometres. Of this distance about 121 kilometres may be said to belong to the Canal proper, with the remainder lying in the Bitter Lakes. There are three main cities on the Canal: Port Said at the northern end, Suez and the associated Port Tewfik at the southern end, and Ismailia approximately midway between (see Fig. 5.1).

52 Maths at Work

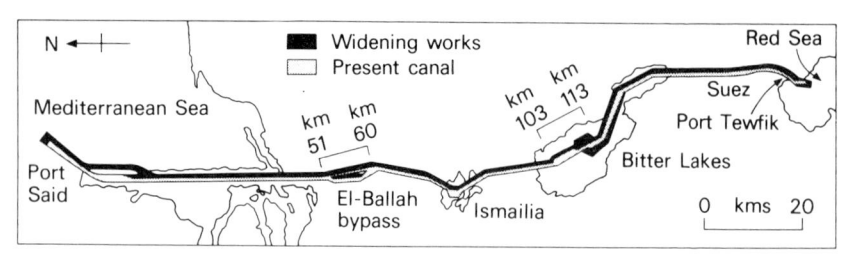

Fig. 5.1 The Suez Canal

Vessels using the canal are charged a toll, and the revenues, of the order of £1 000 000 per day, represent a major contribution to the Egyptian economy. The toll charge for a single ship can be as much as £30 000, so it is essential that the shipping system should operate efficiently and, in particular, that the maximum number of ships possible should be allowed to pass through the canal.

We shall address ourselves to two questions:
(i) What is the maximum capacity of the present Canal?
(ii) How may this capacity be increased?

To answer these questions we need to know a little more of the details of the traffic system operating in the Canal.

The major lengths of the Canal allow only one-way passages of ships, but vessels are allowed to pass one another in two sections, at Bitter Lakes between km 101 and km 116 and at El-Ballah bypass between km 51 and km 60. The movement of ships is organised in convoys. Three convoys per day are utilised, two southbound and one northbound. The first southbound convoy starts from Port Said at 2300 hours, and the north-bound from Port Tewfik at 0500 hours. These starting times enable the convoys to pass one another in the Bitter Lakes, the northbound convoy having a non-stop daylight passage, as far as is possible. This is desirable for safety since the northbound convoy includes tankers carrying crude oil and other dangerous cargoes. The second southbound convoy starts from Port Said at 0700 hours and proceeds to Ballah, where it ties up in the western loop of the bypass to allow the northbound convoy to pass. The second southbound convoy then travels non-stop from Ballah to Port Tewfik.

Each ship is navigated by an official pilot and its time of entry to the canal, its place in the convoy, the speeds at which it travels, and the separation distances from the vessel ahead are all laid down. Signal stations along the canal record the times at which ships pass and relay the information to Ismailia where the progress of each vessel is recorded by movement controllers on a chart known as a transit graph. In this way it is possible for the controllers to gain an overall view of the progression of the convoys and to ensure that speeds and separation distances of vessels are maintained at the specified levels. In the event of a ship having to stop due to engine breakdown, steering failure, bad weather, or other cause, the pilot immediately informs the Movement Control Office and messages are relayed to all following ships, commanding them to halt and tie up at the nearest mooring bollard. It should be appreciated that the physical process of bringing a ship to rest from a speed of 14 kilometres per hour in a confined waterway is not an easy one, and, depending on the size of the vessel, can take several kilometres. The specified separation distances take account of such factors as the size of ship and type of cargo carried. Naturally, vessels carrying petroleum products or other potentially dangerous cargoes are required to maintain larger separation distances than general cargo ships. For example, two general cargo ships would have a minimum interval of five minutes (about one kilometre) between them, while a vessel carrying fissile material would be required to be separated by twenty minutes (about four kilometres) from the vessels ahead and astern.

The allowed speed of a convoy varies between 12 and 14 kilometres per hour, and is determined by a number of factors, for example, the need to ensure that the ship's wake does not damage the banks of the canal.

A diagrammatic representation of a transit graph is shown in Fig. 5.2. The indicated speeds may be increased or decreased (with the controller's permission) by one kilometre per hour and analysis of collected data showed that significantly higher speeds are often apparent.

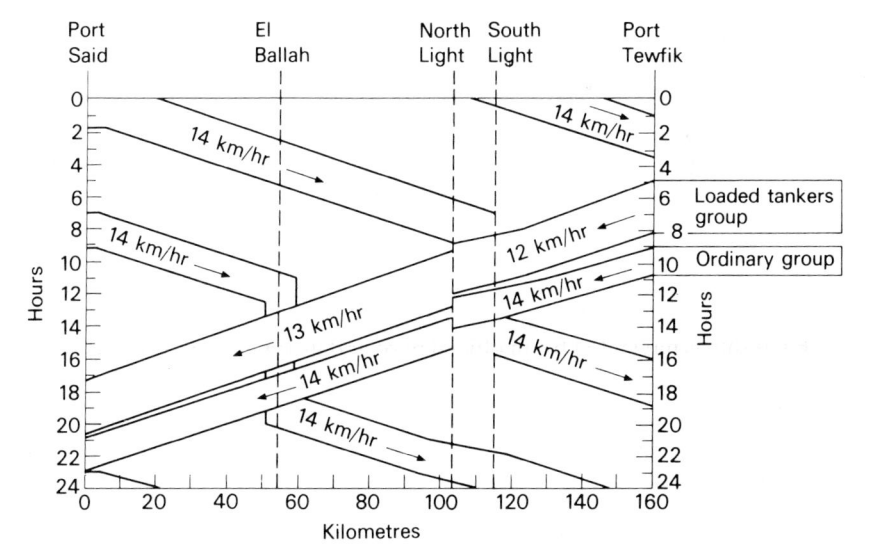

Fig. 5.2 Transit graph for ships moving through the canal

The theoretical capacity of the present Canal

Traditionally the shipping capacity of the Canal has been measured in terms of the number of vessels which are able to complete their transits during a 24-hour period. Many factors affect this measure; these include:
(a) the division of the total number of ships between the northbound and southbound convoys
(b) the convoy system adopted in the Canal
(c) the speeds at which ships are allowed to transit, and the time gaps required between them at various nodes of the Canal
(d) the mix of different categories of ships which transit the Canal.

So as to make the problem more tractable, we now make the assumption that we are concerned with 'standard ships', assumed to transit the canal at a speed of 14 kilometres per hour and to be separated from the vessels ahead and astern by a gap of ten minutes.

In calculating the shipping capacity the following assumptions are made:
(i) a three convoy per day system is in operation, one northbound and two southbound
(ii) the northbound convoy does not stop while transitting the Canal (see page 52)
(iii) the number of ships transitting the Canal is equally divided between northbound and southbound convoys (although records show that slightly more ships pass southwards than northwards).

In addition, the following features relating to the physical layout of the Canal and its operating system must be taken into account:
(iv) the storage capacity of El-Ballah bypass (between km 51 and km 60) is seventeen ships for the second southbound convoy
(v) the storage capacity of Bitter Lakes (between North-Light – km 103.4 – and South-Light – km 112.9) is 36 ships for the first southbound convoy
(vi) southbound convoys begin transitting the Canal from Port Said at km 3.7, and end their transits at Port Tewfik at km 160.3
(vii) the northbound convoy begins its transit of the Canal at Port Tewfik at km 160.3 and finishes at Port Said at km 0
(viii) the gap between the last ship of the second southbound convoy arriving at Port Tewfik (km 160.3) and the first ship of the northbound convoy leaving Port Tewfik should be at least 30 minutes, so that the waiting area at Suez Bay can be cleared by the southbound convoy before the northbound convoy begins its transit through the Canal
(ix) the first ship of the northbound convoy may cross the last ship of the first southbound convoy at km 101, and the last ship of the northbound convoy may cross the first ship of the first southbound convoy at km 116

(x) the last ship of the northbound convoy may cross the first ship of the second southbound convoy at El-Ballah south (km 60).

Given these assumptions, it is now possible to construct a transit graph, based on convoys of standard ships, which can be used to estimate the capacity of the Canal. Thus, in Fig. 5.3(a) the line AB represents the path of the first ship in the first southbound convoy. A is at km 3.7, B is at km 112.9, and the speed of the ship is 14 kilometres per hour. To find the maximum shipping capacity we must clearly utilise the full period of 24 hours. Thus we may draw CD, the path of the last ship of the northbound convoy. Using the information given in the first part of (ix) above, the sum of the numbers of ships in the first southbound and in the northbound convoys may now be determined, and the remaining information can then be used to show that it is possible for the second southbound convoy to transit at its maximum size of seventeen ships.

Some careful calculation (which is left to the reader) allied to this graphical approach should produce a shipping capactiy of about 78 ships for the 24-hour period (see Fig. 5.3(b)).

Let us now formulate the problem algebraically. We use the following notation: l, the number of standard ships in the northbound convoy; q, the number of standard ships in the first southbound convoy; r, the number of standard ships in the second southbound convoy.

We wish to maximise the total number of ships that transit per day, that is

$$l+q+r.$$

Assumption (iii) gives the condition

$$l=q+r.$$

Assumption (iv) imposes the constraint

$$r \leqslant 17.$$

Assumption (v) leads us to

$$q \leqslant 36.$$

Assumption (viii) requires (after some manipulation)

$$r+l \leqslant 57.$$

The first part of assumption (ix) yields the constraint

$$q+l \leqslant 61.$$

The second part of assumption (ix) yields the constraint

$$q \leqslant 47$$

but this is a weaker condition than one obtained earlier, and so can be ignored.

56 Maths at Work

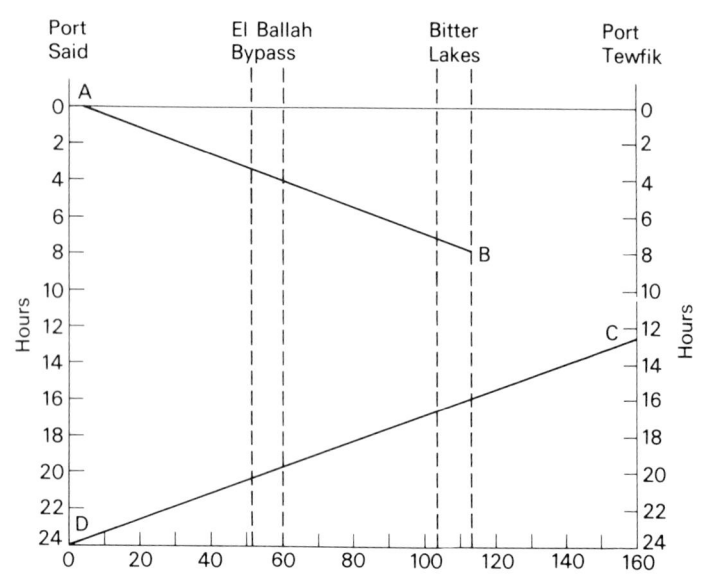

Fig. 5.3(a) Beginning of graphical solution to capacity exercise

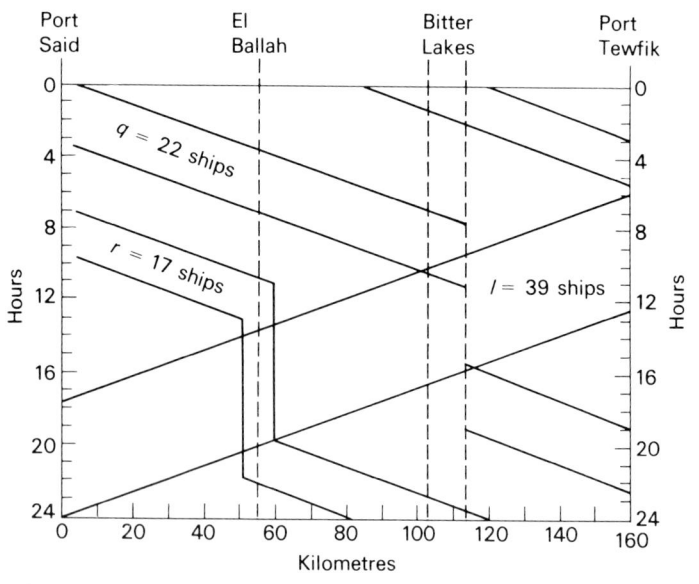

Fig. 5.3(b) Completed graphical solution to capacity exercise

Finally, we have the non-negativity conditions

$$l \geq 0, \quad q \geq 0, \quad r \geq 0.$$

The problem is now a simple linear programming one, although strictly speaking we also need to impose integer values on the variables. We leave it to the reader to verify that the solution is, in fact, $l=39$, $q=22$, $r=17$.

The problem as posed is, of course, a simplification of the real-life situation. In order to convert the theoretical capacity from standard ships to real ships it was necessary to find how the performance of real vessels compare with those assumed for standard ships. To this end a substantial amount of data was collected from the Canal Zone relating to such factors as speeds and separation distances of different types of vessel at several positions along the Canal. The conversion procedure is rather complex, due to the number of factors involved, and lack of space does not permit consideration here. The interested reader may consult reference 2 at the end of the chapter for further details. However, it is worthwhile noting here that it was found that:
(a) if all ships were general cargo vessels, the capacity would be 84 real ships per day
(b) if ten per cent of the northbound convoy were loaded tankers and the remaining vessels were general cargo vessels (a typical mix at present), then the capacity would be 78 real ships per day.

We can see that working in terms of standard ships has led to an estimate of shipping capacity which accords well with the real-life situation. For the remainder of this chapter, in order to make reasonable comparisons, we shall consider capacity to be measured in terms of standard ships.

Forecasts indicate that the present capacity will be exceeded in the early 1980s, and that by 1990 the average number of vessels wishing to transit will exceed 90 (standard ships) per day. It is thus clear that urgent steps must be taken to increase the capacity of the Canal, such increases being closely linked with the plans for enlarging the Canal to accommodate supertankers.

Increasing the capacity of the Canal

There are several ways in which the capacity of the Canal may be increased, for example
  (i) building additional bypasses so that opposing convoys may pass each other over greater distances than at present
  (ii) changing the mode of operation of traffic, in particular by altering the cycle time of 24 hours

(iii) permitting increased speeds of transit and/or reducing separation distances between vessels in a convoy
(iv) allowing small ships to pass each other at any position in the Canal.

The most important of the suggestions put forward for increasing the capacity are (i) and (ii) above, and we now consider the effects of these.

The effect of additional bypasses

There are a large number of development schemes which may be used as a means of increasing the capacity of the Canal. The ultimate achievement would be to provide dual waterways (side by side) for the whole length of the Canal. The cost of providing such a dual waterway (which, it can be readily checked, would increase the capacity of the Canal to 288 standard ships per day) would be enormous, and although the idea remains the ultimate objective of the SCA, full dualling will not be achieved in the foreseeable future. In the meantime less ambitious schemes will be undertaken in stages, and these will form an integral part of the final dualling of the Canal. It should be emphasised that these schemes have been proposed not only from the point of view of increasing the capacity but also for various operational and engineering reasons.

Scheme 1 A bypass (to be known as the Port Fouad Bypass) would be constructed at the northern end of the Canal to provide a direct exit to the Mediterranean Sea from a point near km 12 in the Canal, thus enabling vessels to avoid the congestion of Port Said harbour. This effectively reduces the overall length of the Canal by 12 kilometres. In addition, a bypass would be built to the north of Lake Timsah between km 73 and km 86, and southbound vessels would be able to moor in the Lake to allow northbound vessels to pass. The storage capacity at Lake Timsah would be 20 standard ships. This situation allows an additional southbound convoy to be added to the operational system described earlier. Figure 5.4 shows the details of the system, with the new southbound convoy travelling to the Timsah bypass and waiting until the vessel of the northbound convoy has passed km 86 before it proceeds directly to Port Tewfik.

Using the same notation as on page 55, and letting p be the number of standard ships in the new southbound convoy, the problem is to maximize $l+q+p+r$ subject to the following constraints:

$$l = q+r+p \qquad q \leqslant 36$$
$$q = 68-l \qquad p \leqslant 20$$
$$r \leqslant 17 \qquad r \leqslant 55-l$$
$$l>0, \quad q>0, \quad p>0, \quad r>0.$$

The shipping capacity of the Suez Canal 59

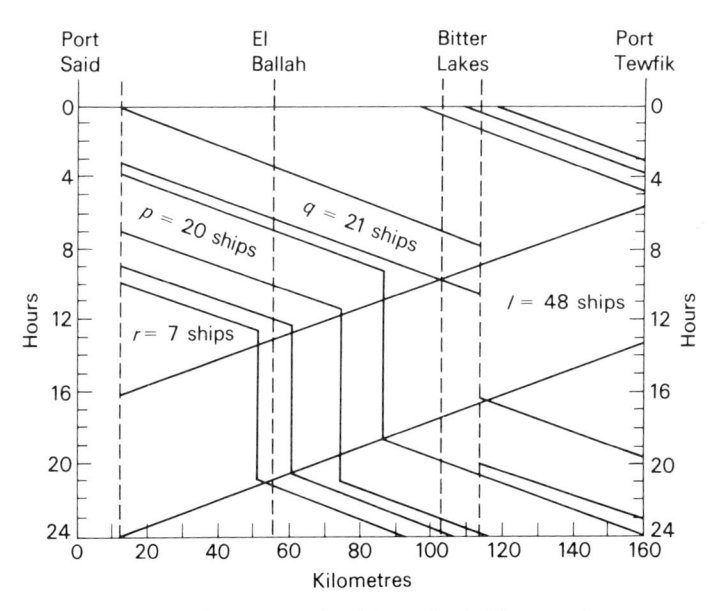

Fig. 5.4 Scheme 1: maximum capacity 96 standard ships

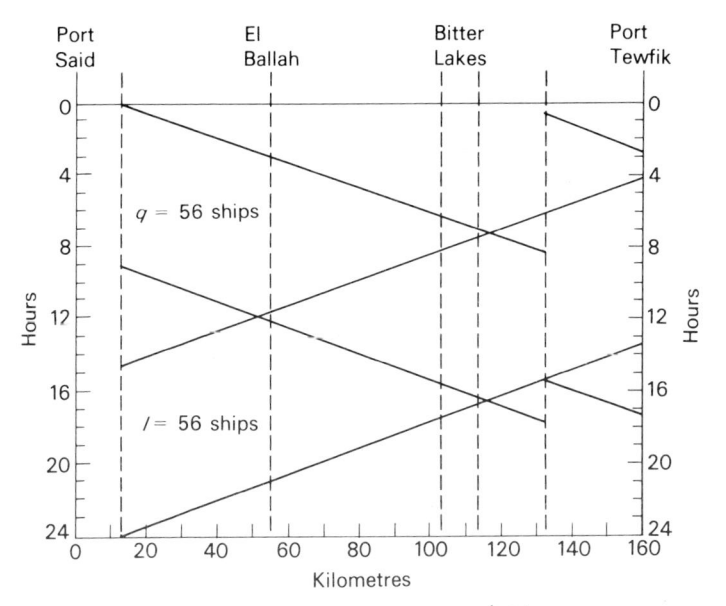

Fig. 5.5 Scheme 2: maximum capacity 112 standard ships

60 Maths at Work

Solving this integer programming problem, the capacity of this scheme is found to be 96 standard ships, with $l = 48$, $q = 21$, $p = 20$, and $r = 7$. Figure 5.4 illustrates how this capacity is achieved.

Scheme 2 As before, the Port Fouad bypass would be in operation, but in addition there would be a continuous section of dual Canal between km 51 and km 113. In this case it is necessary to use one convoy per day in each direction, as shown in Fig. 5.5. The capacity of this scheme is 112 standard ships per day.

The effect of altering the cycle time

We define the cycle time of operations as the interval between the departure times from Port Said of successive first southbound convoys, i.e. the cycle time is the period elapsing before the set of operations repeats itself. Figures 5.2 to 5.5 illustrate operations of the Canal based on a 24-hour cycle. It may be observed from these diagrams that for quite substantial periods of time any given point of the Canal will have no convoy passing. For example, from Fig. 5.2 at km 30 there are no vessels passing for about 11 of the 24 hours available, representing about 45 per cent of the cycle. Such 'dead time' is, of course, caused by the restrictions on passing. It would clearly be more efficient if this 'dead time' could be embedded in a longer operating period and this has prompted the idea of increasing the cycle time. It is shown below that this change in operational procedure can produce a dramatic increase in the shipping capacity. A major advantage of this method of increasing the capacity is that it has no capital cost associated with it, unlike the schemes discussed above which require massive capital investment.

To illustrate the effect of increasing the cycle time from 24 hours we consider a situation where a 48-hour cycle is used in the existing Canal. Figure 5.6 shows how it is possible to accommodate 204 standard ships in the 48-hour period, giving a capacity of 102 standard ships per 24 hours. A feature of the convoy system used is the introduction of a southbound convoy having non-stop passage from Port Said to Port Tewfik. It should be noted that in this case the amount of 'dead time' at any point in the Canal has been substantially reduced when expressed as a proportion of the cycle time. For example, at km 30 the total length of time when there are no vessels passing this point is a little over 14 hours, or less than 30 per cent of the cycle time.

When supertankers are introduced to the Canal it will be necessary to enlarge the Bitter Lakes area to allow these vessels to tie up safely in case of emergencies such as breakdown of a vessel ahead, bad weather, and accidents. This means that the storage capacity of the Bitter Lakes will not be

The shipping capacity of the Suez Canal 61

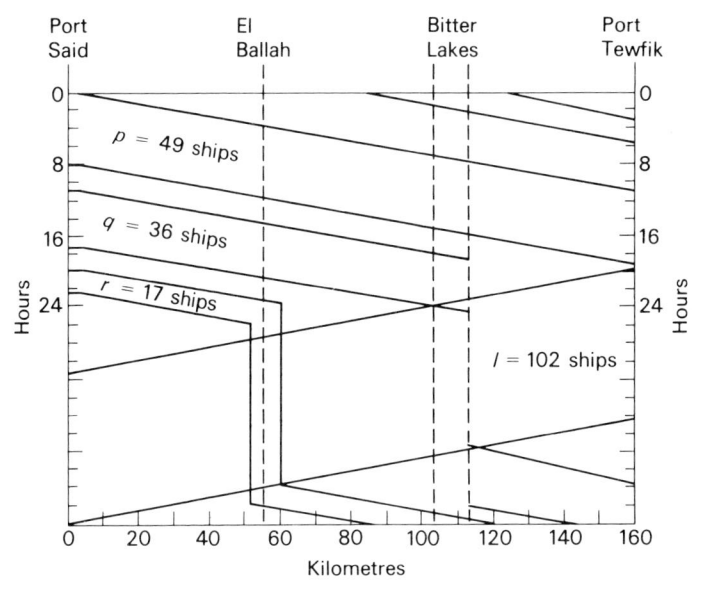

Fig. 5.6 Cycle time 48 hours. Maximum capacity 204 standard ships

restricted to 36 standard ships as postulated in the equations of page 55. Removal of this constraint results in a further increase in capacity to 111 standard ships per 24 hours, which is comparable with the better of the schemes discussed on pages 58–60.

There is no reason of course why the cycle time should be fixed at 48 hours. In general, for an n day cycle, where n is not necessarily an integer, the capacity using a three convoy system as shown in Fig. 5.2 is given by $(144 - 66/n)$ standard ships per 24 hours. This follows from solution of the following programming problem:

Maximize $l + q + r$ subject to:

$$l = q + r \qquad r \leqslant 17$$
$$q = 144n - 83 - l \qquad r \leqslant 144n - 87 - l.$$

Figure 5.7 is a graphical representation of the relationship between capacity and cycle time. It should be noted that the increase in capacity tails off rapidly for cycle times greater than two days.

From the above comments it appears highly advantageous to increase the cycle time from 24 hours if we wish to increase the capacity of the Canal. However, such a proposal has a number of disadvantages from an operational viewpoint. For example, if a 36-hour or 48-hour cycle were to be used, vessels arriving at either end of the Canal would not know precisely when the next convoy would be leaving; this is in contrast to the present system where

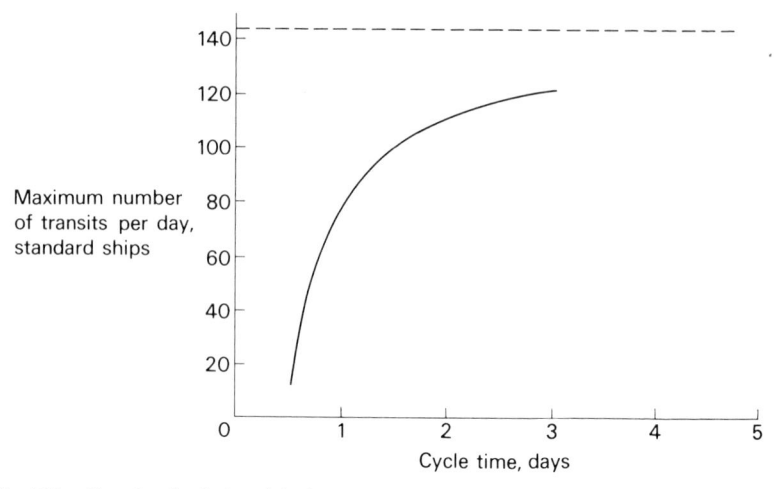

Fig. 5.7 Graph of relationship between capacity and cycle time

it is known that convoys depart at specified times each day and vessels can arrange their arrival times at the Canal to take best advantage of the situation. Clearly if vessels turn up at random with a 48-hour cycle operating, there could be substantial delays before they join the next available convoy. However, various methods of counteracting such disadvantages have been considered (for example, a timetable could be circulated to the shipping world based on a 36- or 48-hour cycle) and it is confidently expected that most objections to an operational system having a 48-hour cycle could be overcome.

Summary

Estimating the shipping capacity of the Suez Canal is a complex procedure depending on a large number of factors. For comparison purposes the capacities of the existing Canal and its proposed developments have been calculated in terms of standard ships. To cater for the levels of traffic forecast for the next twenty years or so it is probably necessary to raise the shipping capacity to a figure in excess of one hundred standard ships per day. It has been shown that this may be achieved by constructing additional bypasses to provide greater lengths of dual waterway. The most ambitious of these schemes raises the capacity to 112 standard ships per day. However, as we have seen, it is also possible to increase the capacity of the canal by the simple expedient of expanding the cycle time of operations to 48 hours — a change which raises the capacity to 111 standard ships per day with little or no capital expenditure.

References

1. Griffiths, J. D. (1977) 'The development of the Suez Canal', *Maritime Policy and Management*, 4(3): 155–166
2. Griffiths, J. D. and Hassan, E. M. (1977) 'The maximum shipping capacity of the Suez Canal', *Maritime Policy and Management*, 4(4): 303–317
3. Sewell, T. F. D. (1976) 'Towards new transit regulations on an enlarged canal', *The Dock and Harbour Authority*, July: 80–82
4. Sewell, T. F. D. (1978) 'Factors involved in developing the Suez Canal', *Bulletin Permanent International Association of Navigation Congresses*, 3: 1–18

6

Brian Lloyd

Runs and sums: the application of mathematics to the analysis of running records

Anyone interested in athletics must often have wondered about the way records have continued to topple. Can substantial improvements continue to be made? What is it that distinguishes, say, Ovett and Coe from the outstanding middle-distance runners of the past?

Not unexpectedly, human running records have provoked considerable mathematical analysis, for they represent a marvellous body of interesting data: records exist over distances ranging from 50 yards to 623 miles, and from five seconds to six days. These data are displayed in Fig. 6.1, which gives records for male runners over a variety of distances. For convenience, the distances have been partitioned into six classes. The way in which the resulting graphs approximate to straight lines is immediately evident. Figure 6.2 shows how running records have steadily improved over the last century and contains conjectures for records to be achieved in the next 20 years.

If one wants to develop a general theory for running it is essential to take into account simultaneously the whole range of records. It is, therefore, desirable to exhibit the data of Fig. 6.1 in a single graph. Clearly it would be useless to attempt to plot times ranging from five seconds to six days on the same linearly scaled axis! For that reason I have chosen in Fig. 6.3 to use logarithmic scales for time and distance. The straight line shown is a good representational summary of our biological data. We note that when the times are very small or very large the plotted points fall below the line. This is a problem that we shall later have to investigate.

Meanwhile we can summarise the information of Fig. 6.3 using a regression line, that is, a line which has the property that the sum of the squares of the distances of the plotted points from the line is a minimum. Each set of points yields two different lines depending upon our choice of independent variable. Thus we have

$$\log t = A + B \log y \tag{1}$$

and
$$\log y = C + D \log t, \tag{2}$$

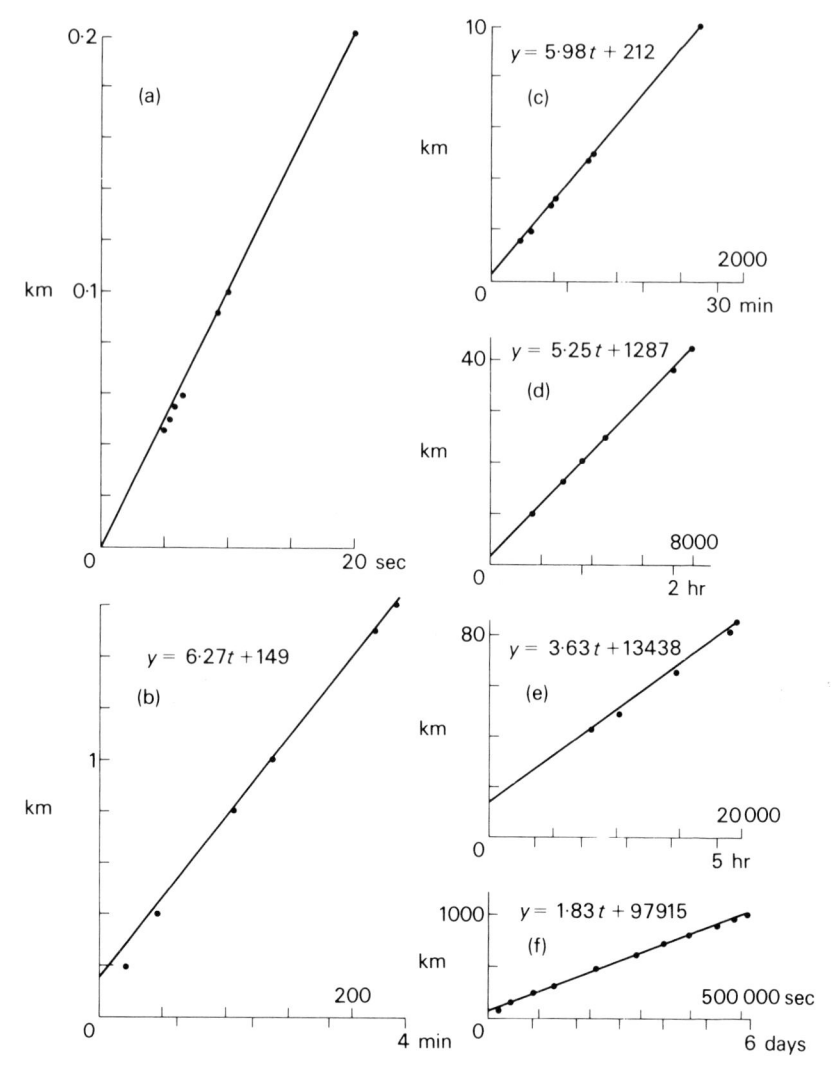

Fig. 6.1 Records for male runners, 50 yd to 623 miles, at August 26, 1965. Distance in km plotted against time in seconds on linear scales. Equations are calculated in terms of *metres* for lines through fastest points (Lloyd 1966)

Runs and sums 67

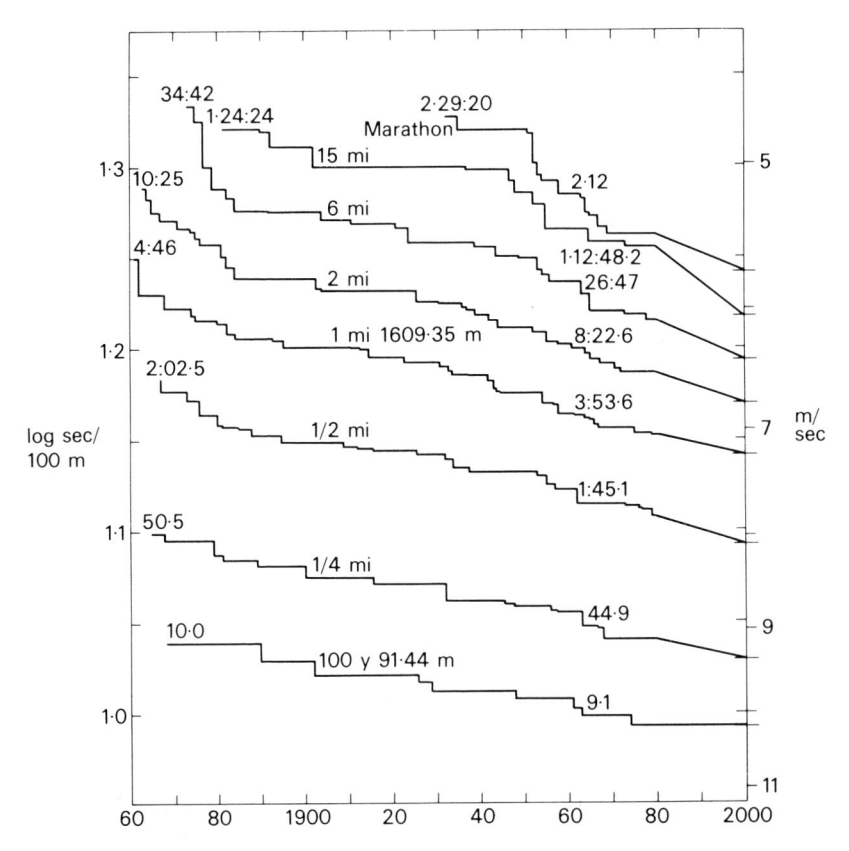

Fig. 6.2 Time trends in male running records, 1861–1965–1980–2000? The logarithm of the average time in seconds taken to run 100 m is plotted against the calendar year. The corresponding velocity in m/s on a logarithmic scale is shown on the right-hand ordinate. Times of the first and the 1965 records are written against the stepped line for each race. Points for 2000 are conjectural

where A, B, C, and D are constants, and t is the time taken to run a distance y.*

---

* Whereas mathematicians often prefer to restrict the use of letters to denoting numbers, e.g. let t be the number of seconds to run a distance y metres, scientists often include the dimensions 'within' the symbol for the variable, e.g. t is the time (measured in seconds) to run the distance y (measured in metres). Thus a scientist will write $y = vt$, where y has dimension L (length), t has dimension T (time), and v has dimension LT^{-1}. If, however, one takes logarithms and writes $\log y = \log v + \log t$, y, v, and t must be regarded as numbers. In all the calculations which follow, distance is measured in metres and time in seconds.

68 Maths at Work

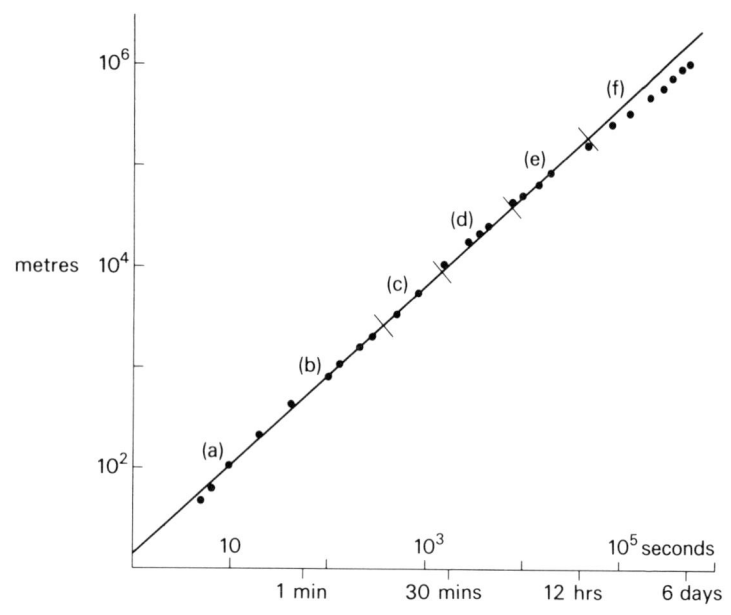

[Figure: log-log plot of distance in metres (10² to 10⁶) versus time in seconds (10 to 10⁵), with points labelled (a) through (f) lying approximately on a straight line.]

Fig. 6.3 Records for male runners, 50 yards to 623 miles, at 26 August 1965. Distance in metres plotted against time in seconds, both on logarithmic scales. Note approximate rectilinearity. Small letters correspond with the lines of Fig. 6.1. Line drawn by eye (Lloyd 1966)

Table 6.1 gives values for the parameters A, B, C, and D calculated from contemporary records in 1881 and 1981 (in the latter case for males (M) and females (F)).

Table 6.1 Comparative parameters: 1881 and 1981

	r	A	B	C	D
1 1881 (M) 100 yd to 100 mi	0.99988	−1.2687	1.1453	1.1083	0.8729
2 1981 (M) 100 m to 100 mi	0.99978	−1.2682	1.1243	1.1290	0.8890
3 1981 (F) 100 m to 50 mi	0.99973	−1.2374	1.1306	1.0957	0.8840

* The 100 mi record dates from 1882 and the marathon from 1896.

In Table 6.1 r is the correlation coefficient – a measure of the linearity of the plotted points. The correlation coefficients are, in fact, very nearly 1 – which corresponds to all the points lying on a straight line. The differences between the three lines are small, but are highly significant both statistically and scientifically.

Equation (1) gives the best prediction of time t from distance y, and by eliminating y between a pair of such equations we can predict one set of times from another, e.g. women's from men's. Thus (with subscripts corresponding to lines in Table 6.1)

$$t_3 = 1.09093 \; t_2^{1.0055}$$

and
$$t_1 = 1.05048 \; t_2^{1.0186}.$$

These equations are merely summaries of the relationships between the data. The relationship between t_2 and t_3 derives, of course, from the 1981 records. It would be interesting to see how the constants in that equation have changed over the decades for which data are available, and to prophecy whether (and when) women will eventually emulate Atalanta and overtake men!

Equations such as (1) and (2) are empirical, and provide only slight clues as to mechanism. They are also 'wrong', in that the previously mentioned deviations from the exact straight line in Fig. 6.3 are not due to experimental error or random scatter: the exact configuration of Fig. 6.3 needs an examination of mechanisms to 'explain' it.

Nevertheless, examination of equation (2), for example, allows some further insight into our problem. By rearranging,

$$\log y - \log t = C + (D-1)\log t;$$

that is,
$$\log v = C + (D-1)\log t,$$

where v is the runner's average speed. Table 6.1 shows that D ranges from 0.87 to 0.89, and taking a round figure of 0.88 we get, for a given year or sex,

$$\log v = C - 0.12 \log t,$$

in which C is a parameter increasing as records improve, and a constant for a given set of records. From this we can draw the obvious but important conclusion that, except perhaps for the shortest races, the longer a race takes, the lower is its average speed. This points to the important notion, first deduced by the Nobel prize-winning physiologist A. V. Hill (1927), that the energy needed for running comes partly from a store of energy and partly from a supply of energy which can be drawn on up to a constant maximal rate which efficient runners utilise to the full. Hill's concept is encapsulated in the equation describing the energy E available to a runner

$$E = S + Rt \tag{3}$$

where S denotes the initial store of energy and R the maximal constant supply (measured in energy per unit time, i.e. power).

We then need to consider the relation between power and running speed. This is a controversial subject, and one which is very difficult to investigate experimentally, but the most probable relationship (Lloyd 1966) is the simplest one, that

$$P = A + bmv \tag{4}$$

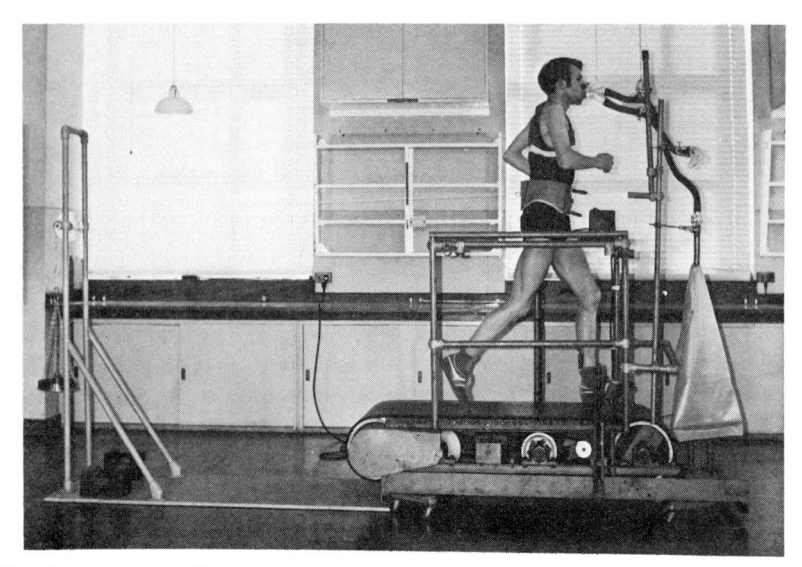

Fig. 6.4 A treadmill experiment to measure the conversion of metabolic energy into external work by John Valentine, a long distance runner

in which P is the total power expended by the runner, A is the power needed at zero speed (the standing metabolic rate) and bmv is the additional power needed to propel a runner of weight mg at speed v. The physiological parameter b represents energy per unit body mass per unit distance, so that bm has the dimensions of a force, the same force operating against the runner whatever his speed. Efficient runners have low values of m and b, and so, for given P and A, are capable of developing a high v. The effective runner will also develop a high P.

Now we can relate equations (3) and (4), for if we integrate equation (4) we obtain

$$E = \int_0^t P\,dt = \int_0^t A\,dt + \int_0^t bmv\,dt = At + bm \int_0^t \left(\frac{dy}{dt}\right)dt$$

$$= At + bmy.$$

If the run has been maximal, so that equation (3) applies, we can say

$$At + bmy = S + Rt$$

and
$$y = S/(bm) + t(R-A)/(bm). \qquad (5)$$

This equation states that for a set of maximal-effort runs in which S and R are fully used, y is a linear function of t, with an intercept $S/(bm)$ representing the distance which can be covered with energy coming from the store only.

We now have to compare this equation with the data and, if appropriate, modify or embellish it to account for the various factors entering into running records.

Let us now try to reconcile our new equations with the data displayed in Fig. 6.1 and to offer physiological explanations for the observable phenomena.

Looking at Fig. 6.1 we can see that the points representing the short races, up to 800 m, lie under the straight line of graph (b). It is apparent that the store of energy S cannot be spent instantaneously by the runner, who cannot fly through 150 or 200 m in zero time, and we posit, as a simple hypothesis, that the store delivers energy according to the equation

$$-\frac{dS}{dt} = \gamma S \qquad (6)$$

where γ is some constant. This is an exponential process, as seen in radioactive decay and first order chemical reactions, in which the rate of change (positive or negative) of a substance or a population is proportional to its quantity or size.

The equation can be integrated to give

$$S = S_0 e^{-\gamma t} \qquad (7)$$

so that at zero time the store has its original value S_0, and at infinite time is zero, all of S_0 having been used. The amount used at time t is $S_0(1 - e^{-\gamma t})$.

We can, therefore, improve equation (5) by replacing S by $S_0(1 - e^{-\gamma t})$ to obtain

$$y = S_0(1 - e^{-\gamma t})/(bm) + t(R - A)/(bm). \qquad (8)$$

Subtracting equation (8) from equation (5) gives

$$\Delta y = S_0 e^{-\gamma t}/(bm)$$

where Δy represents the extent to which the points lie below the straight line of graph (b).

Taking logarithms we get

$$\ln \Delta y = \ln(S_0/(bm)) - \gamma t \qquad (9)$$

and the linearity of an actual plot is shown in Fig. 6.5.

This good agreement between theory and practice is partly a function of the judicious choice of the straight line in graph (b), and is by no means a proof that the mechanism of the exponentially declining store is correct. As in almost all discussions of kinetic mechanisms, disagreement between theory and practice rules out the theory, whereas agreement allows the theory to survive as a working hypothesis, usually to be put to further test.

$$\Delta y = 164\ e^{-0.0397 t}$$

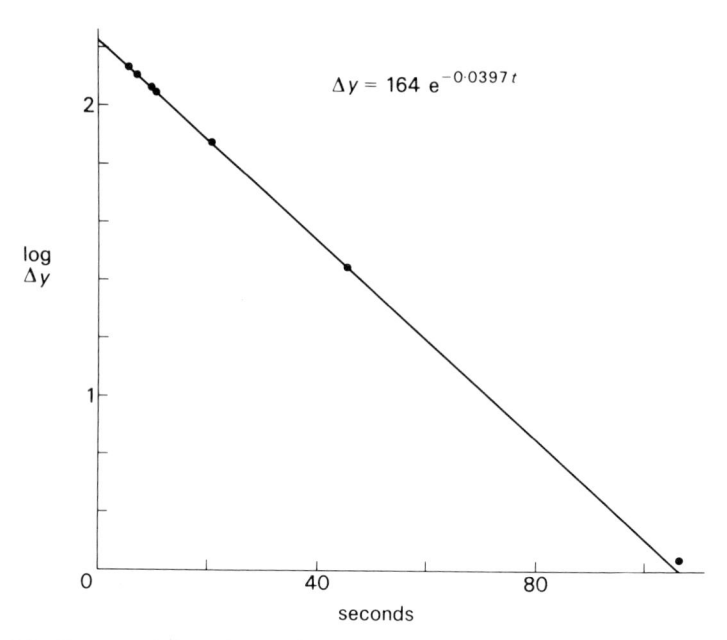

Fig. 6.5 Exponential rundown of short-term store of energy. Δy is the vertical difference between the points of Fig. 6.1(a) and (b) and the line in Fig. 6.1(b). See equation (9). (Lloyd 1966)

So far we have regarded the runner as needing energy only to cover the ground, as if he or she were running on a treadmill with a flying start. In fact, the runner has to accelerate his or her body from rest. Some energy, then, is not available for covering the ground, but must be converted into kinetic energy. The amount of energy thus required will be $\alpha m v^2/(2\varepsilon)$, where α is a unit conversion factor, ε is the efficiency of conversion of metabolic energy into kinetic energy, and v is speed.

The runner also has to overcome air resistance. It has been shown that air drag, which is turbulent, is proportional to cross-sectional area, a, air density, ρ, and the square of speed, v^2 (Hill 1928); i.e. it is $ka\rho v^2$ (where k is a constant). So the work done by the runner in a short interval of time is $ka\rho v^2 \cdot v\delta t$. Over the whole course of the race, from the start up to time t, the work done is $\int_0^t ka\rho v^3 dt$ (or $ka\rho v^3 t$ if v is assumed constant), and the metabolic energy spent is $\int_0^t ka\rho v^3 dt/\varepsilon$, ε again being the efficiency of energy conversion.

The value of the parameter ρ (air density) will be lower at a higher altitude. Thus, for example, its value in Mexico City (venue of the 1968 Olympic Games) is approximately 0.75 that at sea level.

For races of 200 m and above, part of the race track is curved, and on curves the runner has to generate the resulting horizontal centrifugal force, as well as support his own weight vertically. If the radius of the curve is r, the centrifugal force is given by mv^2/r. The combined resultant force, therefore, has magnitude $\sqrt{(m^2g^2 + m^2v^4/r^2)}$. This last term can be rewritten as $mg\sqrt{(1 + v^4/(g^2r^2))}$, which is approximately equal, by the binomial theorem, to $mg(1 + v^4/(2g^2r^2))$. Here $mgv^4/(2g^2r^2)$ is the increase in the effective weight of the runner due to the track's being curved. For running round a circular track the term bm of equation (4) is thus multiplied by $1 + v^4/(2g^2r^2)$, so that

$$P = A + bmv(1 + v^4/(2g^2r^2))$$

and
$$E = At + bmy + bm \int_0^t v^5/(2g^2r^2) dt.$$

The last term is small, and little error is introduced by replacing it with $bmv^4y/(2g^2r^2)$, in which v is the average speed (or the actual speed since the variation is so small), so that, for running on a track of which the curved fraction is f, we may multiply bm by the factor $(1 + fv^4/(2g^2r^2))$. The argument is still incomplete, since the runner expends energy according to his or her mass (e.g. in accelerating the limbs) as well as weight, but the correction obtained from this factor corresponds closely with the differences in times for 200 m runs on straight and curved tracks (about 0.3 seconds).

We are now in a position to equate total energy supply and total energy expenditure in our runner. We introduce a non-dimensional factor q (value 1 at sea level) to allow for the effects of altitude on oxygen supply, on which R is largely dependent.

$$\text{Supply} = qRt + S_0(1 - e^{-\gamma t}).$$

$$\text{Expenditure} = At + bmy(1 + fv^4/(2g^2r^2)) + \alpha mv^2/(2\varepsilon)$$

$$+ \int_0^t k\alpha\rho v^3 dt/\varepsilon; \tag{10}$$

but supply = expenditure, i.e.

$$y = t(qR - A)/B + S_0(1 - e^{-\gamma t})/B - \alpha mv^2/(2\varepsilon B)$$

$$- \int_0^t Cv^3 dt/(\varepsilon B) \tag{11}$$

in which $B = bm(1 + fv^4/(2g^2r^2))$ and $C = k\alpha\rho$.

Analysis of existing data suggests an appropriate value for bm is 64.8 cal/m for a 72 kilogram man, for $\alpha m/(2bm)$ is 0.133, and $C/(bm)$ is 0.0010125 when $a = 0.5 \text{ m}^2$ (Lloyd 1967). If we assume $q = 1$, the remaining parameters ε, $R - A$, S_0 and γ may be found graphically. However, they are best obtained by setting equation (11) up on a computer to give values of y for record values of t. These values of y are then compared with the known distances for records, and an iterative procedure can be used to alter the values of these parameters until the fit, expressed as the sum of the squares of the deviations between observed values and those derived from the equations, is minimised.

An elementary form of this procedure was used by Mr Moran and myself in 1966 on an analogue computer, and we found that the results for men between 50 yards and 1500 metres were fairly well fitted when $S_0/B = 212$ m, $\gamma = 0.0499$ s^{-1}, $(R-A)/B = 6.847$ m s^{-1} and $\varepsilon = 0.5$. The output for speed against distance for the analogue is shown in Fig. 6.6, the lower curve being scaled down for comparison with experimental data obtained for two different runners in 1927 and 1963. The surprising result is the high value of 0.5 indicated for ε, the efficiency of conversion of metabolic energy into external work, which led Mr (now Dr) R. M. Zacks and myself to attempt to measure it directly (Lloyd and Zacks, 1972(a)). The correct value for ε is still under debate.

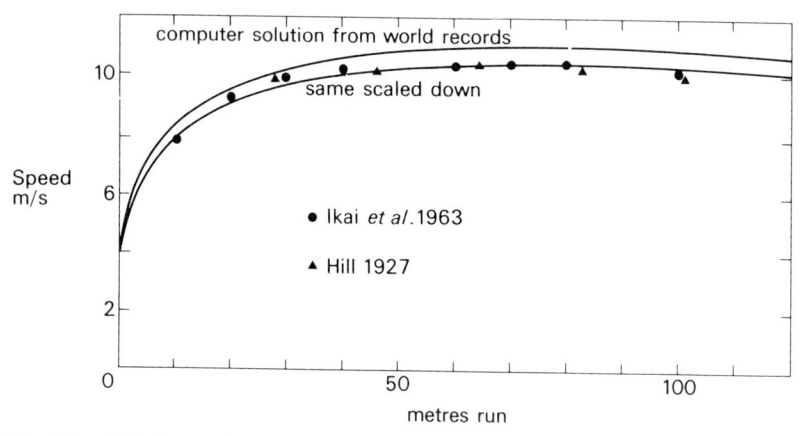

Fig. 6.6 This figure shows two actual tracings of speed against distance obtained from a PACE TR 20R analogue computer set up to solve equation (11). The upper trace represents the solution, the lower trace being scaled down to pass approximately through the points of Hill (1927) and of Ikai et al. (1963), obtained experimentally from first-class sprinters (Lloyd 1967)

Mr Zacks and I (Lloyd and Zacks, 1972(b)) have also used equation (11) as the basis for an investigation of the optimum speed–time pattern for a given race. Figure 6.7, in which v_s represents a steady, coasting speed, indicates two possible 'profiles' for a race. The runner whose profile is illustrated by path A has accelerated as quickly as possible to a maximum velocity and then gradually slowed down to a limiting velocity while still running flat out. This procedure ensures maximum usage of energy, but, because of the air drag

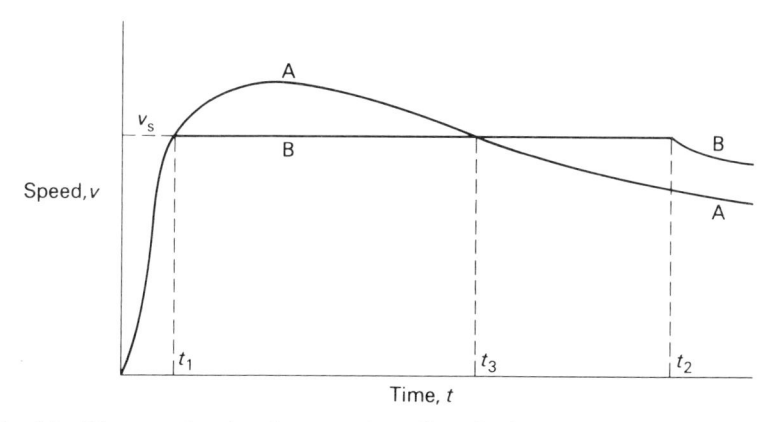

Fig. 6.7 Diagram showing time–speed profiles of a flat-out run A and a run B with steady (coasting) speed v_s. The time taken from start to reach v_s is t_1, and the times at which v_s can no longer be maintained are t_3 and t_2 on the flat-out and steady-speed runs respectively (Lloyd and Zacks 1972(b))

term in v^3, is also maximally wasteful of energy. Path B incorporates a period of coasting followed by flat-out running. While runner B wastes less energy than runner A, he also uses less and may not be faster. Mr Zacks programmed a digital computer to calculate race times at various coasting speeds. For races of 400 m and below there was no optimum, but for greater distances the optimum became progressively lower and more pronounced, indicating, for example, 800 m lap times of 48 and 55.8 seconds for a total of 1:43.8 (not attained until 1973!). Some of the results obtained are shown in Fig. 6.8.

The equation was also used with the help of Dr D. F. Mayers to predict the effect of altitude, on the assumption that R, which is partly based on oxygen uptake, would be reduced by 2.5 per cent at Mexico City, and that drag would be reduced by 25 per cent. The results are given in Table 6.2 (cf. Lloyd, 1967).

Table 6.2 The effect of altitude

Distance (metres)	100	200	400	800	1500
Prediction (seconds)	9.77	19.67	43.96	104.23	215.54
Actual result	9.9	19.8	43.8	104.3	214.9

Equation (11) has thus proved useful for describing the effects of air resistance, altitude, and track curvature, for optimisation, and for covering the problem of the start. It can also be used for wind resistance, but it fails to describe the time–distance relationships beyond the mile; the points shown in graphs (c), (d), (e), and (f) of Fig. 6.1 definitely miss the line in graph (b), and the values of R that apply to them diminish as race distances increase.

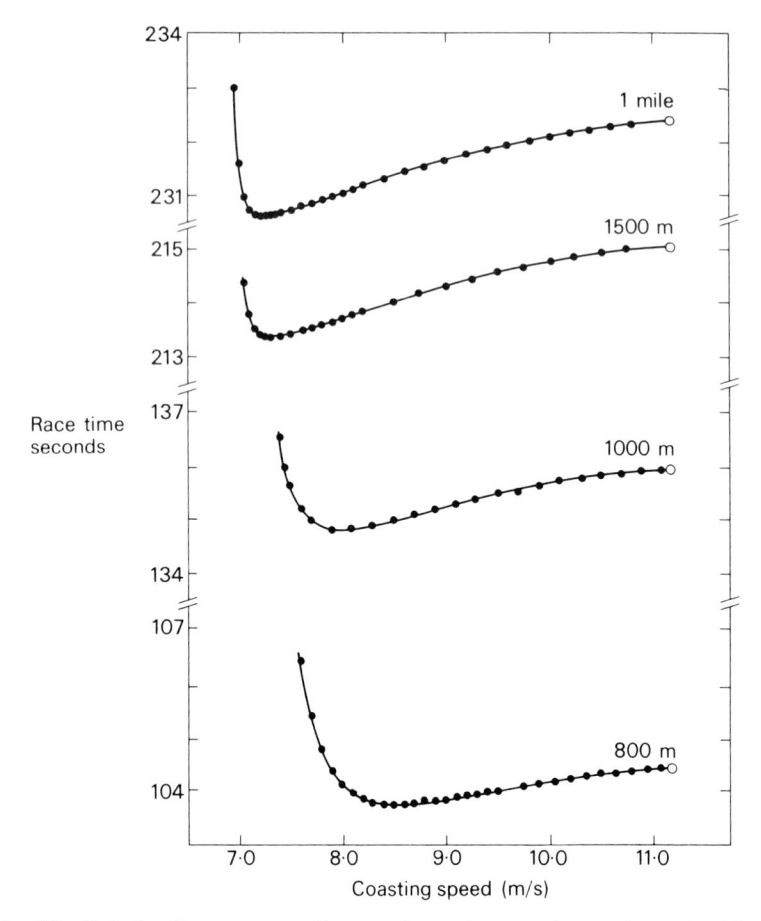

Fig. 6.8 Relation between race times and coasting speed v_s as determined by computer analysis, for distances of 800 m, 1000 m, 1500 m, and 1 mile; open circles denote flat-out runs (Lloyd and Zacks 1972(b))

It occurred to me when working on this problem in the summer of 1980 that R, instead of being truly constant, might be compounded of a lower rate of supply which went on indefinitely, R_i, and a large store, U, which broke down exponentially at a very slow rate. Thus the energy yielded in time t would not be Rt but rather $R_i t + U_0(1 - e^{-\lambda t})$. This idea was tested by a process similar to that described for equation (9). Again the very good straight-line plot obtained indicated that the hypothesis was worth persevering with.

Building this new correction into the energy balance equation, but omitting the curvature term and altitude factor, leads (with the introduction

Runs and sums 77

Table 6.3 Extrapolations of world records for men to the year 2000

Race distance (metres)	Actual time 1980	Extrapolated time 2000
100	9.95 (alt*)	9.82
200	19.72 (alt*)	19.63
400	43.86 (alt*)	42.60
800	1:42.4	1:38.8
1500	3:31.4	3:25.9
1609.35 (Mile)	3:48.8	3:42.7
3000	7:32.1	7:20.7
5000	13:08.4	12:36.9
10 000	27:22.3	26:03.8
42 195 (Marathon)	2h 8:34	2h 2:21
160 935 (100 miles)	11h 30:51	10h 38:9
Distance covered in 1 hour	Actual 1980 20 944 m	Extrapolated 2000 21 988 m

* alt: at altitude

Table 6.4 Extrapolations of world records for women to the year 2000

Distance (metres)	Time Actual 1980	Extrapolated 2000
60	7.2	6.87
100	10.88	10.77
200	21.71	21.35
400	48.60	45.49
800	1:53.5	1:44.42
1500	3:52.47	3:42.13
1609.35 (Mile)	4:21.7	4:00.94
3000	8:27.2	8:02.27
5000	15:08.8	13:52.84
10 000	31:45.4	28:46.31
42 195 (Marathon)	2 h 27:33	2 h 14:36.8

of new simplified coefficients) to the equation

$$y = s(1 - e^{-\gamma t}) + u(1 - e^{-\lambda t}) + pt - 0.133\, v^2/\varepsilon$$
$$- 0.0010125 \int_0^t v^3 \mathrm{d}t/\varepsilon. \qquad (12)$$

Considerable work with Dr T. Gethins using this equation on the computer, has suggested that of the six parameters for men, s (215.1), u (51 250), λ (0.0000737), and ε (0.75) do not seem to have changed over the century. γ (0.0404) seems not to have changed over the last half-century, whereas p, reflecting the capacity to use oxygen, seems to have increased from under 2 to 2.78, and by linear extrapolation against time will reach 3.06 in 2000 A.D. The comparable values for women are s 251.2, u 51 250, λ 0.0000633, ε 0.75, γ 0.029, p 2.38 in 1980 and 2.95 in 2000. We are thus able to suggest possible record times for the year 2000 and these are given in Tables 6.3 (for men) and 6.4 (for women).

To obtain these forecasts we have had to use sets of six parameters, representing such factors as the efficiency of converting metabolic energy to external work and the capacity to use oxygen, each set being derived from records established by ten or so athletes. No individual has, or probably could have, parameters that match any one such set. It is indeed possible, perhaps likely, that in a population of athletes some parameters are negatively correlated. It would be interesting to obtain the parameters for individual athletes and to see the effects of training and development on particular parameters.

References

1. Hill, A. V. (1927) *Muscular Movement in Man: the Factors Governing Speed and Recovery from Fatigue*, McGraw-Hill, New York
2. Hill, A. V. (1928) 'Air resistance to a runner', *Proc. Roy. Soc. (Biol.)*, 102: 380
3. Ikai, M., Shibayama, H. and Ishii, K. (1963) 'A kinesiological study of sprint running', *Jap. Res. J. Physl. Educ.*, 7: 59
4. Lloyd, B. B. (1966) 'The energetics of running: an analysis of world records', *Brit. Ass. Advmt. Sci., Lond.*, 22: 515
5. Lloyd, B. B. (1967) 'Theoretical effects of altitude on the equation of motion of a runner', in R. Margaria (ed.), *Exercise at Altitude*, Excerpta Medica Foundation, Amsterdam, pp. 65–72
6. Lloyd, B. B. (1982) 'Athletic achievement – trends and limits', in G. Thomas and B. Davies (eds), *Science and Sporting Performance*, Oxford University Press, Oxford
7. Lloyd, B. B. and Zacks, R. (1972a) 'The mechanical efficiency of treadmill running against a horizontal impeding force', *J. Physiol.*, 223: 355
8. Lloyd, B. B. and Zacks, R. (1972b) 'Theoretical optimization of time–velocity relationships in running short and middle distances', *Arch. Fisiol.*, 69: Suppl. p. 494

7 G. Maycock

Traffic flow in roundabouts

Roundabouts are familiar to road users in the UK as simple, maintenance-free means of traffic control at road junctions. They are one of the safest forms of junction available to the practising traffic engineer. This chapter describes how mathematical methods are used to design roundabouts so that their ability to handle traffic (their traffic capacity) matches the expected traffic flow in some future year. Such numerical design methods are important economically because if the junction is over-designed (too large for the traffic wishing to use it), money is wasted on unnecessary construction costs, and if the junction is under-designed, traffic queues will form and users will be subjected to excessive delays.

Design background

Modern roundabouts come in all shapes and sizes. Figure 7.1 shows a single-level 'conventional' roundabout. Here the approach roads join a common

Fig. 7.1 A single-level 'conventional' four-arm roundabout

80   Maths at Work

Fig. 7.2 A three-arm 'mini roundabout'

circulating carriageway around a central island which is usually between 30 and 60 metres in diameter. Sometimes roundabouts similar to that illustrated in Fig. 7.1 form part of a more complex interchange where one or more of the approach roads 'flies over' (or under) the roundabout. Roundabouts which form a part of a motorway interchange are of this type, and some can have central island diameters as large as 200 metres. At the other extreme of size are 'mini-roundabouts'. Figure 7.2 shows a mini-roundabout at a small three-way junction in which the central island is no more than a white disc painted on the road. In between the roundabouts illustrated in Figs 7.1 and 7.2 there is a 'continuum' of designs each of which has a varied mixture of geometric features – island diameter, width of circulating carriageway, approach road width, amount of 'flaring' at the entry, and so on – all of which may affect the traffic handling capability of the design.

Before considering just what geometric features do affect the traffic handling capability of a roundabout, it is of background interest to consider why the designs should be so diverse. The first 'traffic circles' were used in France and America shortly after the turn of the century, but they were taken up seriously in England in the following decades. Design rules for roundabouts were formalised in the 40s and 50s, and these rules were based on the 'weaving' principle. Prior to 1966 there was no 'give-way' rule at roundabouts; traffic entering the roundabout had equal status with that circulating around the central island. The operating principle of these early designs was that the entering and circulating streams of traffic merged together in the roundabout, weaving downstream of the entry so as either to be in a position to take the next exit (on the left) or to continue circulating

Fig. 7.3 A 'locked' roundabout (Leeds 1962) prior to the introduction of the 'Give way to the right' rule

around the island to exits further round. This system worked well enough whilst the traffic flows were not very high, but when the roundabouts became busy, there was a tendency for the roundabout to 'lock', as shown in Fig. 7.3. Traffic wishing to enter the roundabout (or leaving it for that matter) is prevented from doing so by a stationary queue of vehicles completely encircling the central island.

One way of reducing the probability of 'locking' is to increase the size of the roundabout, and during the 50s and early 60s roundabouts were built with long parallel-sided 'weaving sections' (the sections between entries and exits) often around non-circular central islands. However, during this period, the search for a solution to the 'locking' problem was on in earnest. Various methods using traffic signals were tried, but the simplest and most effective turned out to be the now familiar 'give way to traffic from the right' rule (called the 'priority' rule from now on). The priority rule meant that traffic already in the roundabout had the right of way, and could therefore always exit freely from the roundabout. Approaching traffic only entered the roundabout when there were gaps for them in the circulating flow, otherwise they queued in the approaches. The priority rule, which was introduced nationally in November 1966, was therefore a radical change in the way roundabouts operated.

Having solved the locking problem, it was then possible to reduce the central island size without the risk of the junction blocking. Even before the priority rule was adopted generally in the UK, experiments on roundabouts with very small central islands (soon to be called 'mini-roundabouts' – it was the era of the mini-skirt!) had been undertaken (in 1964). The first mini-roundabout was tried on a public road in 1968 and in the following decade they were to be taken up by many local authority traffic engineers as a simple and cheap means of improving both the traffic capacity and safety at a range of existing junctions.

Roundabout flow — definitions

In order to describe in mathematical terms what happens at a roundabout, we shall first consider flow in an individual entry. Later in the chapter we shall consider the roundabout as a whole.

Figure 7.4 shows a single entry to a roundabout in which traffic is queueing to enter the circulating carriageway. The figure is in fact a 'snapshot' of the entry at an instant of time, for in reality vehicles are continuously moving into the roundabout circulation from the head of the queue (taking gaps between circulating vehicles), whilst the tail of the queue is being replenished by vehicles arriving from the approach road. Thus the queue can be thought of as being generated by the difference between the number of vehicles which arrive at the rear of the queue within a given time, and the number which discharge into the roundabout in the same time. The former is called the 'demand' flow (q) and the latter the 'saturated entry' flow (q^s) – a 'saturated entry' being one at which there is a queue present. Both q and q^s are measured

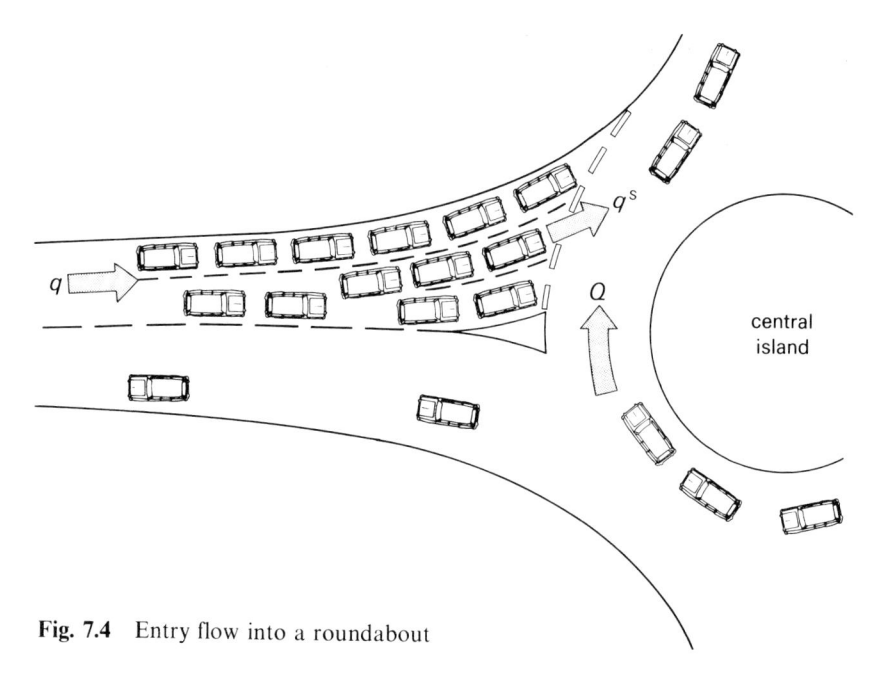

Fig. 7.4 Entry flow into a roundabout

Traffic flow in roundabouts 83

in units of vehicles per unit time (usually per hour), and are averaged over a sufficiently long period of time (at least one minute and preferably much longer) to smooth out the effects of individual vehicle departures.

When calculating junction capacity, flow, in vehicles per hour, is not an adequate measure because it does not properly take into account the difference between a private car and a goods vehicle. For this reason, in the context of junction capacity, pcu's (passenger car units) are often used, in which case a goods vehicle (a vehicle with more than four tyres) is regarded as being the equivalent of two cars. Thus the flow of x cars and y goods vehicles per hour becomes a combined flow of $x+2y$ pcu's per hour.

If q (demand flow) $> q^s$ (saturated entry flow) a queue will form. (In fact, the queue will grow at an average rate of $q-q^s$ vehicles each hour; however, for the present purpose we are not concerned with the actual queue length.) It is important to note that under saturated conditions, q and q^s are not generally equal; q^s is the smaller of the two. If $q < q^s$, the entry is said to be 'unsaturated' and there will be periods of time when the queue falls to zero. Under unsaturated conditions, all the traffic arriving from the approach enters the roundabout with only temporary delays, and the flow joining the roundabout circulation equals the demand flow q.

Now q^s (the saturated entry flow) will result from individual drivers accepting gaps between vehicles already circulating in the roundabout. These circulating vehicles will form the 'circulating flow' designated Q in Fig. 7.4. It is clear that as Q increases, the time gaps between circulating vehicles will on average decrease, so that fewer drivers waiting at the give-way line will be able to enter the roundabout; q^s will thus decrease.

The simplest relation that might connect Q and q^s is a linear one, and it (fortunately) happens that the equation,

$$q^s = F - fQ \tag{1}$$

illustrated in Fig. 7.5, proves a good practical representation of traffic behaviour at real roundabout sites. We shall consider the implications of this in the next section.

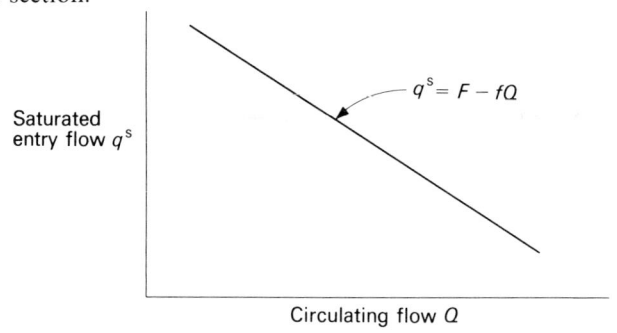

Fig. 7.5 Relationship between entry flow and circulating flow

Roundabout entry flow — measurement and prediction

In order to design a roundabout to cope with a particular level of traffic flow, a designer must be able to determine the entry/circulating flow relationship (Fig. 7.5) for each entry of a particular design from the geometric features of the layout. Research at the Transport and Road Research Laboratory has resulted in the establishment of relationships of the form given by equation (1), where the constants F and f are determined by the roundabout entry geometry, road widths, 'flares', etc. The derivation of such predictive relationships has involved two techniques:
(a) track experiments
(b) public road observations.

Fig. 7.6 An experiment in progress on the TRRL test track (September 1980)

Figure 7.6 shows a track experiment in progress on the Transport and Road Research Laboratory's test track at Crowthorne. The part of the test track used for traffic experiments consists simply of a large open area on which full scale junction designs can be laid out using moveable white kerb markers. Members of the public, with their cars, are hired from the local area to drive through the test junctions. All the parameters of the tests are controlled — traffic flows, turning movements, queueing conditions, and layout geometry. By changing the geometry from test to test, varying the volume of the circulating flow (Q) within each test, and measuring the corresponding saturated entry flows (q^s), it is possible to trace out the entry/circulating flow relationships of Fig. 7.5. Fig. 7.7 shows two

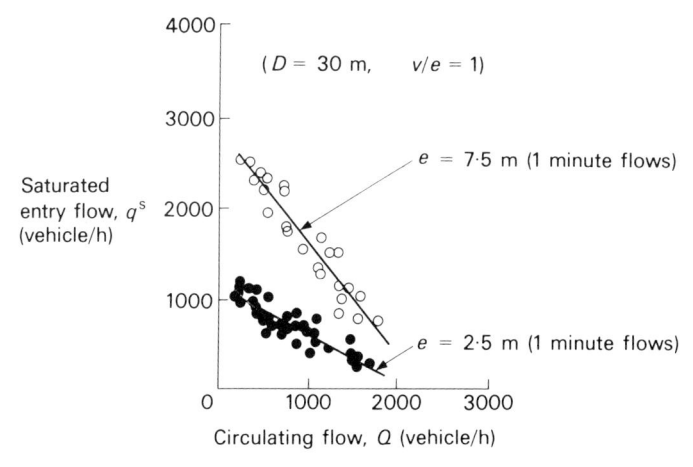

Fig. 7.7 Entry flow–circulating flow relationships obtained on the TRRL test track

examples obtained during track tests in the summer of 1976, and illustrates the effect of varying one geometric parameter, the width of entry, e. The roundabout under test was a typical small roundabout with an overall diameter of 30 m, and the figure shows the entry/circulating flow relationships for the two widths of entry 2.5 m and 7.5 m (i.e. one lane or three lane entries). The diagram illustrates how well defined the track test results are, and gives an indication of the linearity of the entry/circulating flow relationship. The track test technique has been used to study the effect of the principal geometric variables, namely, entry width, entry flare (in the case of entries which widen towards the give-way line), approach road width, width of the circulating carriageway, and overall roundabout size.

Of course, the track tests are bound to be artificial to some extent, since the test drivers are not a random sample of all road users, and test driving conditions are rather special. So the track tests are used solely to indicate what the dependencies should be between the traffic and geometric variables, and the resulting relationships are calibrated by means of public road studies.

The public road studies consist of finding a large number of roundabout entries which are operating at capacity (i.e. with queues — usually during either a morning or an evening peak) and recording, on a minute-by-minute basis, pairs of values for saturated entry flow q^s and circulating flow Q. The sites must cover as wide a range of geometries as possible, from mini-roundabouts to large 'conventional' roundabouts. Guided by the relationship obtained on the test track, multiple linear regression methods (using a standard statistical computer package) are then used to extract from the public road data the best relationship for predicting q^s. In the case of the roundabout studies, 86 sites were covered and something like 11 000 saturated minutes of roundabout entry operation studied.

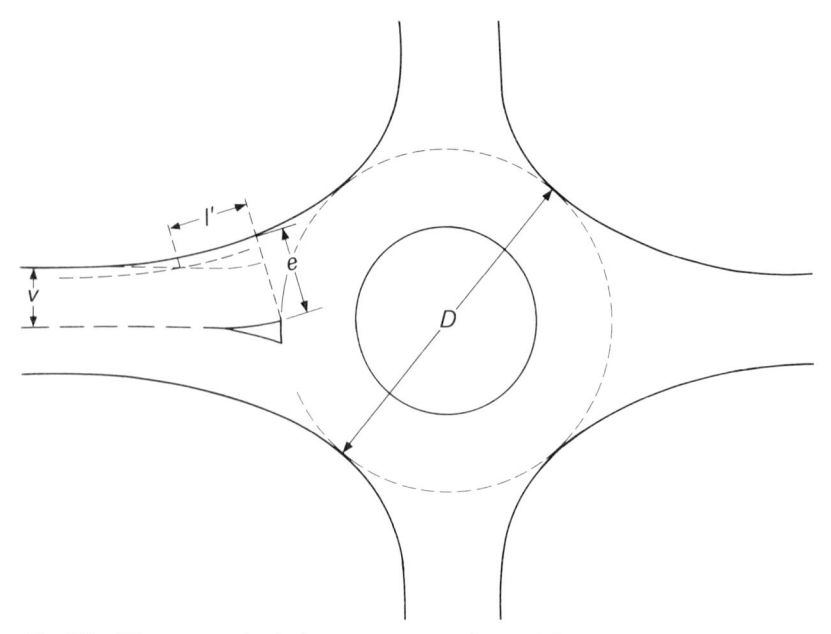

Fig. 7.8 The geometric design parameters of roundabouts

The final predictive equation was

$$q = k(F - fQ) \qquad (2)$$

where k is a correction factor which takes account of two minor geometric variables (the entry angle and the entry radius) and which may be taken as 1 for the 'average' site,

$$F = 303 \, x_2$$
$$f = 0.21\{1 + 0.5/(1 + \exp((D-60)/10))\}(1 + 0.2 \, x_2)$$

where
$$x_2 \text{ (the effective entry width)} = v + \frac{e-v}{1+2S}$$
and
$$S \text{ (the sharpness of flare)} = 1.6\frac{(e-v)}{l'}.$$

e, v, l', and D are defined in Fig. 7.8.

(For a further description of the derivation of this formula and for more precise definitions of the geometric parameters, the reader is referred to reference 2.)

Three features of the above formula are worth emphasis.

(a) The effective entry width*, x_2, is the major determinant of roundabout entry capacity. The characteristics of x_2 can be seen by reference to the algebraic definition given above in terms of e, v, and S. The sharpness of flare factor, S, is a measure of the rate at which the extra width provided by a flare over the normal approach road width (i.e. $e-v$) is developed (see Fig. 7.8). Sharp flares have large values of S (up to a practical maximum of about 3) and gradual flares have small values of S (down to 0). So the effective entry width, x_2, equals the approach road width (v) plus the extra width ($e-v$) multiplied by an 'efficiency of use' factor $\left(\dfrac{1}{1+2S}\right)$. The 'efficiency of use' factor varies from 1 when $S=0$ (i.e. the extra width is very effectively used when the flare is infinitely gradual, in which case $x_2 = e$, the entry width) to about 0.14 when $S=3$ (the extra width is very inefficiently used for sharp flares, in which case $x_2 \to v$, the approach road width).

(b) The overall size of the roundabout defined in terms of D, the inscribed circle diameter (see Fig. 7.8), has been incorporated in the expression for the slope of the entry/circulating flow relationship (f) in a way which reflects the public road observations that for identical entry geometries, large roundabouts have flatter entry/circulating flow relationships than do smaller roundabouts. The form of this correction factor is such that it is asymptotic to observed values at both high and low extremes of the value of D.

(c) There are some geometric variables (notably width of the circulating carriageway and visibility distances) which are not included in the above formula. This does not mean that such dimensions are not important in design, indeed geometric design standards published by the Department of Transport specify what value these parameters should take. It does mean, however, that for roundabouts designed according to the accepted geometric standards, the particular variables omitted from the formula do not contribute significantly to the prediction of entry/circulating flow relationships.

The roundabout as a whole

On page 82 we defined and discussed flow at one entry of a roundabout and indicated how the entry/circulating flow relationship may be predicted from the geometry. But by the very nature of the operation of a roundabout, the

---

* Note that entry width is regarded as a continuous variable, it having been demonstrated by track and public road studies that 'saturation flow' is roughly proportional to width and is not greatly affected by lane markings. This somewhat surprising result emphasises the importance of basing models on practical data.

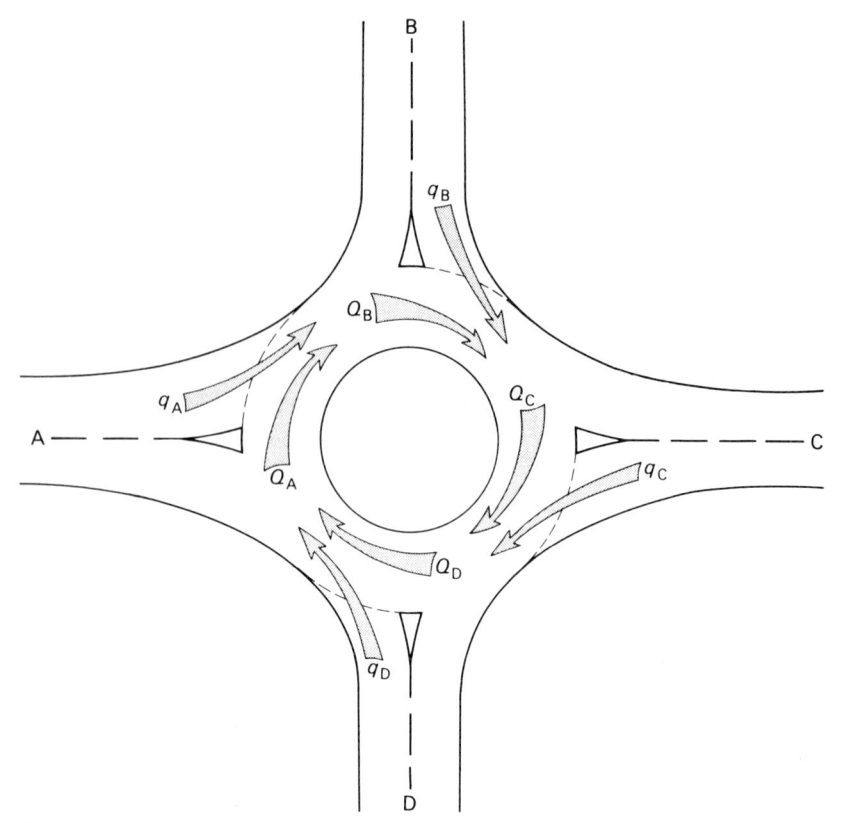

Fig. 7.9 Interacting flows on a four-arm roundabout

entries do not operate independently. Consider the four-arm roundabout illustrated in Fig. 7.9. We will designate the arms as A, B, C, D, the entry flows (the q's) as q_A, q_B, q_C, q_D, and the corresponding circulating flows as Q_A, Q_B, Q_C, Q_D.

Once vehicles from an entry lane have joined the circulating carriageway, they become part of the circulating flow for subsequent entries. The actual values of the circulating flows Q_A, Q_B, Q_C, and Q_D will thus depend on the actual entry flows and the turning movements drivers wish to make. We will quantify the turning movements in terms of the average proportions of the entering traffic which will take the first, second, third, etc. exit. We will denote these proportions by $p_{N,M}$ where N and M represent the labels appropriate to the entry and exit arms respectively. Thus, for example, the left turn proportion from arm A on the four-arm layout of Fig. 7.9, will be $p_{A,B}$, and the right turn proportion from arm D will be $p_{D,C}$, etc. U-turns would be designated $p_{A,A}$ etc.

Traffic flow in roundabouts 89

Clearly then, for arm A (Fig. 7.9):

$$p_{A,B} + p_{A,C} + p_{A,D} + p_{A,A} = 1$$

Now, if the traffic entering from arm A is q_A (or perhaps q_A^s if the entry is saturated), then the actual traffic flow for each of the turning streams from arm A are $q_A p_{A,B}$, $q_A p_{A,C}$ etc or $q_A^s p_{A,B}$ etc for saturated conditions. Similarly for other entries. It is now possible to write down the values of the circulating flows crossing any entry in terms of the flows entering the other arms of the roundabout and the turning proportions, by determining which turning streams combine to form the relevant value of Q. For example, assuming that there are no U-turners (for descriptive simplicity), Q_A consists of the straight-through movement from arm D (i.e. $q_D p_{D,B}$) and the right turn movements from arms C and D (i.e. $q_C p_{C,B}$ and $q_D p_{D,C}$). Algebraically:

$$Q_A = q_C p_{C,B} + q_D (p_{D,B} + p_{D,C}).$$

We may now substitute this value of Q_A in the entry/circulating flow equation (equation (2)) for arm A:

$$q_A^s = F_A - f_A Q_A$$

where F_A and f_A are the arm-specific values of F and f obtained by substituting the geometric parameters for arm A into equation (2) (and we have taken $k = 1$).

Assuming that the roundabout is fully saturated (i.e. all arms are queueing), we would obtain for arm A:

$$q_A^s = F_A - f_A(q_C^s p_{C,B} + q_D^s (p_{D,B} + p_{D,C})).$$

Similar expressions would be obtained for the other arms, so that for a four-arm roundabout with no U-turners, rearranging the above form of the equation slightly, would give:

$$q_A^s + f_A p_{C,B} q_C^s + f_A (p_{D,B} + p_{D,C}) q_D^s = F_A$$

$$f_B(p_{A,C} + p_{A,D}) q_A^s + q_B^s + f_B p_{D,C} q_D^s = F_B$$

$$f_C p_{A,D} q_A^s + f_C (p_{B,D} + p_{B,A}) q_B^s + q_C^s = F_C$$

$$f_D p_{B,A} q_B^s + f_D (p_{C,A} + p_{C,B}) q_C^s + q_D^s = F_D.$$

The above set of simultaneous equations can be solved to provide estimates of q_A^s, q_B^s, q_C^s and q_D^s. These values will be the entry flows for a fully saturated roundabout of given geometry and for a specified set of turning movements. Obviously if the geometry of any arm changes, or the turning movements change, a different set of entry flows would result.

Now, in practice it is rare for all entries to a roundabout to be queueing at once, although it does occasionally happen. If, having calculated the saturated entry flows, q^s, as above, it is discovered that demand flow, q, on one or more entries is less than q^s, then the original assumption that those entries were saturated was wrong: those entries for which $q < q^s$ are unsaturated. When an entry is unsaturated, the flow into the roundabout simply equals the demand flow, and the entry/circulating flow dependency disappears. The equation appropriate to the unsaturated arm (say arm N) in the above set of simultaneous equations is replaced by

$$q_N^s = q_N \text{ (demand)}$$

and the new set of equations could be solved to obtain estimates of the roundabout entry flows.

Computer methods

The last section set out how the entry flows in a fully saturated roundabout could be calculated algebraically. It also suggested how, in principle, it is possible to deal with the situation when one or more of the arms is unsaturated. However, the algebraic solution of the unsaturated case can lead to complications in the way the equations are formulated and solved, because reducing the entry flow at one arm once it has been discovered to be unsaturated will alter the capacities available to all other entries, and the problem becomes interactive. For computer application, therefore, it is more practical to use the iterative technique described below.

Consider the roundabout shown in Fig. 7.9, for which the entry/circulating flow relationships have been determined for each entry using equation (2). Start at entry A, and assume initially that $Q_A = 0$. Calculate q_A^s from the entry/circulating flow relationship for arm A (it will equal simply F_A in this case). If this entry flow is greater than the demand flow, q_A, for that arm (a constant figure specified as input), take the value of q_A as the actual entry flow from arm A. Subtract from the actual entry flow (q_A^s or q_A, whichever is the less) the traffic turning left from arm A (i.e. $q_A p_{A,B}$) and the remainder becomes Q_B. Having now obtained a value for Q_B, the entry flow from arm B can be obtained as q_B^s (calculated from the entry/circulating flow relationship for arm B) or q_B (demand), whichever is the less. Subtracting left-turners from arm B gives an estimate of Q_C. So the process moves around the roundabout several times, recalculating at each cycle revised estimates for both q's and Q's until convergence is achieved, that is, until the differences between successive estimates are practically negligible. Normally only three or four iterations are required. From the 'final' values of Q_N, an estimate of q_N^s can be obtained by substitution in the appropriate entry/circulating flow relationship.

The algorithm described in the previous paragraph for calculating capacities has been incorporated into a computer program called ARCADY

(Assessment of Roundabout Capacity And DelaY). The program (see reference 1) not only calculates flow in any specified roundabout using the methods described in this chapter, but also calculates average queue lengths. The calculation of queue lengths requires detailed information about the way traffic flows during a peak period vary with time, and is beyond the scope of this chapter. (For a full treatment of queues and delays at road junctions, the reader is referred to reference 3.) However, calculations of saturation flows, queues and delays, can be used by designers both to optimise the physical layout of the roundabout, and to strike the correct 'economic' balance between construction cost on the one hand and traffic delays on the other. Accordingly, the techniques outlined in this chapter form a part of the Department of Transport's recommended method for the design and appraisal of roundabouts.

[*This chapter was contributed by permission of the director of the Transport and Road Research Laboratory.*]

References

1 Hollis, E. M., Semmens, M. C. and Denniss, S. L. (1980) 'ARCADY: a computer program to model capacities, queues and delays at roundabouts', *Department of the Environment, Department of Transport, TRRL Report LR 940*, Crowthorne (Transport and Road Research Laboratory)
2 Kimber, R. M. (1980) 'The traffic capacity of roundabouts', *Department of the Environment, Department of Transport, TRRL Report LR 942*, Crowthorne (Transport and Road Research Laboratory)
3 Kimber, R. M. and Hollis, E. M. (1979) 'Traffic queues and delays at road junctions', *Department of the Environment, Department of Transport, TRRL Report LR 909*, Crowthorne (Transport and Road Research Laboratory)

8

Ian Flindell

Sound mathematics: measuring noise annoyance

Major developments such as new airports and motorways have a considerable potential for causing noise annoyance, yet to protect people against noise can be very expensive. A balance has to be struck between permitting and preventing noise. Unfortunately, people differ in their opinion on what constitutes a noise annoyance. It is important, then, to be able to assess and to model how a typical community reacts to different degrees of noise exposure.

What makes this area of research interesting is that there are many ways of measuring noise exposure and people's reactions to it. Those who study community noise will, therefore, need to know about the physics of sound, psychology, and mathematical modelling. This chapter describes in simple terms some known features of community noise and presents an example of recent work carried out at the Institute of Sound and Vibration Research, Southampton University, to develop models for predicting overall annoyance responses to environments in which more than one potentially objectionable noise source is present.

The problem

Community noise is an area where research is still necessary. A simple decibel reading of the noise level due to an aircraft flying overhead will rarely be sufficient to predict how people will feel about the noise. What are the effects of the duration of the noise and how many times does it occur in the day? Is it predominantly low or high frequency? Are there any other noises which dominate it?

Also important are questions relating to the people exposed to the noise. What are they doing when the noise is present? Are they trying to sleep, carrying out everyday chores, or perhaps a bit of do-it-yourself work with an electric drill? These are just some of the parameters that could be taken into account in a mathematical model which attempts to relate community response to noise exposure.

The role of this research is to formulate suitable models and then test them by means of field surveys or laboratory experiments. The objective is normally to find the simplest model that will relate community response to noise exposure. Field surveys are carried out by interviewing a large number of people and finding out the average response to noise at various measured noise exposure levels. In laboratory experiments people are asked to listen to precisely controlled noises and their responses are measured. Field surveys have the advantage that actual responses are obtained, whereas it is often difficult to be certain that the results of laboratory experiments can be applied to practical experience. However, the results of field surveys can be contaminated or confounded by other variables, for example, the socio-economic class of the respondents, which is often reflected in the geographical area in which the noise occurs. Laboratory studies can, to some extent, avoid such a bias as there can be greater control of these other variables.

The major difficulties in research stem from the problems of measurement and from the need to devise improved models. The task of dreaming up a new model is a creative one but can be considerably assisted by a study of existing models. The task of measurement is painstaking but benefits from a methodical approach.

Annoyance

There are many effects of noise, each of which requires a different model to relate response to noise exposure. In this chapter we shall concentrate on annoyance registered by the community as a whole. Annoyance measures enable an integrated judgement to be made of all the many specific interferences and disturbances that noise causes. For example, one person might consider it important that the noise interferes with his ability to listen to his hi-fi system, whereas another might be more worried about difficulties in going to sleep. People can express degrees of annoyance without displaying the physical symptoms of being annoyed, often because they have had to force themselves to live with noise nuisance through having no alternative. In laboratory experiments people don't actually get annoyed! They merely compare the noise exposures against their experience and make relative judgements of the annoyance potential of the noise to which they are subjected.

The most direct way of measuring annoyance is to use a rating scale which has named or numbered categories, ranging from no annoyance to extreme annoyance. The laboratory subject or field survey respondent is asked to select a category which best corresponds with his or her degree of annoyance. The average annoyance of a group of subjects or respondents can be determined by taking the mean or median of the individual annoyance ratings. (Category scales using words have to have numbers assigned to each category. This procedure can introduce distortion to the analysis of results, particularly if the category names have not been chosen carefully. For example, is 'quite a lot' closer to 'very much' than to 'a little', or is it exactly in between?)

Simple models

Models to relate general community annoyance to noise exposure can be simple or complex, depending on the number of noise exposure parameters that are taken into account. The simplest model that can be proposed is that annoyance is proportional to noise level. More complex models take into account the frequency components of the sound, the number and duration of noise events, and even the number of noise sources present (aircraft and road traffic noise, for example).

Fig. 8.1 illustrates the simple model that annoyance is proportional to noise level. (Noise levels are normally measured in decibels (db).) Sound waves consist of rapid fluctuations in air pressure, which propagate in a similar fashion to the waves formed when a stone is thrown into a pond, although at a much faster rate. Now the average pressure in any sound wave

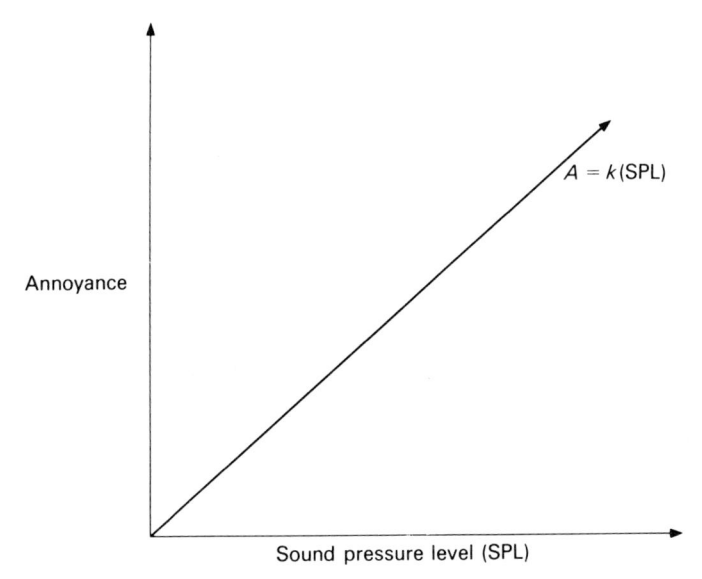

Fig. 8.1 A simple model of annoyance

is zero, because positive and negative halves of the wave cancel out when averaging. To avoid the problem of the average pressure being zero, the rms (root mean square) pressure is used. The unit of rms pressure is the pascal, one pascal being an rms pressure of one newton per square metre.

The ear has a very wide sensitivity range to different rms pressures. The quietest sound that a healthy young adult can hear is approximately 0.00002 pascals, and the threshold of pain is reached somewhere above 20 pascals, thus covering a range of 1 000 000 to 1. The energy, or power, of a sound wave is proportional to the rms pressure squared, thus the sensitivity of the human ear covers a power range of 10^{12} to 1.

Now, the ear is sensitive to a change of 0.0001 pascals at very low sound levels but a change of even 0.1 pascals would not be detectable at very high levels because the ear is sensitive to proportional changes rather than absolute changes. The use of the decibel scale conveniently accommodates this phenomenon, and is designed such that a five decibel change sounds approximately the same at all sound levels.

Sound pressure level (SPL) expressed in decibels is given by:

$$\text{SPL} = 10 \log_{10} \left(\frac{p}{p_0}\right)^2 \text{ decibels} \quad (1)$$

where p = rms pressure (pascals) and p_0 = reference rms pressure (taken to be 0.00002 pascals). Thus the SPL is simply the logarithm of the ratio of the rms pressure of a sound to a reference rms pressure, multiplied by a convenient constant. Fig. 8.2 illustrates the typical SPLs and rms pressures of a selection of sounds.

Sounds can have different frequency components present. They may be of predominantly high or low frequency, or of all frequencies. The human ear, however, is not equally sensitive to all frequencies. It is most sensitive to tones at around 3 to 4 kHz, that is tones having frequencies of 3000 to 4000 cycles per second. A curve called the A-weighting curve is normally used in order to describe this differential frequency sensitivity. An electrical filter is built into most sound level meters (instruments for measuring SPLs) in order to make the instrument less sensitive to very low and very high frequencies. The shape of the curve of frequency sensitivity is shown in Fig. 8.3.

We can, then, improve our simple model by taking relative frequency sensitivity into account, and by assuming that annoyance is proportional to the A-weighted SPL. (We shall make use of the A-weighting curve throughout the rest of this chapter.) The time-varying A-weighted SPL is given by $L_A(t)$ where

$$L_A(t) = 10 \log_{10} \left(\frac{p_A}{p_0}\right)^2$$

p_A being the A-weighted rms pressure.

Sound mathematics

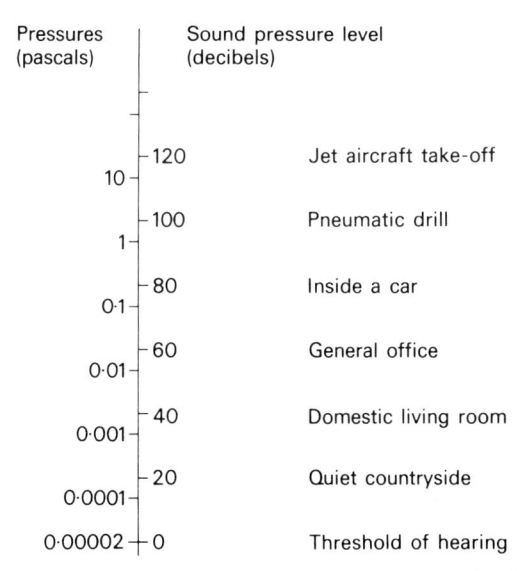

Pressures (pascals)	Sound pressure level (decibels)	
10	120	Jet aircraft take-off
1	100	Pneumatic drill
0·1	80	Inside a car
0·01	60	General office
0·001	40	Domestic living room
0·0001	20	Quiet countryside
0·00002	0	Threshold of hearing

Fig. 8.2 Typical sounds, sound pressures, and sound pressure levels

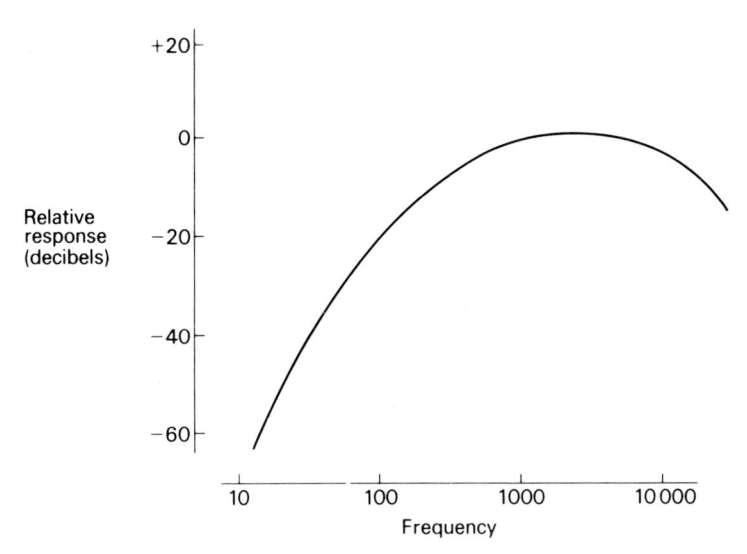

Fig. 8.3 A-weighting filter

Most sounds vary in SPL with time. Aircraft and railway noise, for example, are rarely audible all the time, even at sites very near to airports or railway lines, whereas distant road traffic noise tends to have a relatively constant SPL. The Equivalent Continuous Sound Level (L_{Aeq} — the subscript A denotes the use of the A-weighting) is the result of averaging the SPLs over an 18- or 24-hour day to give a single figure noise descriptor. The L_{Aeq} (measured in decibels) is given by:

$$L_{Aeq} = 10 \log_{10} \left[\frac{1}{T_2 - T_1} \int_{T_1}^{T_2} 10^{(L_A(t)/10)} dt \right] \quad (2)$$

where $[T_1, T_2]$ is the time interval being considered.

Thus to obtain L_{Aeq} one integrates the A-weighted rms pressure (pascals) squared over the time interval being considered, finds the average per unit time, and then converts back to decibels by taking the logarithm. It is left as an exercise for the reader to examine the relationship between $10^{(L_A(t)/10)}$ and the A-weighted rms pressure squared (pascals squared).

The L_{Aeq} is in fact the steady noise level which would have the same energy over the given time period as the sound under consideration. Fig. 8.4 illustrates the relationship between L_{Aeq} and typical aircraft and road traffic noises. The next more complex model, therefore, is based on the assumption that annoyance is proportional to the L_{Aeq} of the noise.

The overall L_{Aeq} of any environment where there is more than one noise present can be found from equation (2) by rewriting it so that

$$10^{(L_{Aeq}/10)} = \frac{1}{T_2 - T_1} \int_{T_1}^{T_2} 10^{L_A(t)/10} dt.$$

Hence for a number of different noises we have

$$10^{(L_{Aeq_1}/10)} + 10^{(L_{Aeq_2}/10)} + \ldots = \frac{1}{T_2 - T_1} \int_{T_1}^{T_2} (10^{L_{A_1}(t)/10} + 10^{L_{A_2}(t)/10} + \ldots) dt$$

and so

$$10 \log_{10}(10^{(L_{Aeq_1}/10)} + 10^{(L_{Aeq_2}/10)} + \ldots) = 10 \log_{10} \left(\frac{1}{T_2 - T_1} \int_{T_1}^{T_2} (10^{L_{A_1}(t)/10} + \ldots) dt \right)$$

Now the integral on the right is, from equation (1), just L_{Aeq} overall, and so we obtain

$$L_{Aeq} \text{ overall} = 10 \log_{10} [10^{(L_{Aeq_1}/10)} + 10^{(L_{Aeq_2}/10)} + \ldots] \quad (3)$$

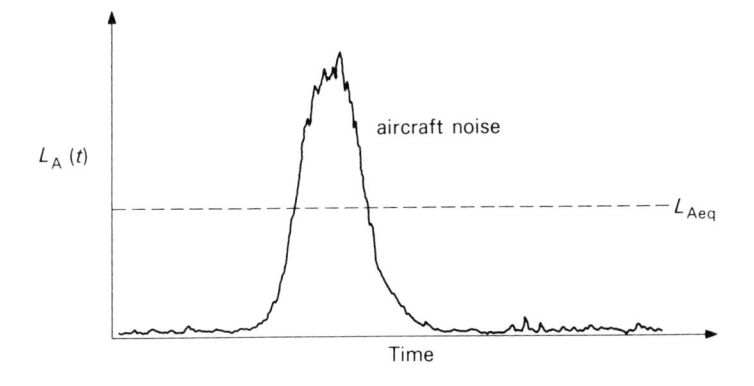

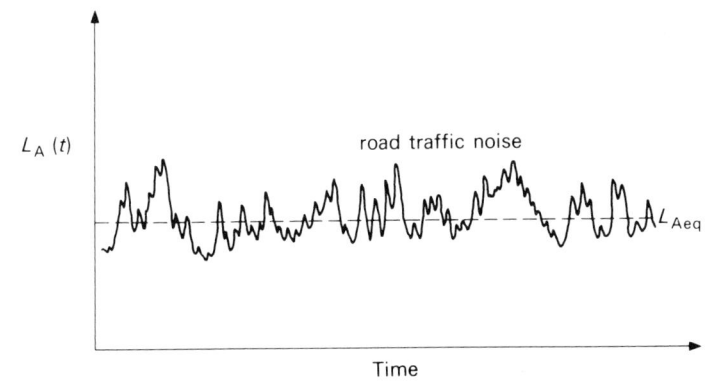

Fig. 8.4 L_{Aeq} and typical noises

where L_{Aeq_1}, L_{Aeq_2}, ... are the L_{Aeq}s of the various noise sources.

This formula represents the addition of the intensities of the separate noises. (Intensity is the rms pressure squared.) In physical terms the intensity of any combination of noises is simply the sum of the intensities of the contributing noises.

Unfortunately, we know from the results of various field studies that annoyance is not the same for different noise sources which have the same L_{Aeq}. Further, overall annoyance where there is more than one noise source is greater than implied by the overall L_{Aeq}. Therefore L_{Aeq} is not a complete answer to the many problems of noise assessment. The next section describes more complex models that have been devised to improve on L_{Aeq}.

Complex models

Powell, working at the NASA Langley research centre in Virginia, USA, devised a summation and inhibition of annoyance model (see reference 1) in order to account for the enhanced annoyance of multiple noise source environments. His model assumed that the annoyance due to each noise source would be inhibited by the presence of other noise sources and the overall annoyance would be the sum of these separate inhibited noise source annoyances. The equations governing inhibition and summation were very complex and need not be produced here. However the model is illustrated by the lower curve in Fig. 8.5. The 'cusps' are artefacts of the mathematical expression of Powell's model and are not important.

One can represent relative annoyance due to different noises by drawing contours of 'constant annoyance' as in Fig. 8.5, in which corrected L_{Aeq}s (see below) for each of two noise sources are measured along the axes. Starting at the left hand side of the graph, overall annoyance is completely dominated by source 1 because source 2 is at a very low level. As we move to the right, source 2 gradually starts to have more influence until, at the point of subjective equivalence of the two noise sources (shown by the straight line), both have to be at lower L_{Aeq} levels than either source alone would have to be in order to give the same annoyance. Then moving further still to the right, source 2 completely dominates the overall annoyance. Fig. 8.5 also shows the different effects of the Powell model and the overall corrected L_{Aeq} model.

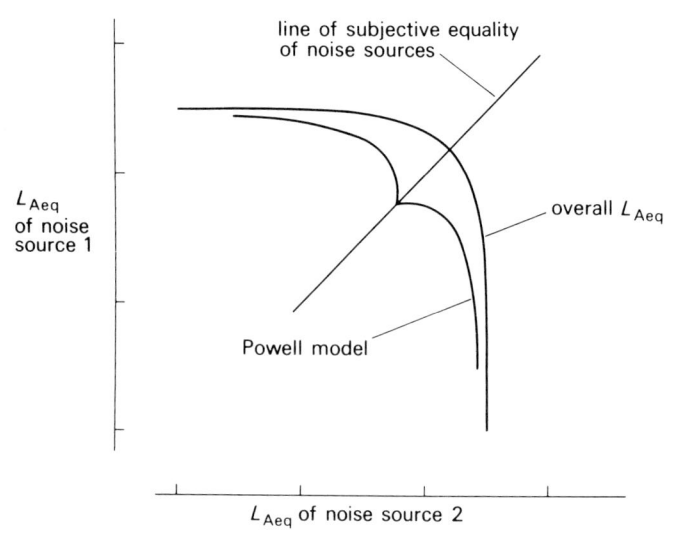

Fig. 8.5 Contours of constant annoyance

For example, on the line of subjective equality of noise sources, the Powell model gives the same overall annoyance as the L_{Aeq} model at lower levels (which in turn implies a prediction of higher annoyance at the same noise level).

Fig. 8.5 also shows the overall L_{Aeq} of two contributing noise sources. This figure assumes that the two noise sources produce equal annoyances at similar L_{Aeq}s. In fact, different noise sources tend to produce different annoyances at similar L_{Aeq}s. This can be taken into account by subjectively weighting the L_{Aeq}s. For example, suppose that road traffic noise gives an annoyance of x at an L_{Aeq} of y, and aircraft noise gives an annoyance of x at an L_{Aeq} of z. The corrected L_{Aeq} for the aircraft noise, is obtained by adding $(y - z)$ to the aircraft noise L_{Aeq}. Hence, the two noise sources produce similar annoyances at similar corrected L_{Aeq}s (assuming of course, that the correction for the road traffic L_{Aeq} is zero).

The overall corrected L_{Aeq} is now given by

$$L_{Aeq} \text{ overall} = 10 \log_{10}(10^{(L_1 + D_1)/10} + 10^{(L_2 + D_2)/10} + \ldots) \qquad (4)$$

where $L_1, L_2, \ldots$ are the L_{Aeq} levels of sources 1, 2, … and $D_1, D_2, \ldots$, the subjective weightings to the L_{Aeq} levels of sources 1, 2, ….

The Powell model can also be applied by using corrected L_{Aeq}s for each of the contributing noise sources. The subjective weightings are illustrated in Fig. 8.6 for road traffic and railway noise. It is possible to carry out

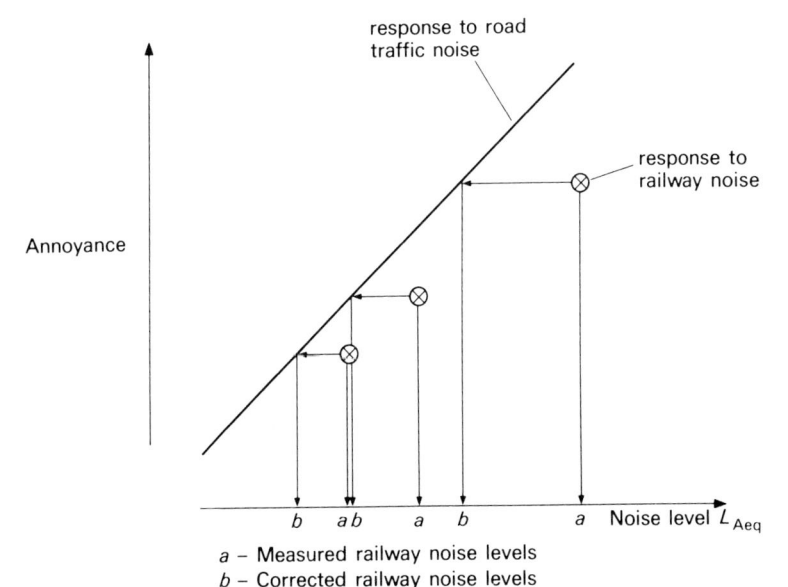

Fig. 8.6 Subjective weightings

experiments involving people's annoyance reactions to a range of exposure levels from two noise sources to see which model fits the data better. Generally speaking, the model which gives the greater correlation coefficient between the noise exposure measure and the subjective response measure is the better model. There are certain problems involved in interpreting correlation coefficients however, and the reader should always be cautious now that correlation analysis is available on most scientific calculators.

Experiments

Experiments can be carried out in order to compare the models. A simulated domestic living room is furnished and provided with concealed loudspeakers. Volunteers sit in the room and are exposed to tape-recorded noises. After listening to the noises for, typically, ten minutes, they are asked to complete an annoyance questionnaire. Each volunteer listens to a number of different noises. The order of presentation of the noises is varied for different volunteers according to a pre-arranged scheme in order to avoid biassing the results.

In such an experiment we used noises of road and railway traffic. These were recorded at varying distances from the sources in order to achieve a range of recorded noise levels. The results, shown in Fig. 8.7, tended to support the use of the Powell model as opposed to overall corrected L_{Aeq}.

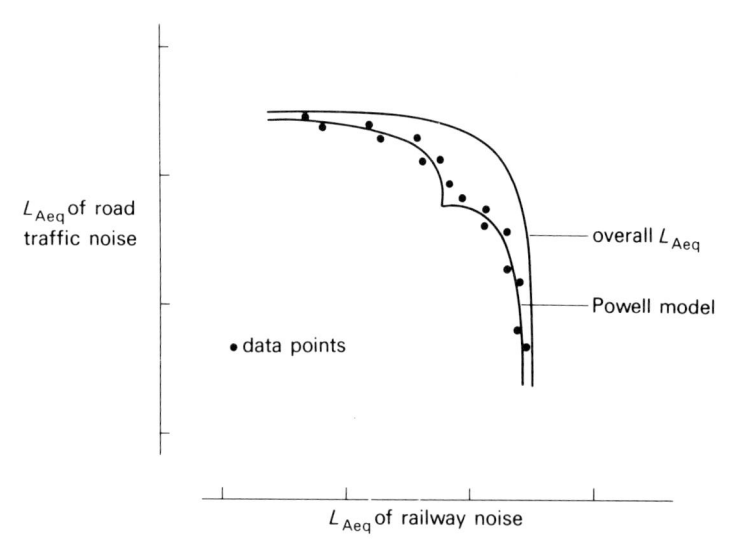

Fig. 8.7 Results of experiment on contours of constant annoyance

However, as stated above, the Powell model is very complex and it was therefore decided to search for a simpler model which would fit the data as well or even better. The resulting model was termed Community Annoyance Potential (CAP), in deference to Dr C. A. Powell, who devised the Powell model.

The CAP model

This model is based on the commonsense assumption that below a certain noise exposure level annoyance is minimal, and above a much higher noise exposure level annoyance is at a maximum. The overall corrected L_{Aeq} and Powell models work in decibels and thus imply that annoyance increases by the same amount when going from 60 to 70 dB as when going from 20 to 30 dB or from 100 to 110 dB. The CAP model has an S-shaped relationship between annoyance and noise exposure (expressed in decibels) so that increases at very high or very low noise levels make relatively little difference to the annoyance responses. It is illustrated in Fig. 8.8. CAP for a separate noise source is given below.

$$\mathrm{CAP} = \frac{10^{(L_A - 66)/(10\sqrt{2})}}{10^{(L_A - 66)/(10\sqrt{2})} + 1} \tag{5}$$

where L_A is the decibels level of the noise source.

Thus CAP has the convenient property that it is very small when L_A is small, equals 0.5 when L_A is 66 dB, and is close to 1 when L_A is large. It is not

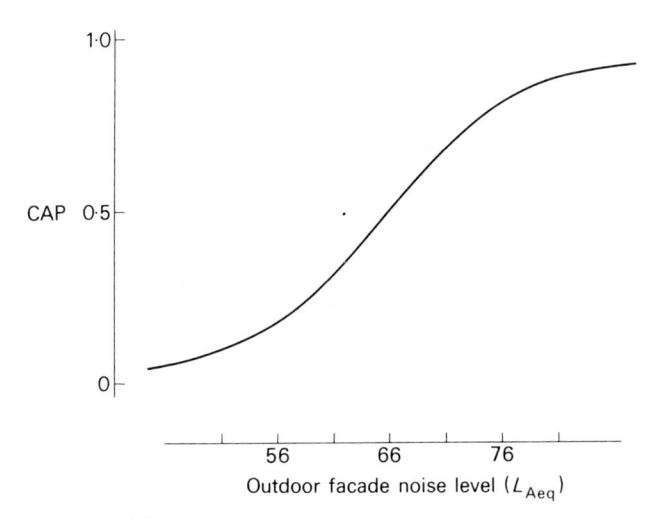

Fig. 8.8 CAP model

necessary to use decibel measures, the CAP can be calculated directly from the average rms pressure (pascals) using a reference level of 0.04 pascals instead of 66 dB. The reader is invited to derive the expression for CAP using average rms pressure instead of decibel measures.

The CAP model assumes that the overall annoyance response to two or more noise sources is proportional to the sum of the average rms pressures (pascals) from the noise sources. The CAP overall can be calculated from the CAPs of the separate noise sources (CAP_1 and CAP_2) by using the equation given below (the reader might also like to check this!).

$$CAP\ overall = \frac{\left(\left(\frac{CAP_1}{1-CAP_1}\right)^{1/\sqrt{2}} + \left(\frac{CAP_2}{1-CAP_2}\right)^{1/\sqrt{2}}\right)^{\sqrt{2}}}{\left(\left(\frac{CAP_1}{1-CAP_1}\right)^{1/\sqrt{2}} + \left(\frac{CAP_2}{1-CAP_2}\right)^{1/\sqrt{2}}\right)^{\sqrt{2}} + 1} \quad (6)$$

This equation can be programmed without difficulty into a pocket calculator in order to find CAP overall from CAP_1 and CAP_2. However, it is exceptionally difficult to find a solution for either CAP_1 or CAP_2 given the other two unknowns. If any reader wishes to attempt such a solution they should first derive the following equation to obtain the average rms pressure ($\overline{rms\ p_A}$) from CAP.

$$\overline{rms\ p_A} = 0.04 \times \left(\frac{CAP}{1-CAP}\right) \quad (7)$$

where 0.04 relates to 66 dB SPL.

A much easier method of finding a solution for either CAP_1 or CAP_2 when CAP overall is known is to use a nomogram. This is shown in Fig. 8.9. The nomogram has three scales for CAP_1, CAP_2, and CAP overall. Any two scales should be picked off at the appropriate points, then a straight line through the two defined points gives the appropriate value on the third scale where it crosses that scale.

The CAP model was tested to see how well it fitted the laboratory study data for road and railway traffic noise. Fig. 8.10 shows equal annoyance contours for the CAP model, the Powell model, and the overall corrected L_{Aeq} model. Remember that the Powell model fitted the data better than the overall corrected L_{Aeq}. It will not escape attention that the CAP model closely approximates to what the Powell model would be if its 'cusps' were smoothed out. In fact, the CAP model fits the data slightly better than the Powell model because of the elimination of the cusps, and gives a slightly higher correlation coefficient.

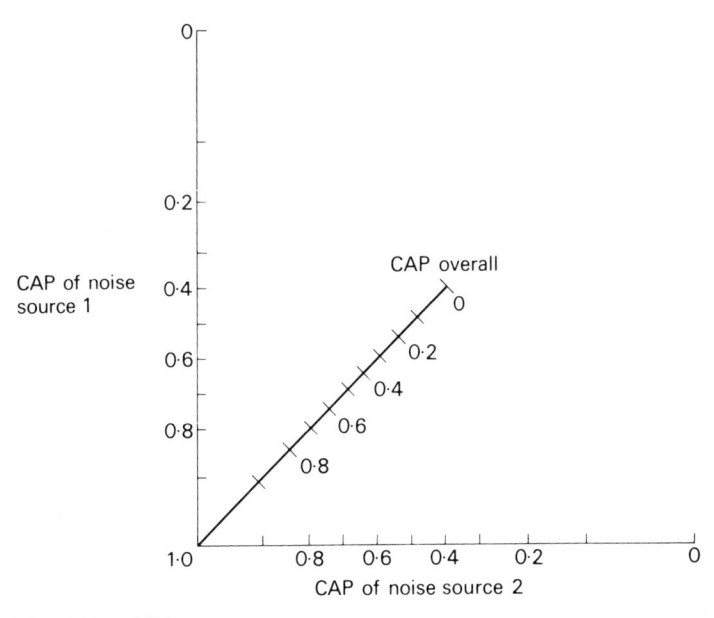

Fig. 8.9 CAP addition nomogram

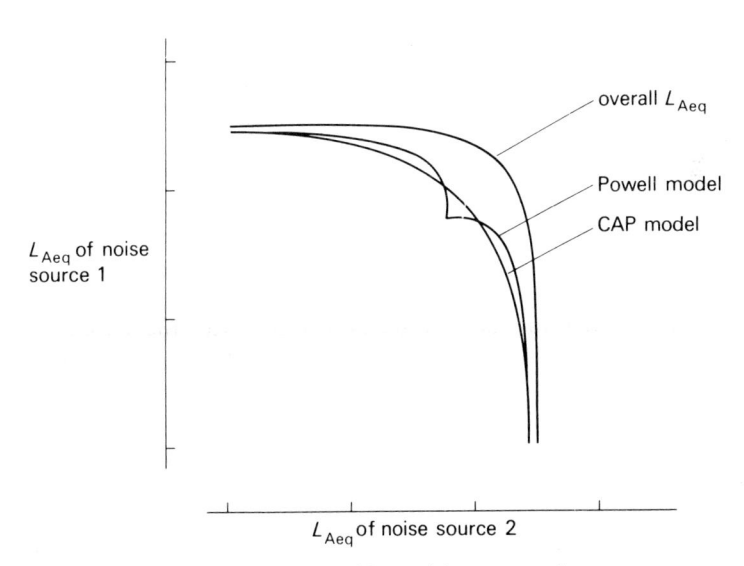

Fig. 8.10 Overall L_{Aeq}, Powell and CAP models compared

The general model

It is not good practice to adopt any new procedure for noise assessment solely on the basis of the results of one laboratory experiment, so the new model was tested in a further experiment and by reanalysing other published data. The CAP model was supported by some data but not by others. In the latter cases it was possible to devise plausible hypotheses to explain the discrepancies. Unfortunately, these hypotheses required further work in order to test them, work which has not yet been carried out.

However, a valuable step forward was made during the process of data reanalysis. The assumptions behind the CAP model were (a) that there is an S-shaped relationship between annoyance and noise exposure expressed in decibels, and (b) that overall annoyance is proportional to the sum of the average rms pressures of each noise source. Now, the overall L_{Aeq} model assumes that overall annoyance is proportional to the sum of the average intensities of each noise source, and reflects the purely physical addition of noises. The CAP model reflects a psychological addition of the annoyances caused by the noises, such that the annoyance of any combination is greater than implied by the physical sum of the intensities.

It occurred to me that the assumption of an S-shaped relationship between annoyance and noise exposure was not terribly important, since most noise problems occur within the approximately linear portion of the CAP curve. The assumption that annoyance is proportional to the sum of the average rms pressures, rather than rms pressure squared, led to yet another model. This is merely the CAP model expressed in decibels but has the advantage of being very similar to the widely used L_{Aeq}. A new measure, pressure L_{Aeq} (pL_{Aeq}), is defined by:

$$pL_{Aeq} = 20 \log_{10} \left[\frac{1}{T_2 - T_1} \int_{T_1}^{T_2} 10^{(L_A(t))/20} dt \right]. \quad (8)$$

Notice it is exactly the same as equation (2) for L_{Aeq} except that all the multipliers and divisors change from 10 to 20.

The pressure sum (psum) is given by:

$$\text{psum} = 20 \log_{10} \left[10^{(pL_{Aeq_1})/20} + 10^{(pL_{Aeq_2})/20} + \ldots \right]. \quad (9)$$

Again equation (9) is the same as for overall L_{Aeq} (equation (3)) except that all the multipliers and divisors change from 10 to 20. The procedure is used by first evaluating the pL_{Aeq}s of all separate noise sources present, and then adding the pL_{Aeq}s together using the psum formula. The resulting expression in equation (9) correlates as highly as the CAP model with overall annoyance, yet avoids the use of complex equations or nomograms. Subject to the further work mentioned above, it is very likely that this new procedure may actually be adopted in noise control regulations in the future.

Reference

1 Powell, C. A. (1979) 'A summation and inhibition model of annoyance response to multiple community noise sources', *NASA Technical Paper 1479*, (United States National Aeronautics and Space Administration, Scientific and Technical Information Branch).

9

Stephen Shennan

Disentangling data

Why on earth should an archaeologist want to use mathematics? This is a question which is frequently asked when people hear that archaeologists have been known to make use of mathematical techniques. To understand the reasons it is necessary to examine the way in which archaeologists make inferences about the past, and indeed what it is they try to infer.

The public view of archaeology tends to concentrate on a very limited part of it, the part which is most visible. The most obvious of an archaeologist's activities is excavation, and the problems which arise here are such things as understanding marks in the soil, recording where finds come from, disentangling and recording the layers in a stratified deposit, or just organising the labour force. These are the kinds of operation with which most people imagine the archaeologist is concerned.

Prior to excavation the question arises as to how the sites which are to be excavated are discovered in the first place. The remarkable efficacy of aerial photography in certain circumstances is widely known, but survey on the ground is equally important. Remains of ancient pottery and flint tools are, in many places, simply lying on the surface waiting to be picked up by those who know what to look for. After survey or excavation the objects recovered are catalogued, cleaned, studied, and put in museums, a sight with which everyone is familiar.

The description I have just given immediately prompts a series of questions: What is it all for? Why does the archaeologist go to all that trouble? What are his or her aims? Given those aims, how does the archaeologist use excavation or survey records and catalogues of finds, to make inferences about the past?

I would like to begin by looking at aims. Until relatively recent times archaeologists were mainly concerned with putting things in chronological order, establishing sequences of different types of pots, different types of houses, or different types of metalwork, for example. Once such sequences were established, the reasons for the changes were not investigated. Instead, on the basis of a largely implicit theory of the reasons for cultural change established at the beginning of this century, they were assumed. In European

Fig. 9.1 Radiocarbon dating

One of the ways in which statistical concepts came into archaeology was through the use of radiocarbon dating, a method devised by the American scientist Willard Libby in the 1940s for which he later received the Nobel Prize.

Atoms of the radioactive isotope of carbon ^{14}C are formed in the upper atmosphere of the earth and enter the food chain in the course of photosynthesis as plants assimilate atmospheric carbon dioxide. Living organisms are in equilibrium with the atmospheric concentration of ^{14}C, but when death occurs intake ceases and the ^{14}C in the surviving tissues, such as wood or bone, starts to decay at a constant rate. The quantity of ^{14}C left in the tissue is then directly proportional to the time which has elapsed since the tissue died. As radioactive decay is a random process there is a limit to the accuracy of radiocarbon dates, depending on the number of radioactive breakdowns recorded by the counter in a finite period. The errors are expressed in the form of the standard deviation and all dates are officially published as a mean with an associated standard deviation value.

King Arthur's Round Table in the Great Hall of the castle at Winchester (pictured here) was recently dated by this technique. The date has not yet been officially published but it appears that the table dates not to Arthurian times, the fifth or sixth centuries A.D., but to the first half of the fourteenth century A.D.

(The above account of radiocarbon dating is derived from Burleigh, R. (1980), 'Dating and dating methods', in A. Sherratt (ed.), *The Cambridge Encyclopaedia of Archaeology*, Cambridge University Press, 416–432)
Photograph E. N. Lane

Disentangling data 111

prehistory, specific innovations were assumed to derive from the more advanced civilisations of the Near East, and here and in other parts of the world general changes in assemblages of archaeological material were assumed to result from the replacement of one people and its culture through invasion by another people from elsewhere, which brought in its own culture. It was very often a case of 'passing the buck': every specialist in a particular period and area would always claim that everything came from next door, of which very little was known because of lack of research.

About 25 years ago things began to change. The appearance of radiocarbon dating — an absolute method of dating which was independent of archaeologists' ideas — meant that dating became rather less of an archaeological problem. Furthermore, the results which it brought contradicted a lot of the archaeologists' ideas about dating. If these were incorrect, then the assumptions on which they were based were open to doubt. The suspicion began to arise that the archaeological record was much more complicated than had been thought. In particular, an attack was mounted on the idea that changes in the archaeological record were simply the result of a changing sequence of peoples, each with their own ideas about, for example, how pots should be made, or houses should be built. An argument was put forward which sounds very sensible and straightforward now, although it was revolutionary in its context. It was suggested that the archaeological record is the result of past human behaviour, that the behaviour was affected by many different factors, but that there is no reason in principle why, from a study of the material remains, it should not be possible to reconstruct the behaviour and infer the reasons for it. No reason in principle perhaps, but of course there were and are plenty of difficulties in practice.

What I would like to do is to show which procedures were involved in attempting to realise these aims in a particular case, focussing particularly on the question of whether the variation observed in the archaeological material can be explained in terms of the social organisation of the people who created the archaeological remains which we have recovered. In recent years, attempts to reconstruct the pattern of social change in prehistory, when we have no written records, have become increasingly numerous, as it has been realised how important it is for an understanding of our past. This seems, and is, a daunting task, when we consider peoples known from modern anthropological studies, where all the richness of life is present, and contrast what is known about them with the archaeological evidence which they might leave. Nevertheless, examination of such cases does give us some hope. For example, we learn that in many societies, individuals of differing age, sex, and social status are characterised by different types of dress and ornament, and that often these items are deposited with them in their graves when they die. If an archaeologist were to excavate such burials he might be able to say

112   Maths at Work

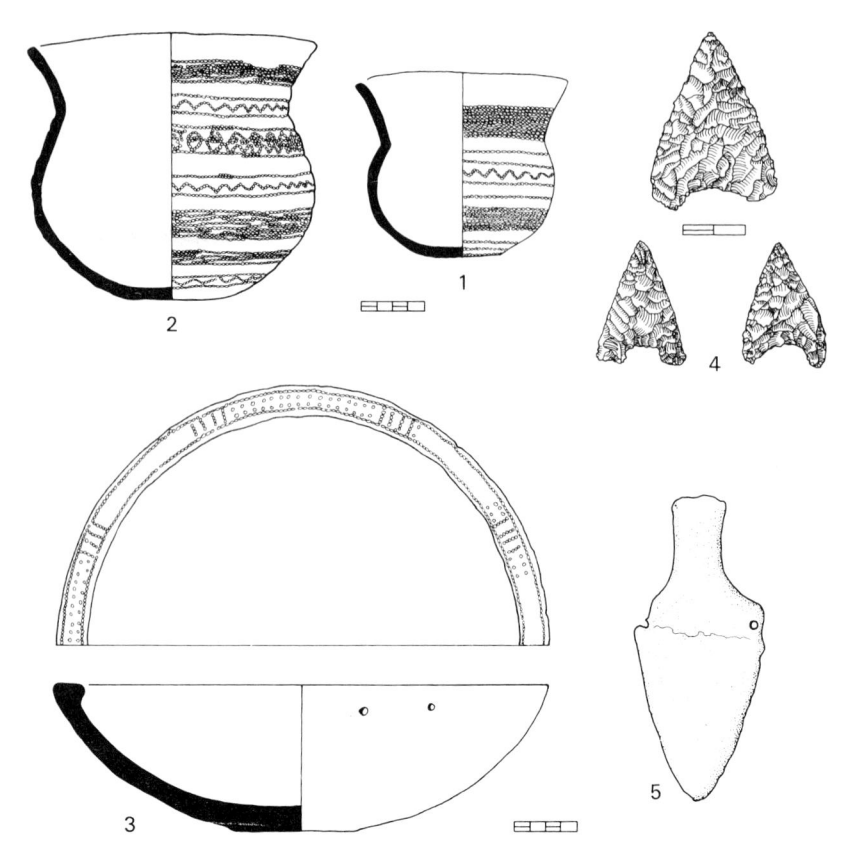

Fig. 9.2(a)   Bell beaker grave inventory Kobylnice, Moravia

something about the nature and the extent of social divisions of different kinds within the society.

I would like to describe the investigation of precisely such a case. It involves a set of graves in what is now Czechoslovakia, dating from around 2500 B.C., a time when copper and bronze were just coming into use. The burials, which have been excavated over the past 100 years, contain skeletons, usually only one but sometimes more. With the skeletons were buried a number of different grave goods. All the graves contain the same range of items but they have different combinations and some have more than others. Two of the different combinations are illustrated in Fig. 9.2(a) and (b); the most characteristic type of item is a kind of pot known as a bell beaker (Fig. 9.3).

Disentangling data 113

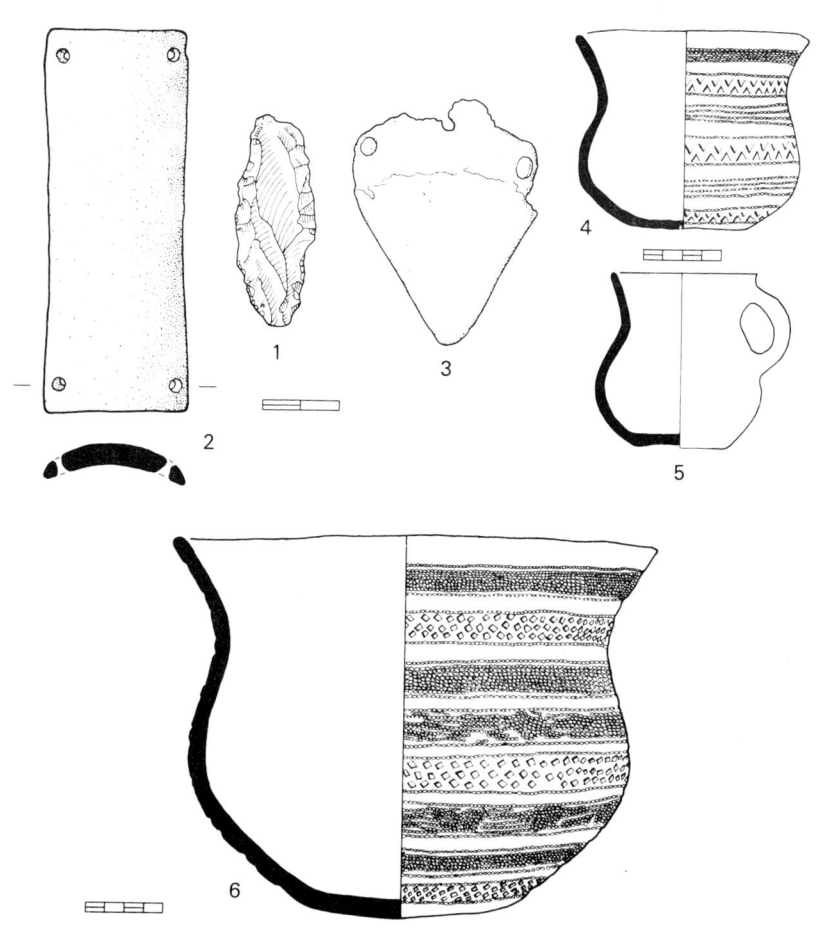

Fig. 9.2(b) Bell beaker grave inventory: Letonice, Moravia

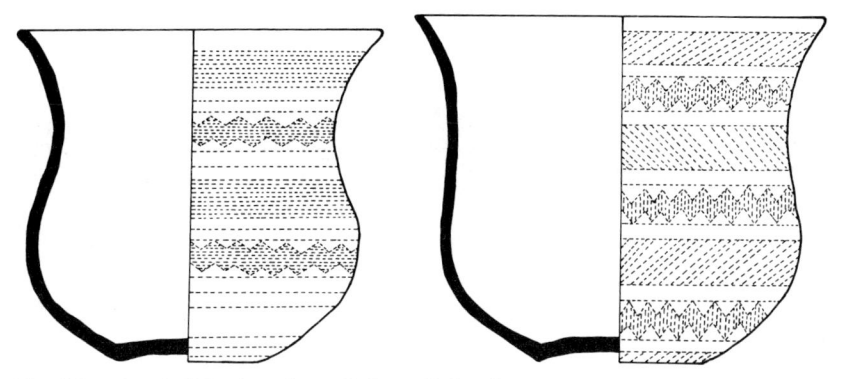

Fig. 9.3 Two bell beakers from Bylany, Bohemia

How do we set about seeing if there is any order within such a set of data? There is obviously a great deal of variation present; furthermore, as there are several hundred graves, there is no way in which we can look at all the lists of grave contents at once and come to some intuitive conclusion about them. It simply is not possible; we need some systematic method.

One obvious way of looking for patterning would be to see if there are any particularly consistent associations of certain items with others. These might indicate what the people who carried out the burials regarded as particular 'kits' of goods for burial.

If we make a list of types and number the graves, we can record for each type the number of the grave in which it occurs, as in the example below.

Table 9.1 Types found in graves

Type	Graves in which type occurs
Decorated bell beaker	10, 29, 33, 45, 69, 88, 91, 102
Pottery jug	15, 19, 45, 71, 83, 113, 121, 136, 151
Copper dagger	15, 29, 45, 88

If two types occur in the same grave we can regard that as an association; but it is not satisfactory simply to record the number of associations, since we need to take into account the number of times the two types occur unassociated with one another, and we want to make sure that the figures are comparable from one pair of types to the next. In other words, a standardised index of association is required.

Such indices can be constructed in a variety of different ways; the rationale may be illustrated by means of some of the decisions which have to be made. For example, if two types occur together in the same grave we will certainly consider that an association, but do we want to attach any significance to those cases where both of the types are *absent* from a particular grave? Referring to Table 9.1, pottery jug and copper dagger have in common that neither of them occurs in graves 1–14, 16–18, 20–28, etc. In the present case it was decided that joint absences (or negative matches as they are known) did not have the same status as joint presences (positive matches), so they were excluded from consideration. For any given pair of types, then, the index had to be some ratio of the number of positive matches and the number of occurrences of the types. But what ratio? Here a problem was created by the fact that some of the types occurred much more frequently than others. Thus, if one item occurs 10 times and every time is associated with another item which occurs 50 times, do we take that as a 10/10 association or a 10/50 association? There is an asymmetry involved. One solution is to take an average and to define the association, A_{JK}, between any two artifact types J and K as follows:

$$A_{JK} = \tfrac{1}{2}((N_{JK}/N_J) + (N_{JK}/N_K))$$

where N_J denotes the total number of occurrences of J, N_K that of K, and N_{JK} the number of joint occurrences of J and K.

The measure ranges from 0, when the two types never co-occur, to 1, when they always co-occur.

We can calculate this measure of association for all pairs of artifact types, and obtain a matrix of associations between the various types. This matrix is symmetric, $A_{JK} = A_{KJ}$, and the diagonal elements, A_{JJ}, are, by definition, 1. In the case of the Czechoslovakian copper-age study, 32 different types of objects occurred in the graves, so a 32×32 matrix of associations was obtained.

The next question that arises is what to do with such a matrix. The mass of numbers in a matrix of this size is hardly less confusing than the original data. In fact, a great variety of options exists, all of which can be put into practice by means of existing computer program packages which can be run by means of a few simple commands. A number of these options will now be examined.

One useful way to start is by drawing a graph (in the sense of graph theory, i.e. a collection of points — vertices or nodes — joined in a specified way by edges). In our case the vertices represent the object types, and the two vertices

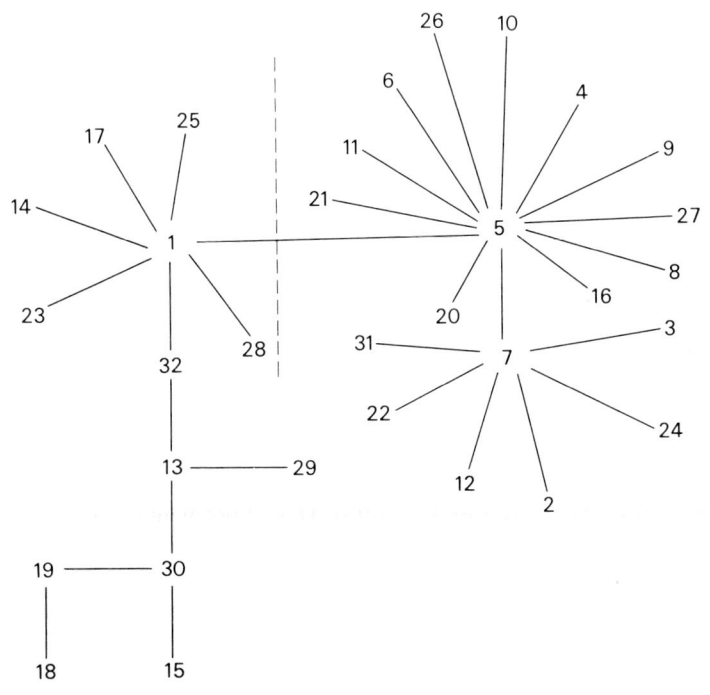

Fig. 9.4 Minimum spanning tree of the relationships between 32 bell beaker artifact types on the basis of their co-occurrence in graves. The dotted line indicates the division of the tree into two groups (see text).

representing the types J and K are joined by an edge which is assigned the 'weight' $1 - A_{JK}$. We now seek a 'minimum spanning tree', i.e. a graph of $N-1$ edges connecting all N vertices, which has no circuits and in which the sum of the weights of the edges is minimal. In other words, we are finding a route through the graph which *maximises* associations. The minimum spanning tree for the 32 types of object in the graves is shown in Fig. 9.4. It suggests the possibility of there being specific sets of items differentially associated with one another. One way to specify such sets is to try to delete edges of the graph with the aim of maximising the similarities within, and the differences between, the resulting groups. In this case, reasonably homogeneous groups are produced by the deletion of the single edge between decorated bell beaker and jug, giving the two groups indicated in the figure.

It is possible to check this result using another method of analysing our association matrix called 'hierarchical agglomerative cluster analysis'. We start off with all our types separate from one another, then link them together in a series of steps, starting with those items which are most closely associated. It is possible to represent the links in the form of a tree (known as a 'dendrogram' in the jargon) with an association or similarity scale up the side (Fig. 9.5).

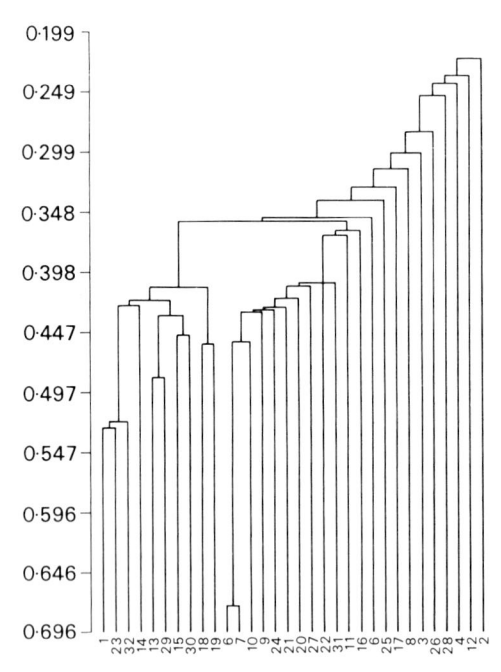

Fig. 9.5 Dendrogram based on the nearest neighbour criterion indicating the relationships between 32 bell beaker artifact types on the basis of their co-occurrence in graves (see text)

A great variety of different criteria with different properties have been proposed for linking up the individuals and groups in the tree. The one shown in Fig. 9.5 is the result of using the nearest neighbour criterion. Individuals are added to a group as soon as they achieve a specified degree of association with any member of the group. Similarly, two groups are joined as soon as any two members achieve a specified degree of association. Eventually, as Fig. 9.5 shows, all the individuals or items are joined up with one another.

In this case one group does seem to stand out from the dendrogram, and in fact is identical to the left-hand group derived from the minimum spanning tree, including such types as decorated bell beaker, arrowhead, copper dagger, etc. Thus, we seem to have some support for the idea that there is some patterning in the associations between the objects.

So far, so good. But suppose some devil's advocate approaches us and says: 'I don't believe those groupings at all. How do you know that they haven't occurred by chance, that they are not simply a function of the frequencies with which the objects occur?' This presents us with a problem, since no very satisfactory statistical tests have been developed for the results of cluster analyses. However, there is one way which at least gives us some help in testing our devil's advocate's suggestion. Suppose we take the frequencies of the objects as given and generate a random permutation of the data. For example, the decorated bell beaker occurs in 98 graves out of 400, so we can generate 98 random numbers between 1 and 400 and say these are the grave numbers in which our decorated bell beakers occur. We can do this for all our object types. By this means it is possible to generate a completely random data set. We can then obtain its association matrix via our coefficient and carry out a cluster analysis on it using the same technique. One result is shown in Fig. 9.6. It can be seen that this time we have no sign of any grouping, which suggests that our devil's advocate is probably wrong, the grouping is real. Ideally, this randomisation process should be done a number of times to compare the patterns, but it is very costly of time and even doing it once gives us a useful basis for comparison.

On the basis of these analyses it seems reasonable to infer that there is some patterning in the associations of the various types. In particular, there appears to be one relatively limited set of mutually associated items, the left-hand group in Fig. 9.4 which corresponds to the group which stands out in the dendrogram (Fig. 9.5), i.e. decorated bell beakers, ear-rings, whetstones, stone axes, arrowheads, flint scrapers and flakes, boar's tusks, copper daggers and wrist-guards. Several of these are types which one might assume *a priori* had a high value because of the rarity of their materials, the distance over which the raw materials and/or the objects themselves must have travelled from their sources, and the effort and skill invested in their manufacture. Furthermore, some of these types are distinct from most of the others

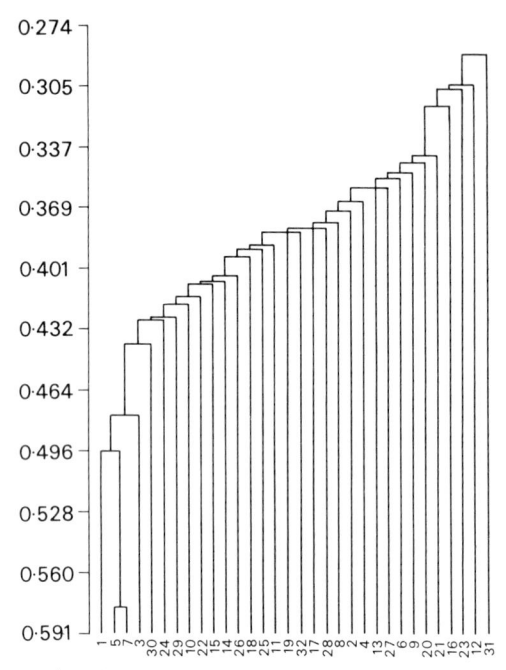

Fig. 9.6 Dendrogram based on the nearest neighbour criterion indicating the relationships between 32 bell beaker artifact types on the basis of a random permutation of their occurrences in graves (see text)

deposited in the graves in that they have a very wide distribution across Europe. Decorated bell beakers, for example, are found from Ireland to Hungary, and from Norway to North Africa. This is most unusual. Moreover, anthropological and historical studies suggest that widespread items tend to be those which have prestige value.

It appears then that we have a basis for suggesting that we have defined a grouping of mutually associated prestige items which were buried with certain individuals when they died but not with others. This leads one to the inference that there may have been differences of rank within copper age society in Czechoslovakia. We are making some progress towards our aim of explaining the variation in the data set and making inferences about past social organisation.

It might be asked, however, whether we have done enough. Is there a possibility, for example, that graves containing the items listed above were earlier in date than those without, in other words, that burial practices had changed through time? A number of tests on independent aspects of the data, not described here, suggested that this was not the case. There did not seem to be a time trend in the data.

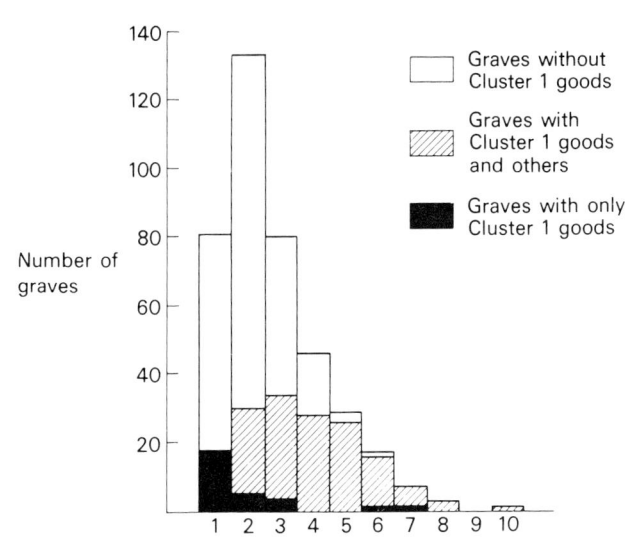

Fig. 9.7 Bar graph showing the number of bell beaker graves containing different numbers of grave goods. Graves with goods of the bell beaker cluster are distinguished from the others.

This was satisfactory, but it still seemed worth trying other avenues which might indicate whether or not the argument concerning the social significance of the group of grave goods discussed above was a valid one. It was reasoned that if these objects were prestige goods associated with higher ranking individuals, then we might expect graves containing them to have more goods than others (see Fig. 9.7). Examination of this question is not completely straightforward, since the more items a grave contains, the greater the probability that it will include one of the prestige group of items. The method of getting round this problem presented below was suggested by Dr P. Prescott.

There are ten different types in the cluster of mutually associated prestige items which has been defined above, while there are 32 different grave goods types altogether. If a grave contains r goods, the probability that it does *not* contain any items from the cluster, assuming a random selection of r goods from the 32 types, is given by

$$\frac{^{22}C_r}{^{32}C_r} = \frac{(32-r)!\,22!}{32!(22-r)!}$$

where $^nC_r = \frac{n!}{r!(n-r)!}$ is the number of different combinations that exist of n items taken r at a time.

It is most straightforward to see why this is so by considering the simple case where $r = 1$. The number of different combinations of 22 items taken one at a time is, of course, 22, and of 32 items it is 32. If we bear in mind that in the case we are considering the 22 are a subset of the 32, then we can see that 22 of the 32 combinations (or 0.6875) will not contain an item from the cluster. Thus, the probability of any individual grave not containing an item from the cluster will be 0.6875 for $r = 1$.

The probability that a grave containing r items contains at least one item from the cluster is given by

$$1 - \frac{^{22}C_r}{^{32}C_r}.$$

These probabilities may be calculated for all values of r which occur.

Once the probabilities have been calculated, they may be used to investigate whether graves containing items from the cluster do indeed tend to have more goods than others. The method may be illustrated by reference to the case where $r = 1$. There are 82 graves containing a single item, so if the goods were randomly distributed we should expect $82(1 - 0.6875)$, i.e. 25.6 graves to contain items from the cluster, compared with an actual value of 17. These calculations may be carried out for all values of r. The results are given in Table 9.2.

Table 9.2 Expected and observed distribution of prestige items

Number of items in grave (r)	Probability of an item from the prestige cluster occurring	Number of graves	Expected number of graves with one or more items from prestige cluster (E)	Observed number of graves with one or more items from prestige cluster (O)	(O−E)
1	0.3125	82	25.6	17	−8.6
2	0.5343	134	71.6	30	−41.6
3	0.6895	81	55.8	33	−22.8
4	0.7966	46	36.6	28	−8.6
5	0.8692	29	25.2	26	+0.8
6	0.9176	17	15.6	16	+0.4
7	0.9493	7	6.6	7	+0.4
8	0.9696	3	2.9	3	+0.1
9	0.9822	0	0.0	0	0.0
10	0.9900	1	1.0	1	0.0

It is immediately apparent from the negative signs in the 'observed–expected' column that for $r = 1, 2, 3, 4$ the number of graves containing items from the cluster is less than that expected. This suggests that there are *fewer* graves containing *at least one* item from the prestige cluster amongst the graves with a *small* number of goods than would be expected if the items belonging to this cluster were randomly distributed. Again, then,

Disentangling data 121

there is support for the idea that there existed a group of higher-ranked individuals within this prehistoric society whose rank was expressed at burial by means of prestige objects.

Having established all this, one may ask whether there are any attributes of the population themselves to which this information can be related. The answer to this is 'yes'. If physical anthropologists or anatomists examine a skeleton, they can establish its age and sex with a reasonable degree of certainty, so long as it is in reasonable condition. The possibility then arises of looking at the distribution of the grave goods in relation to the age and sex of the individual buried with them, where these are known. Let us take a specific example, for graves containing individuals of known sex. (Table 9.3.). The numbers in parentheses are the expected values under the null hypothesis (see below).

Table 9.3 Grave goods in relation to sex of individual buried with them

Decorated bell beaker	Occupant of grave		
	Male	Female	
Present	17 (11.84)	4 (9.16)	21
Absent	14 (19.16)	20 (14.84)	34
	31	24	55

Given this information is there any indication that there is a relationship between the sex of the individual buried and whether or not a decorated bell beaker is buried with them? It looks as though there might be, but do we need to take the figures seriously? We can establish the probability of there being a relationship by means of a chi-squared test. In a case such as the one examined here, this tests the null hypothesis that there is no difference between two samples with respect to their frequency distribution across a set of mutually exclusive categories. We obtain the expected number of male and female graves with and without decorated bell beakers on the assumption that there is no difference between them, and compare these expected values with those which exist in reality.

$$\chi^2 = \Sigma \frac{(O-E)^2}{E}$$

where O denotes the observed frequency in a given category and E the expected frequency for that category.

In this case the calculated value of $\chi^2 = 8.34$, which must be compared with the tabulated values of chi-squared in the chi-squared statistical table, for the appropriate number of degrees of freedom, which in this case is one. The calculated value exceeds the tabulated value for the 0.01 probability level, so we conclude that it is highly improbable that decorated bell beakers are equally distributed between male and female graves. This approach gives us another way of obtaining social information about our burials in terms of the types of distinctions between the sexes made by the people who actually carried out the burials. In fact, this and other tests suggested that the group of prestige items which we have been discussing were restricted to certain adult males.

So far then, by the use of a number of different quantitative techniques, it has been possible to define some patterning in the variation present in our copper age graves, and by means of a mixture of archaeological reasoning and statistical methods, to suggest a substantive interpretation of that variation. There remains one method to look at, which can provide further information about the variation in the graves not accessible by other means, and particularly useful from the point of view of comparing different sets of data.

When we looked at cluster analysis earlier, we were examining a matrix of coefficients of association between objects, based on the graves in which they occurred. But it is also possible to work out an index of similarity between the graves on the basis of the objects which occur in them. Again, the result will be a symmetric matrix of coefficients, this time of the similarities between each grave and every other grave. Furthermore, the same question arises as before concerning which coefficient should be used to describe the similarity. Let us take a hypothetical example:

Attributes	1	2	3	4	5	6	7	8
Grave 1		1		1		1		
Grave 2	1	1		1				

We need a standardised coefficient so that the similarity between graves will be comparable from one pair of graves to the next. It will be convenient if the measure has a lower bound of 0 when there are no similarities between the two graves, and 1 when they are identical. Do we want cases where two graves have in common the lack of some attribute (a negative match) to be taken into account in calculating similarity? In this instance, because a large number of attributes occurred in the data set as a whole, whereas any given grave only possessed a small number of them, it was decided to exclude negative matches from consideration. Similarity was defined as follows:

$$S_{JK} = \frac{N_{JK}}{U_{JK}}$$

where N_{JK} denotes the number of attributes (types) the two graves have in

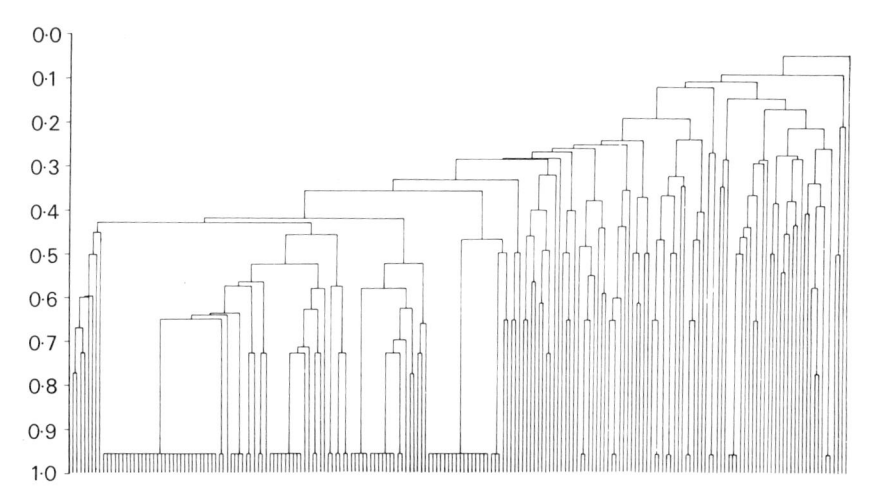

Fig. 9.8 Dendrogram based on the group average criterion indicating the relationships between 200 bell beaker graves on the basis of the items found in them (see text)

common, and U_{JK} the number of attributes (types) represented in the two graves.

For the example illustrated, $S_{12} = \frac{2}{4} = 0.5$.

As before, the next question is: How do we see if there is any meaningful patterning in the matrix? It is even more of a problem now, because in general the number of units — here graves — will be a lot greater than the number of variables — here objects found in them. We might easily have a 100 × 100 matrix.

One way of looking for patterning is again to use cluster analysis, but with such a large matrix, the results, although helpful, can often be confusing (see Fig. 9.8). An alternative is to return to the implications of the archaeological aim that was specified earlier — of explaining the variation in the data. We have seen that there may be a variety of possible sources of such variation. Is there any way in which we can perhaps identify these sources and at the same time obtain a simplified picture from the confusion of similarity coefficients? This idea suggests an avenue which has been tried with some success: obtaining the eigenvalues and associated eigenvectors of the matrix. These quantities result from some fairly complicated matrix algebra which I do not propose to describe here. They do, however, have a fairly straightforward intuitive interpretation which I will try to outline.

We can imagine trying to represent the graves under study as points in a space, such that the similarities between the graves are represented by the distances between the points. In order to represent the relationships accurately we would need a space of many dimensions. We can further imagine that within this space the points will not necessarily be equally scattered in all directions; they may be distributed over a relatively short distance in some dimensions and a considerably longer one in others. It is possible to define the orientation of these different axes or dimensions and the lengths over which the points are distributed along them. Once we have established the orientation of the longest line and its length, we can then define the line which goes through the next longest part of the point scatter, subject to the proviso that it must be at right angles to the first one, and we can obtain its length too. It is possible to go on doing this for as many independent dimensions of our space as exist. These axes and their lengths correspond to the eigenvectors and eigenvalues of the similarity matrix. They will often have a substantive interpretation in terms of the data from which they were derived. We can establish a set of coordinates for our points (here the graves) in relation to these axes, and attempt to interpret them. The axes are independent dimensions of variation in the data and their lengths reflect the importance of the dimensions in accounting for variation in the data. This analytical procedure is known as 'principal coordinates analysis'.

If we plot the rank order of the dimensions against the percentage of variation in the data explained by them, we have a basis for comparing the structure of variation in different data sets which can be used for defining certain aspects of change through time. Thus, it is possible to compare the structure of variation in the copper age bell beaker graves which have been

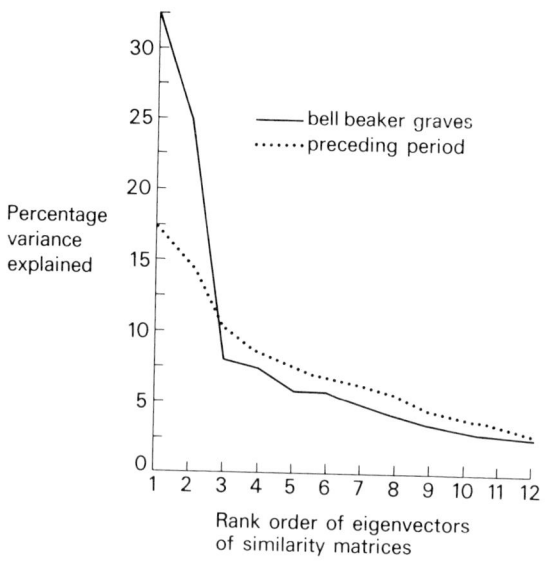

Fig. 9.9 Graph of eigenvectors against the variance explained by them, from principal coordinates analyses of bell beaker graves and graves of the preceding period (see text)

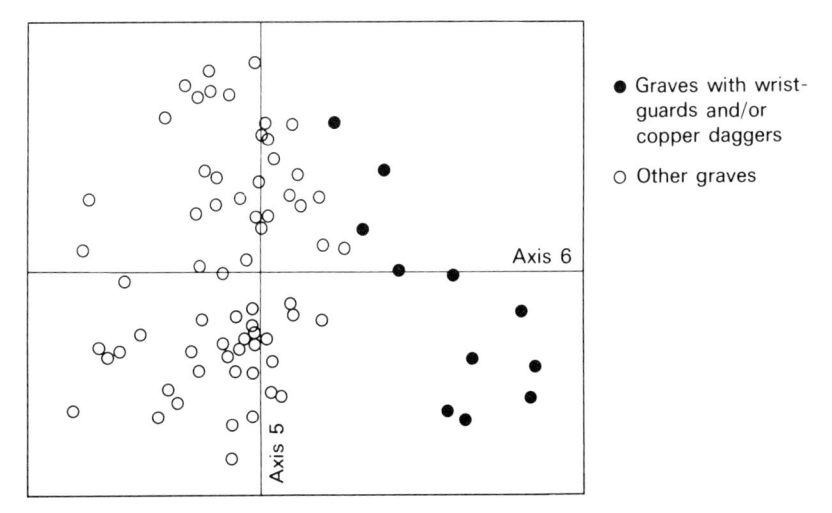

Fig. 9.10 Principal coordinates scattergram of bell beaker graves, axes 5 and 6 (see text)

the object of study here, with that in the graves of the same area in the preceding period (Fig. 9.9). We can see that they seem to have distinctly different patterns. In the bell beaker case a larger proportion of variation in the graves is 'explained' by a smaller number of dimensions than for the earlier graves. In the latter set of data one or two factors are not nearly so dominant, reflecting a situation where the variation is more disordered and its different aspects less highly correlated with one another.

It has already been noted that an attempt may be made to interpret the axes obtained by the analysis substantively. This is done by noting the coordinates of the different graves in relation to the axes and then referring back to the raw data listing to find out the contents of graves at different locations along the axes. In this way it is possible to infer the nature of the trends the different axes represent (Fig. 9.10). By combining these interpretations with the information on the relative importance of the different dimensions, we obtain a further useful tool.

In the case under consideration here, interpretation suggested that among the graves from the period immediately preceding that of the bell beaker data set analysed in this study, male–female distinctions were highly important, while for the bell beaker graves they were of less significance. More important in the latter case was the distinction already noted between the relatively limited number of higher-ranking adult male graves and the rest.

In summary, then, this complex procedure enables us to define patterning in the variation within our data, assess the relative importance of different aspects of that patterning, and define some relatively abstract distinctions in the structure of variation between one set of data and another. These results are susceptible to meaningful interpretation on a comparative basis.

This chapter has illustrated the kinds of aims which archaeologists today attempt to achieve in order to explain the variation they observe in the archaeological record. The realisation of such aims depends to a considerable extent on the recognition and definition of patterning in their observations. Mathematics has a key role in the process of pattern recognition because it brings a power and objectivity to the task which would not otherwise be present. Nevertheless, it should be appreciated that the way in which the data are initially formalised mathematically depends largely on archaeological criteria, and that the validity of the inferences drawn from the mathematically defined patterns depends likewise on archaeological assumptions. It is these two factors, particularly the latter, which are often open to question.

10

R. E. Beard

Spreading the risk

Mathematics is used in many commercial activities. This chapter illustrates some of the features involved by considering one particular commercial activity, namely insurance.

My own background lies in insurance and it may be of interest to sketch in very briefly some of the details. I started at the lowest clerical level in a large insurance company transacting most classes of business, qualified as an actuary and retired some 44 years later from the position of General Manager. There was an interruption of some 4 years when I was with the Admiralty as what may be loosely described as the 'numbers man' for the Fleet Air Arm. After retirement I was first associated with the Department of Mathematics at Essex University and am currently a Special Professor in the Department of Industrial Economics at Nottingham University. Apart from my involvement with the Institute of Actuaries I played a significant part in the foundation and development of an international group, known as ASTIN, which specialises in the application of risk theory to non-life insurance.

The example in this chapter is concerned with non-life insurance. The principles involved are applicable to all classes of business, though the much greater relevance of investment aspects complicates problems dealing with life business.

Now, if I were asked to summarise my experience in as few words as possible, one generalisation would be that society suffers from the curse of the arithmetic mean. Vast quantities of statistical data are collected and have to be compressed so that the human mind can endeavour to grasp the significance of the figures, and for this purpose the arithmetic mean is the universal tool. But this compression necessarily obscures the fact that most measurements involve a spread of values around the mean, the spread arising from real differences between the individual measurements and random fluctuations of one kind or another.

Much of the advancement in the natural sciences during this century has flowed from the recognition of random variation, now largely expressed as the theory of stochastic processes, but for various reasons progress in the social sciences has been slow. One reason is probably the nature of accountancy, which requires quantities to be expressed in precise numerical terms, so uncertainties have to be accommodated in other ways. Another reason is probably political: a reluctance to recognise that individuals have an inherent variability in respect of all characteristics which might be measured.

This aversion to variability, which is reflected in the use of the arithmetic mean, is clearly seen in misunderstandings of the operation of insurance, both by those seeking insurance protection and by the insurers.

The basis of insurance

It is first necessary to point out a basic difference between insurance and other forms of commercial activity. All business boils down to agreements between two parties which are controlled by legislation of one kind or another. In purchasing an article there is an onus on the seller to see that the specification and performance are met and there is an onus on the purchaser to provide the purchase money. In insurance the proposer must provide proper information about the risk so that the insurer can quote an appropriate premium. The insurer must provide for payment if the event as described in the policy arises, provided the premium has been paid. Should it transpire that the risk differed from that described in the proposal the premium quoted could be inappropriate and the law provides that the contract is voidable.

The basis of insurance is the spreading of risk and can be visualised by a number of individuals who each own an item of property subject to destruction by a natural hazard such as fire. If the risks are identical, then an insurance group can be created into which each pays a premium and which can then reimburse those members whose property is destroyed. If statistics are compiled of the experience over a period, a risk premium can be calculated by finding the average annual cost of the claims and dividing this between the members. There is an implicit assumption that the risks are identical and that the occurrence of a fire is a random event.

Suppose, for example, that there are 100 persons in a group of this type each with property worth £1000 which is totally destroyed if a fire should occur. If the chance that a particular property is destroyed is 0.02 (obtained from the statistical records) then, on average, two properties will be destroyed in a year and an appropriate risk premium would be £20 (i.e. 1000×0.02).

However, in a particular year it is unlikely that exactly two fires will occur, there might be 0, 1, 2, ... according to chance. The probability that a particular number of fires arise can in this case be calculated by the binomial theorem, i.e.

$$(0.98 + 0.02)^{100} = (0.98)^{100} + {}^{100}C_1(0.98)^{99}(0.02)$$

$$+ {}^{100}C_2(0.98)^{98}(0.02)^2 + \ldots$$

where the first term on the right hand side gives the probability that no fires occur, the second one fire and so on.

The figures in Table 10.1 can now be calculated. Column three gives the expected cost of 0, 1, 2, ... fires using the probabilities in column two, the total expected cost being £2000. Each person pays £20, so the receipts are £2000 and column four represents the 'surplus' at the end of the year depending on the number of fires. If no fires, one fire or two fires arise, the balance is non-negative, but if more than two fires occur the group will not be in a position to meet its liabilities. To avoid defaulting on its commitments the group then needs some form of buffer which can be drawn upon when the fluctuations are adverse and can be built up when the fluctuations are favourable. One way of doing this is to borrow money by way of capital.

From column two it will be found that the chance of no claims, one claim or two claims is 0.6767, which means that the probability of 'ruin' is about $\frac{1}{3}$. If additional funds of £4000 were available, the fund would be able to meet six claims. Since the probability that more than six claims arise is only 0.004, this would be a much more reasonable situation. However, it would be necessary to pay interest on the borrowed money which must be recovered through

Table 10.1 Number of properties destroyed

	Probability of exactly n fires	Expected cost (£s)	Surplus (£s)
0	0.1326	0	2000
1	0.2707	271	1000
2	0.2734	547	0
3	0.1823	547	−1000
4	0.0902	361	−2000
5	0.0354	177	−3000
6	0.0114	68	−4000
7	0.0031	22	−5000
8	0.0007	5	−6000
9+	0.0002	2	−7000+
Total	1.0000	2000	

increased premiums. If the net interest cost was equivalent to ten per cent p.a. amounting to £400, the premium would have to be increased to £24.

This simple example shows that the premium must include a charge for the cost of smoothing out the random fluctuations in the incidence of claims, in addition to the expected cost, and also that the claims are assumed to arise at random relative to the insured peril. (In addition, of course, a charge must be made for the administrative costs.)

Implicit in the model is the assumption that the results for one year only are being considered. The extension to more than one year is more complicated. For instance if the 'horizon' is two years it is necessary to consider the outcome of the first year and use this as the input for the second year. The calculations will soon become prohibitive by direct means and recourse has to be made to more sophisticated mathematics than we can deal with here. (The solution for an infinite horizon is, in fact, given by an integral equation.)

Reinsurance

Instead of borrowing money to provide a buffer fund, which is equivalent to spreading the fluctuations in time, reinsurance might be used. The principle here is that the reinsurer has a number of contracts with different insurance groups whose experiences are likely to differ, so that adverse fluctuations in some groups are offset by favourable fluctuations in others. Thus, in the situation described earlier, the original insurance group may obtain quotations for the reinsurance of excess claims in a number of ways. It may consider raising £2000 capital, which with the premiums of £2000, would enable it to meet four claims, and get a quotation for reinsuring claims in excess of four (i.e. limiting the maximum claim cost to £4000). The reinsurer has precisely the same problem in fixing his quotation and will include in his estimate of the premium a margin to cover fluctuations as well as the expected claim cost. The cost of this insurance protection and the service charge on the lower capital could be recouped by loading the risk premium.

However, the insurance group could apply the same reasoning as the reinsurer and seek to extend its own activities by creating further groups itself. Assuming independence of the groups, there will be a balancing of fluctuations which will reduce the relative size of the capital required to reduce the ruin probability to an acceptable level, and which will, in consequence, reduce the excess capital required to cover fluctuations. Thus, if four groups were involved representing 400 cases, a similar calculation to that of Table 10.1 shows that at the 0.004 level of ruin rather less than 17 claims would be involved. With total premiums of £8000 the further capital required would be about £9000, relatively speaking, about half the previous figure. As before, insurance protection could be obtained to reduce the amount of capital needed. (The calculations may be affected in practice by the skewness of the claim distribution, in which case simple application of the above procedure can lead to unsatisfactory results!)

The essence of the foregoing is that within an insurance group the contribution of each member should meet the expected claims plus a loading to cover the cost of smoothing out the fluctuations. The claim expectation has to be estimated from the objective information provided in the proposal and from subjective judgement of other non-quantifiable features. Past records can be used, but these have to be projected forward to allow for any trends which might affect the amount of claim. The most important of these factors is the change in the value of money (inflation), since in some important classes of insurance the amount of claim depends on the time of settlement rather than the conditions at the time the policy was effected. This dependence complicates the interpretation of past statistics but it is not possible to deal with this aspect here.

If changes in the value of money are eliminated, then experience shows the shape of the claim distribution is fairly stable in time. Supposing insurance groups could be classified according to the claim distribution, the expected claim cost would be solely dependent on the expected claim frequency rate, assuming no correlation between the frequency rate and the amount. The contribution of individuals would then be proportional to their expected claim frequency.

Application to motor insurance

The last situation is approximately that found in motor insurance. There are complications because there are different types of policy coverage, but the general pattern is that the distribution of amounts of claim is very skew, with a large number of smaller claims and a smaller number of larger claims, some of which may be up to 1000 times the average claim. It will be assumed that the complications can be ignored and that differences between individuals can be measured by the chance that they make a claim.

This chance is a function of many variables which depend on the type of car, the nature of its use and the environment, the age and other characteristics of the driver, and so on. Unfortunately most of the conveniently measurable variables are interrelated, and some means has to be found of eliminating these relations so that it is possible to find the effect of each variable on its own. If this is done, the business can then be classified according to these independent factors. In practice it is found that even then there is still a residual variation which has to be assessed from the frequency of the actual claims experienced. This is allowed for by adjusting future premiums accordingly.

The conclusion is that the effective insurance group is determined by the objective factors and there is a fine adjustment within the group to take care of subjective factors.

The first stage, that is the elimination of the relationships between objective factors, can best be demonstrated by a simple example. In practice, a computer is essential when many factors at different levels of intensity are involved, but the principles are the same.

Table 10.2 Exposure to risk

		Exposed to risk (car years)					
		Factor B					
	Level	*1*	*2*	*3*	*Total*	*Number of claims*	*Rate*
Factor A	1	400	300	1100	1800	404	0.22444
	2	500	400	300	1200	200	0.16667
	3	700	500	800	2000	196	0.09800
Total		1600	1200	2200	5000		
Number of claims		310	186	304		800	
Rate		0.19375	0.15500	0.13818			0.16000

Table 10.2 sets out hypothetical data for an analysis involving two of the above factors, for example age and type of car, each of which is experienced at three levels of intensity. Algebraically we may represent this as follows. Suppose

Q_{a_r} = total number of claims for factor A at level r over all levels for B,
Q_{b_s} = total number of claims for factor B at level s over all levels for A,
λ_r = exposure to risk in car years at level r of factor A (over all B),
λ_s = exposure to risk in car years at level s of factor B (over all A),
λ_{rs} = exposure to risk at level r of A *and* level s of B.

Thus
$$\sum_{s=1}^{3} \lambda_{rs} = \lambda_r, \quad \sum_{r=1}^{3} \lambda_{rs} = \lambda_s, \quad \text{and} \sum_{r=1}^{3} \sum_{s=1}^{3} \lambda_{rs} = N \tag{1}$$

where N is the total number insured. Further, if Q is the total number of claims made, and m is the overall claim frequency rate, then

$$\sum_{r=1}^{3} Q_{a_r} = \sum_{s=1}^{3} Q_{b_s} = Q, \quad \text{and } m = Q/N. \tag{2}$$

The object is to express the expected rates for level r in factor A, a_r, and for level s in factor B, b_s, in terms of the claims actually experienced. These can be obtained from the following set of six equations, one for each level in each factor:

Spreading the risk 133

$$Q_{a_r} = \lambda_r m + \lambda_r a_r + \sum_{s=1}^{3} \lambda_{rs} b_s$$

$$Q_{b_s} = \lambda_s m + \lambda_s b_s + \sum_{r=1}^{3} \lambda_{rs} a_r$$

(3)

By the constraints in equations (1) and (2), one of these equations is redundant and we have five independent equations whilst (assuming m is given) there are six unknowns. Now, if in equations (3) each a_r is increased by a constant δ and each b_s is decreased by the same constant δ, the solution remains unchanged. Therefore we can choose the constant δ so that one of the expected rates, say a_1, is zero, allowing us to solve equations (3) for the other five.

Some additional criterion is then needed to fix the value of δ, and one such is that the expected claims from factors A and B operating alone are equal to those expected using the overall average rate m. This means that the net deviations balance out for each factor and overall.

The essential calculations for the data given in Table 10.2 are set out below. For this example the differences between the calculated values and those obtained from the marginal totals are not particularly large but in practical conditions significant differences can occur.

Example

$1800m + 1800a_1 + 400b_1 + 300b_2 + 1100b_3 = 404$
$1200m + 1200a_2 + 500b_1 + 400b_2 + 300b_3 = 200$
$2000m + 2000a_3 + 700b_1 + 500b_2 + 800b_3 = 196$
$1600m + 1600b_1 + 400a_1 + 500a_2 + 700a_3 = 310$
$1200m + 1200b_2 + 300a_1 + 400a_2 + 500a_3 = 186$
$2200m + 2200b_3 + 1100a_1 + 300a_2 + 800a_3 = 304$

Ignoring the last equation, setting $a_1 = 0$, and assuming that in this problem the overall claim frequency rate $m = 0.16$, we deduce the following equations to be solved for $a_2, a_3, b_1, b_2,$ and b_3:

$ 400b_1 + 300b_2 + 1100b_3 = 116$
$1200a_2 + 500b_1 + 400b_2 + 300b_3 = 8$
$ 2000a_3 + 700b_1 + 500b_2 + 800b_3 = -124$
$500a_2 + 700a_3 + 1600b_1 = 54$
$400a_2 + 500a_3 + 1200b_2 = -6$

The solution is

$a_2 = -0.08, \ a_3 = -0.14, \ b_1 = 0.12, \ b_2 = 0.08, \ b_3 = 0.04.$

Hence:

A claims $1200(-0.08) + 2000(-0.14) = -376$
B claims $1600(0.12) + 1200(0.08) + 2200(0.04) = 376$

which gives $\delta = 0.0752$.

The adjusted factors are therefore (with $m = 0.16$),

$$a_1 = 0.0752 \quad b_1 = 0.0448$$
$$a_2 = -0.0048 \quad b_2 = 0.0048$$
$$a_3 = -0.0648 \quad b_3 = -0.0352.$$

The marginal rates (obtained by deducting 0.16 from the claim rate) are similarly

	Factor	
Level	A	B
1	0.06444	0.03375
2	0.00667	-0.00500
3	-0.06200	-0.02182

It is now possible to translate these values into a points system such that the total points applicable to a given combination of factors can be used to determine the relative premium. It is assumed that the average claim cost is linearly dependent on the mean of the claim distribution multiplied by a factor depending on the value of money.

There is a very sound commercial reason behind the underlying principle of the calculation of equitable premiums between policyholders. For example, suppose that two companies have similar rating structures except for one factor. One company calculates the premium based on the average figure for the particular factor whereas the other discriminates between five levels for this factor. At the lower levels the second company will charge lower premiums and will charge higher premiums at the higher levels. In a competitive market the first company will then lose the lower rated business to the second company and the second company will lose the higher rated business to the first company. Considering their own experience in a routine study of the suitability of their premiums the first company will note a deterioration due to the differential shift and will revise its premiums upwards to a new equilibrium level. This will aggravate the situation and the result will be a further shift in business between the companies. The second company will not detect any change in its experience. This instability will persist until the first company receives all the higher rated business and loses the lower rated business. A number of companies failed a few years ago through inadequate appreciation of this particular aspect, coupled (of course) with the effects of inflation.

Although this chapter is mainly concerned with specific aspects of insurance operation, the principles are applicable to other forms of commercial activity and some of these have been described in the section headed 'Finance' in reference 1.

Reference

1 Lighthill, James (ed.) (1978) *Newer Uses of Mathematics*, Penguin Books.

11

J. R. Nation and T. J. Critchley

Borrowing and lending

In this chapter we shall discuss one particular application of mathematics to banking, compound interest. This is a topic often touched upon at school, but, as we shall see, the banker must consider its use in a variety of situations. Compound interest is, in fact, an important and powerful tool for the solution of many practical problems relating to finance and investment. It is, however, based on fairly straightforward mathematical principles which are easily grasped given familiarity with the notation. Even complex practical problems can be solved quite simply by breaking them down into component parts and simplifying formulae at each step.

Descriptions of interest rates

There are three common methods of applying interest to loans — and of quoting rates of interest. The banker will use all of these and will apply one or a combination of these methods in any practical problem. The customer must be aware of the form in which the interest rate is quoted.

(a) The effective rate of interest (denoted by i)

The concept of an effective rate of interest is crucial to all practical problems. By definition it is the actual decimal rate of increase per unit of loan per period. If the period is a year then the effective rate of interest is equivalent to the annual percentage rate. Often, however, the period is less than a year, for example when one makes monthly repayments on a credit card. The Consumer Credit Act then requires the annual percentage rate also to be specified.

378 *Interest.* *Appendix.*

XI. When it is required to find the present worth of an annuity, by rebating or discounting at a given rate of simple interest, the operation will be as in the following example, *viz.* How much present Money is equivalent to an annuity or rent of 100 *l.* *per annum*, to continue 5 years, rebate being made at the rate of 6 *l.* for 100 *l.* for one year, at simple interest? *Answ.* 425 *l.* 18 *s.* 9 ½ *d.* very near.

Of the present worth of Annuities by discounting at simple interest.

It is manifest that there must be computed the present worth of 100 *l.* due at the first year's end, also the present worth of 100 *l.* due at the second year's end, and in like manner for the third, fourth and fifth year's; all which particular present *worths* being added together, the aggregate or sum will be the total present *worth* of the *Annuity*, to wit, in the example above propounded, $425\frac{8286150}{8821267}$ *l.* that is, 425 *l.* 18 *s.* 9 ½ *d.* very near.

The operation by decimals (which comes near enough to the truth) will be as follows, *viz.*

	l.	*l.*	*l.*	*l.*
1.	106 : 100 ::	100 :	94 .	33962 +
2.	112 : 100 ::	100 :	89 .	28571 +
3.	118 : 100 ::	100 :	84 .	74576 +
4.	124 : 100 ::	100 :	80 .	64516 +
5.	130 : 100 ::	100 :	76 .	92307 +
	Answ.		425	.93933 +

Here

410 *Interest.* *Appendix.*

TABLE VI.

Which shews the present worth of one Pound Annuity, to continue any term of years under 31, and payable by yearly payments, compound Interest being computed at any of these, rates, to wit, 4, 5, 6, 7, 8, 9, 10, 11, *and* 12 per cent. per annum.

Years.	4	5	6	7	8	9	10	11	12
1	.96153	.95238	.94339	.93457	.92592	.91743	.90909	.90090	.89285
2	1.88609	1.85941	1.83339	1.80801	1.78326	1.75911	1.73553	1.71252	1.69005
3	2.77509	2.72324	2.67301	2.62431	2.57709	2.53129	3.48685	2.44371	2.40183
4	3.62989	3.54595	3.46510	3.38721	3.31212	3.23971	3.16986	3.10244	3.03734
5	4.45182	4.32947	4.21236	4.10019	3.99270	3.88965	3.79078	3.69589	3.60477
6	5.24213	5.07569	4.91732	4.76653	4.62287	4.48591	4.35526	4.23053	4.11140
7	6.00205	5.78637	5.58233	5.38928	5.20636	5.03295	5.86841	4.71219	4.56375
8	6.73274	6.46321	6.20979	5.97129	5.74663	5.53481	5.33492	5.14612	4.96763
9	7.43533	7.10782	6.80169	6.51523	6.24688	5.99524	5.75902	5.53704	5.32824
10	8.11089	7.72173	7.36008	7.02358	6.71008	6.41765	6.14456	5.88923	5.65022
11	8.76047	8.30641	7.88688	7.49867	7.13896	6.80519	6.49506	6.2065	5.93769
12	9.38507	8.86325	8.38384	7.94268	7.53607	7.16072	6.81369	6.49235	6.19437
13	9.98964	9.39357	8.85268	8.35765	7.90377	7.48690	7.10335	6.74987	6.42354
14	10.56312	9.89864	9.29498	8.74546	8.24423	7.78614	7.36668	6.98186	6.62816
15	11.11838	10.37965	9.71224	9.10791	8.55947	8.06068	7.60608	7.29087	6.81086

Fig. 11.1 'Interest' has occupied an important position in mathematics for many centuries as these two pages from Wingate's *Arithmetic* (Shelley's edition of 1713) show.

(b) The nominal rate of interest ($i^{(p)}$)

Banks, building societies, and other financial institutions frequently use a 'nominal' rate of interest which expresses the total interest payable in a period (usually a year) per unit sum invested. Thus a bank will advertise that it pays interest at, say, 12 per cent on deposit accounts. Such a rate is, however, meaningless without an accompanying statement relating to the frequency with which interest is paid during the period, half-yearly, quarterly or whatever. This frequency is denoted by the superscript (p).

For example, if interest is 10 per cent per annum payable quarterly, then $i^{(4)} = 0.10$ and $i = i^{(4)}/4$, or 0.025 ($2\frac{1}{2}$ per cent) per quarter. Hence, for an annual nominal rate of interest of ten per cent payable quarterly, the *effective* period is a quarter and the effective interest rate is $2\frac{1}{2}$ per cent per quarter. Expressed annually, the *effective* interest rate for the same example would be 10.38 per cent per annum, due to the compounding effect under consideration.

(c) The flat rate of interest

Hire purchase companies and banks often quote a flat rate of interest to would-be borrowers, something which can be misleading when the customer attempts to compare the relative merits of two apparently similar loans. The flat rate is a rate charged on the *initial* amount of the loan and therefore does not take into account the reducing balance of the loan over the repayment period.

For example, if the flat rate per annum is, say, 12 per cent and repayments are monthly over two years, then one per cent per month is charged on the value of the initial loan for each of the 24 months. The effective rate of interest is therefore much greater (in this case approximately 23 per cent per annum).

Fundamental results and notation

In this section we shall describe some fundamental theory and obtain some basic results. We shall assume that the time period is one year and the effective rate of interest is i per annum. In practice, though, any convenient period may be chosen and the same methods used.

(a) Accumulations

A customer who deposits money in a bank, will wish to know how that initial payment will grow with the years. This can be readily calculated. £100 accumulates to £$100(1+i)$ at the end of one year. £$100(1+i)$ reinvested for a further year accumulates to £$100(1+i)^2$ at the end of the second year. In general £X accumulates to £$X(1+i)^n$ at the end of the nth year.

(b) Present values (discounting)

It may happen that a borrower wishes to repay immediately a fixed sum due in some years' time. What adjustments should be made to the sum to be repaid?

If £X accumulates to £$X(1+i)$ after one year, then £X is the present value of £$X(1+i)$ due in one year. Hence £$X/(1+i)$ is the present value of £X due in one year. This formula is usually simplified by denoting $1/(1+i)$ by v. Using this notation, we can, for instance, see that the present value of £100 due in n years at an effective rate of interest of i per annum is £$100v^n$.

(c) Nominal rates of interest

To facilitate understanding and to help in more complicated problems, it is usually advantageous to convert nominal rates into effective rates. This can be done as follows:

If the nominal rate is $i^{(12)}$ per annum then we know that interest is paid monthly at an effective rate of $i^{(12)}/12$. Clearly, then

$$\left(1+\frac{i^{(12)}}{12}\right)^{12} = 1+i$$

i.e.

$$i = \left(1+\frac{i^{(12)}}{12}\right)^{12} - 1$$

and

$$i^{(12)} = 12[(1+i)^{1/12} - 1].$$

In general,

$$i^{(p)} = p[(1+i)^{1/p} - 1],$$

a very important relationship for the more complex practical problems.

Putting our formulae to use

Let us now see how our formulae can be extended to deal with some more complicated problems, such as the repayment of loans by regular payments. Again we assume an effective rate of interest of i per annum although in practice, as before, any convenient effective period may be chosen and the same methods applied.

First we introduce some further useful notation. Let us consider the result of saving £100 a year for a number of years. Here it is useful to distinguish between the two cases: depositing the payment at the *end* of each year, that is, paying in *arrears*, and making the payment at the *beginning* of each year, that is, paying in *advance*.

The accumulation of £100 p.a. *in arrears* for n years

$$= £100[1 + (1+i) + (1+i)^2 + \ldots + (1+i)^{n-1}], \text{ a geometric series,}$$

$$= £100\left[\frac{1-(1+i)^n}{1-(1+i)}\right] = £100\frac{(1+i)^n - 1}{i}$$

$$= £100\, S_n, \text{ where } S_n = \frac{(1+i)^n - 1}{i}. \tag{1}$$

The accumulation of £100 per annum *in advance* for n years

$$= £100[(1+i)+(1+i)^2+ \ldots +(1+i)^n]$$

$$= £100\left\{(1+i)\left[\frac{1-(1+i)^n}{1-(1+i)}\right]\right\} = £100\left\{(1+i)\left[\frac{(1+i)^n-1}{i}\right]\right\}$$

$$= £100\ddot{S}_n, \text{ where } \ddot{S}_n = (1+i)\left[\frac{(1+i)^n-1}{i}\right]$$

Clearly

$$\ddot{S}_n = (1+i)S_n = S_{n+1} - 1$$

and

$$S_n = v\ddot{S}_n .$$

Similarly, we can also calculate present values based on payments made annually in arrears or annually in advance. In the former case we have the present value of £100 per annum *in arrears* for n years

$$= £100(v+v^2+ \ldots +v^n) = £100 \frac{v(1-v^n)}{1-v}$$

$$= £100\, a_n, \text{ where } a_n = \frac{v(1-v^n)}{1-v} = \frac{1-v^n}{i} . \tag{2}$$

Again, the present value of £100 per annum *in advance* for n years

$$= £100(1+v+v^2+ \ldots +v^{n-1}) = £100 \frac{(1-v^n)}{1-v}$$

$$= £100\, \ddot{a}_n, \text{ where } \ddot{a}_n = \frac{1-v^n}{1-v} .$$

Clearly

$$\ddot{a}_n = (1+i)a_n = 1 + a_{n-1}$$

and

$$a_n = v\ddot{a}_n .$$

Moreover,

$$a_n = v^n S_n$$

$$S_n = (1+i)^n a_n .$$

Such ideas can be employed to answer questions such as: 'What is the regular annual repayment (in arrears) to secure a loan of £1000 repayable over ten years at ten per cent per annum effective?'

Solution 1 (*Discounting*)

Let the annual repayment be £X per annum. Then the present value of a series of annual repayments of £X must equate to £1000.
Hence

$$£X a_{10} = £1000 \text{ at } 10\% \text{ p.a.}$$

$$X = 1000/a_{10}.$$

(The value of a_{10} is tabulated, though it can easily be calculated using formula (2).)

$$£X = £162.74 \text{ p.a.}$$

Solution 2 (*Accumulating*)

If the annual repayments are £X per annum, they must accumulate to the value of £1000 in ten years time. Hence

$$£X \, S_{10} = £1000 \, (1+i)^{10} \text{ at } 10\% \text{ p.a.}$$

$$X = 1000 \, (1+i)^{10} / S_{10}.$$

(The value of S_{10} is tabulated, though it can easily be calculated using formula (1).)

$$£X = £162.74 \text{ p.a.,}$$

giving an identical solution to Solution 1.

Whilst either method is permissible, Solution 1 is preferable since it is marginally simpler. In more complex problems there are even greater merits in using the discounting methods.

Most practical problems involve the same approach as was used in the above example with the addition of one or two complications. These complications are normally of two kinds:

(a) A nominal rate of interest per annum is quoted as opposed to an effective rate.

(b) Loan repayments are made at a frequency differing from the effective interest period.

Let us consider each of these in turn and apply them to the above problem.

(a) Nominal rate of interest per annum quoted

The problem considered above might have been: What is the regular quarterly repayment (in arrears) to secure a loan of £1000 repayable over ten years at ten per cent per annum payable quarterly?

Solution
Step 1 Determine the effective interest period and the effective interest rate.
Since the nominal rate $i^{(4)} = 10$ per cent, the effective period is a quarter and the effective rate is $2\frac{1}{2}$ per cent or (0.025) per quarter.
Step 2 Determine the number of effective interest periods in the term of the loan. This is obviously $4 \times 10 = 40$ quarters.
Step 3 Use Solution 1 above, using 40 quarters at $2\frac{1}{2}$ per cent per quarter. Hence

$$£X \, a_{40} = £1000 \text{ at } 2\frac{1}{2}\% \text{ per quarter}$$

$$£X = £1000/a_{40} = £39.84 \text{ per quarter.}$$

(b) Differing repayment and effective interest periods

Before proceeding with an example, let us consider the problem generally when repayment periods are more frequent than effective interest periods.

Let us assume that repayments are made p times during an effective interest period. Ideally we would like to compute the equivalent lump sum value (payable at the end of the interest period) of these payments, then apply this as a factor and proceed using Solution 1 above. In other words if i is the effective rate of interest per period, and repayments of $£X/p$ are made p times during this period, then the required value is

$$£\frac{X}{p}[(1+i)^{1-1/p} + (1+i)^{1-2/p} + \ldots + 1]$$

$$= £\frac{X}{p}\left[\frac{(1+i)-1}{(1+i)^{1/p}-1}\right] = £\frac{Xi}{p[(1+i)^{1/p}-1]} = £\frac{Xi}{i^{(p)}}$$

(see page 138).

We can now answer the following typical practical question: 'What is the regular *monthly* repayment to secure a loan of £1000 repayable over ten years at ten per cent per annum payable quarterly?
Step 1 Define the effective period, which in this case is a quarter.
Step 2 Calculate the effective rate of interest per quarter:

$$i^{(4)}/4 = 10/4\% = 2\frac{1}{2}\% \; (0.025) \text{ per quarter.}$$

Step 3 Determine the number of effective periods in the ten years duration: $10 \times 4 = 40$ quarters.
Step 4 Since repayments are monthly (i.e. three times a quarter) we will need to use the factor $i/i^{(3)}$ formulated at the beginning of this section.

Step 5 Proceed to the solution.
Hence
$$£Xia_{40}/i^{(3)} = £1000 \text{ at } 2\tfrac{1}{2}\% \text{ per quarter}$$
where £X/3 is the monthly repayment.
$$£X = £1000/(ia_{40}/i^{(3)}) = £39.508745.$$
So £X/3 = £13.17 per month.

Compound interest tables

The solution of most practical problems is made much simpler by the use of tables or computers. The latter can often be more profitably used by breaking problems down into component parts for which tabulated functions exist. Random manual checks can then be made to test that programs are working properly. The most useful tables include values of $(1+i)^n$, v^n, S_n, a_n, i, $i^{(p)}$ and $i/i^{(p)}$, for various i, p and n. In addition to these functions a number of others are found to have practical value.

(a) **The rate of discount 'd'**

The rate of discount is a measure of the allowance to be made for payment in advance of a sum due at the end of the year. More formally, it is the rate of discount, allowable immediately on each unit sum receivable at the end of the year, equivalent to an interest rate i.
Hence
$$d = 1 - v = 1 - \frac{1}{1+i} = iv \quad \text{and} \quad d(1+i) = i.$$

(b) **The nominal rate of discount '$d^{(p)}$'**

$d^{(p)}$ is used to denote the annual rate of discount payable p times per year equivalent to d payable immediately.
$$(1-d) = \left(1 - \frac{d^{(p)}}{p}\right)^p.$$

True actuarial discount is, however, rarely used in practice, although the ratio $i/d^{(p)}$ is useful for simplifying payments made in advance. For example, the present value of a unit per annum, payable quarterly in advance (denoted by $\ddot{a}_n^{(4)}$) is equivalent to $ia_n/d^{(4)}$, a function which is tabulated.

The commercial bill broker tends to disregard such mathematical niceties and will, for example, if the commercial rate of discount is three per cent, assess the discount on a three months bill for £100 as £(100 × 0.03/4), and on a six months bill as £(100 × 0.03/2). The *effective* rate of discount per annum will, therefore, differ. In the former instance it is $1-(1-0.03/4)^4$, in the latter $1-(1-0.03/2)^2$.

(c) Force of interest 'δ'

So far we have assumed that interest is paid at fixed intervals — our model has been a discrete one. Occasionally it is useful to construct a model in which interest is assumed to be paid continuously. (Compare, for example, discrete (recurrence relation) and continuous (differential equation) models for the growth of populations.)

If we have a nominal rate of 1 (i.e. 100%) per annum, then

$i^{(1)}$ causes £1 to accumulate to £$(1+1)$ after one year,

$i^{(2)}$ causes £1 to accumulate to £$(1+\frac{1}{2})^2$ after one year,

$i^{(12)}$ causes £1 to accumulate to £$(1+\frac{1}{12})^{12}$ after one year,

$i^{(n)}$ causes £1 to accumulate to £$(1+1/n)^n$ after one year.

The effect of adding interest continuously is found, then, by determining $\lim_{n\to\infty}(1+1/n)^n$. It is, of course, the number e.

In general, a nominal rate of δ per annum will, if added continuously, cause £1 to accumulate to £e^δ at the end of one year. Thus, the force of interest, δ, corresponds to an effective annual rate of interest of i where $i = e^\delta - 1$. Hence,

$$e^\delta = 1+i, \qquad \delta = \ln(1+i)$$

and

$$e^{-\delta} = 1-d = v, \qquad \delta = -\ln v.$$

The function i/δ, which is useful for loans repayable continuously in advance, is also tabulated.

Some further practical problems

When calculating the level repayments of a loan, for example, a mortgage on a house, we should be aware that each repayment is made up of a capital and an interest repayment. Furthermore, for the duration of the loan, the interest element decreases (since some of the capital has been repaid) and therefore the capital element increases.

In practice, we very often need to know the interest and capital elements of each loan repayment separately, and the total interest paid during the term (for example, for taxation purposes).

Let us take a simple example of a loan of £1000 repayable annually in arrears over five years at ten per cent per annum effective.

The annual repayment is the solution to $£Xa_5 = £1000$ at ten per cent, whence $£X = 263.797$ (say £263.80).

We know that the interest element at the end of the first year is $(0.1 \times £1000) = £100$ and therefore, by subtraction, the capital element is £163.80.

We can therefore produce the loan repayment table as follows:

Table 11.1 Loan repayments

End of year	Capital paid (£)	Interest paid (£)	Total repayment (£)	Loan outstanding (£)
0	–	–	–	1 000.00
1	163.80	100.00	263.80	836.20
2	180.18	83.62	263.80	656.02
3	198.20	65.60	263.80	457.82
4	218.02	45.78	263.80	239.80*
5	239.82*	23.98	263.80	–

* Error in pence due to rounding

On closer inspection of this table it is seen that the capital elements increase in geometric progression. Furthermore, if we require to know, without producing the full table, what the capital element of the fourth annual repayment is, we can calculate it as $£163.80(1.1)^3 = £218.02$, which agrees with the tabulated figure. In general, capital contained in the rth annual payment equals the capital in the first payment multiplied by $(1+i)^{r-1}$.

In addition, the capital outstanding after r repayments is the present value (at that time) of the remaining $(n-r)$ payments; $£Xa_{n-r}$. For example, the capital outstanding after two payments in the above illustration is $£263.80a_3 = £656.04$, which apart from a rounding error, agrees with the tabulated value.

These methods of calculation are very useful in practice for loans repayable over a large number of years, when compilation of the full repayment schedule is not required.

To complete the picture:

$$\text{total interest paid during the term} = £X(n - a_n),$$
$$\text{total principal repaid} = £Xa_n,$$
$$\text{total amount repaid} = £Xn.$$

The preceding example concerns straightforward annual repayments at an effective annual rate of interest. As we saw earlier most practical problems are more complicated, but nevertheless similar methods can be employed. In general terms, if the loan £A is to be repaid over n years by instalments payable p times yearly with an effective annual rate of interest i, then:
(a) the *interest* contained in the tth payment is

$$£A(1-v^{(n-(t-1)/p)})/(pia_n/i^{(p)})$$

(b) the *principal* contained in the tth payment is

$$£A(v^{(n-(t-1)/p)})/(pia_n/i^{(p)})$$

(c) the *principal* outstanding after the tth payment is

$$£Aa_{n-t/p}/a_n.$$

As a final worked example let us consider a typical problem connected with the repayment of a hire–purchase flat rate loan.

'What is the level monthly payment for a loan of £1000 repayable over two years at ten per cent flat rate, and what is the effective rate of interest paid?'
Step 1 Calculate the total interest paid over the two years:

$$£(0.10 \times 1000 \times 2) = £200$$

Step 2 Calculate the total repayment:

$$£200 + £1000 = £1200$$

Step 3 Calculate the level monthly repayment:

$$£\frac{1200}{24} = £50 \text{ per month}$$

Step 4 Calculate the effective rate of interest per annum, which is the solution to

$$£\left(50 \times 12 \times \frac{i}{i^{(12)}} \times a_2\right) = £1000 \text{ at } i \text{ p.a.}$$

We are now faced with the problem of solving this equation for i, which cannot be done simply. The most practical method is to find by trial and error two tabulated values which straddle £1000, and then interpolate between them.

Substitution of $i = 19\frac{3}{4}$ per cent yields £999.9618, while substitution of $i = 19\frac{1}{2}$ per cent yields £1002.0373.

Simple straight line interpolation therefore provides an approximate value for i of 19.745 per cent. This method is suitable for most practical purposes, though it may not always conform to the conditions of the Consumer Credit Act.

More accurate results can be achieved using techniques of numerical analysis, for example, the Newton–Raphson method.

The subject of compound interest, then, has many applications — and there are others which we have not been able to describe here, for example, the calculation of life assurance premiums, discounted cash flows, and the calculation of gross redemption yields on fixed interest securities. We have opted in this chapter to concentrate attention on the important area of loan repayments, a topic affecting the daily lives of so many people. Our examples should have demonstrated how a good basic understanding of the subject is a very useful weapon in the armoury of anyone working in the commercial world, particularly in banking.

Philip Prescott

12 The design and analysis of a consumer preference test

As an applied statistician I am sometimes asked to help with practical problems arising in industry, market research, or medicine. During the last few years enquiries have ranged from the effects of drugs in clinical trials to the heights of waves hitting oil platforms in the North Sea to, more recently, the attitudes of head teachers to health education in schools. However, the practical application of statistical methods that I should like to describe here involves a recent study of consumer preference for a particular kind of apple pie — the sort of apple pie sold as a lunchtime snack or convenient dessert.

The question to be answered was: 'Which kind of apple pie is preferred by most people?' This seems a simple enough question, but finding an answer involves a considerable amount of careful thought and planning.

Before giving details of the experiment, I must point out that for obvious reasons the confidentiality of the main results and the anonymity of the manufacturer concerned must be respected, so perhaps I should begin with the usual film-credit disclaimer. 'Although this is a true story, some of the facts have been changed, and any resemblance to real apple pies is entirely coincidental.'

My objective is to give a brief outline of the main steps involved in setting up a practical trial of this kind. We shall see that some of the steps require mathematical ideas, some require statistical concepts, but most of the steps are based on simple common sense.

What is an apple pie?

To begin to answer the question that was originally posed it is necessary to identify the product. What are the ingredients of an apple pie and can these ingredients be varied to improve the acceptability of the product? The manufacturer already produced a particular type of pie and had a good idea which ingredients could be economically varied. Behind the original question is a more detailed one: 'Should the ingredients of the presently manufactured pie be changed to improve its customer acceptability, and if so which ingredients are important and what should the recipe be?'

Let us begin by examining the question of what constitutes an apple pie. Having consulted several cookery books at home, I was surprised to find that the recipes for apple pie were all different. There was no general consensus of what the ingredients should be. Two examples will indicate the wide variations amongst the ingredients listed.

The first is taken from Sonia Allisons's *The Love of Cooking* and is absolutely basic. The recipe is:

Apple pie (serves 4 to 6)
$2\frac{1}{2}$ lb ($1\frac{1}{4}$ kg) cooking apples
4 to 8 oz (100 to 200 g) castor sugar

short crust pastry
beaten egg for brushing
extra castor sugar for decoration

The ingredients are simple — apples, pastry, and sugar and very little else. Nevertheless the end result looks delicious.

In contrast to this, the recipe for 'Traditional English Apple Pie' in Robert Carrier's *Great Dishes of the World* contains a number of additional ingredients. (Carrier discloses, incidentally, that the English apple pie dates from at least the thirteenth century!)

$1\frac{1}{2}$ lb cooking apples
juice of $\frac{1}{2}$ lemon
pastry for shell and top
4 oz granulated sugar
2 oz dark brown sugar
1 tablespoon flour
$\frac{1}{8}$ level teaspoon grated nutmeg

$\frac{1}{4}$ level teaspoon powdered cinnamon
grated peel of $\frac{1}{2}$ orange
grated peel of $\frac{1}{2}$ lemon
2 oz chopped raisins and sultanas
1–2 tablespoons orange juice
1–2 tablespoons butter

We see that the extra ingredients may be divided into three groups: (a) lemon and orange, (b) spices, i.e. nutmeg and cinnamon, and (c) dried fruit, i.e. raisins and sultanas.

It is evident from these two examples that the contents of an apple pie vary considerably, and what we are seeking is that combination of ingredients which produces the pie preferred by most people.

The factors involved in the preference test

Apart from the basic ingredients of apples, sugar, and pastry, also considered in the test were lemon, dried fruit, and spices. These may be regarded as three *factors* whose *levels* or amounts may be varied in the recipes. The precise levels used in the actual test are confidential but it is sufficient to regard the levels as 'presence' or 'absence' in each case. There are therefore eight possible combinations of these factor levels producing eight different recipes.

In addition to these content factors, two presentation variables were also to be included as factors. Firstly, the pies could be presented with a *closed pastry case* or with a decorative *open lattice-work* top. Secondly, the amount of water included in the filling could be adjusted to give a dry or moist appearance.

Thus we have five factors each at two levels as follows:

Table 12.1 Factors that can be varied in apple pies

Factor	Level	
	low	*high*
A: lemon	absent	present
B: pastry covering	open	covered
C: dried fruit	absent	present
D: spice	absent	present
E: water	dry	moist

Five factors each at two levels implies $2^5 = 32$ product versions. For example we could have each factor at its low level: no lemon, open pastry, no dried fruit, no spice, dry filling, or we could have a pie with lemon, open top, no fruit, spice and moist filling, and so on. Evidently a simple notation is required to identify each particular combination of factor levels being used. There are two such notations in common use. The first associates 0 with the low level of a factor and 1 with the high level, so that the second example above would be coded 10011. This notation is particularly easy to extend to cases of factors at more than two levels. However the notation I prefer for experiments with factors at two levels only is as follows. For each factor use a blank for the low level and the corresponding factor letter (in lower case) for the high level. So, for example, 'lemon, open top, no fruit, spice, moist' is denoted by *ade*. The combination of all factors at the low level is denoted by (1). In this way all 32 possible combinations can be represented as follows:

(1)	d	e	de
a	ad	ae	ade
b	bd	be	bde
ab	abd	abe	abde
c	cd	ce	cde
ac	acd	ace	acde
bc	bcd	bce	bcde
abc	abcd	abce	abcde

The design of the preference test

Now that the product versions have been identified, we must face the practical problems of determining which of these 32 versions of apple pie is preferred by most people.

Clearly, in order to obtain results which are applicable to prospective purchasers of the pies, the test must be carried out using members of the public representative of the population at which the product is aimed and must involve asking people to taste the pies and give their preferences.

Obviously it is not practical to ask anyone to taste and compare all 32 product versions, so we need to decide how many different apple pies any individual should be asked to compare. We also need to know how many individuals should be included in the experiment and what kind of preference measure should be used. These questions are interlinked in that the answer to one question will affect the answers to the others. The fact that there are 2^5 possible versions suggests that the number of products compared by an individual should be a power of 2, that is 2, 4, 8, or 16. Many consumer tests involve a simple comparison of two products at a time in the form of a round-robin which would involve comparisons of all possible pairs. Using this procedure with 32 products would involve too many pairings, in fact there are 496 ways of pairing 32 products. On the other hand, asking someone to taste 8 or 16 pies was felt to be unreasonable. It was decided therefore to base the experiment on asking each individual to compare *four* of the product versions.

Although several measures of preference could be envisaged, it was thought that a simple ranking of the four products would be most appropriate and reasonably straightforward to apply. Each respondent would be asked to place his or her four products in order of preference by allocating ranks r_1, r_2, r_3, r_4 to them; equal ranks were permitted if no distinction was made between some of the product versions. The ranks were then converted to scores by setting the score for the pth product, s_p, equal to the number of products ranked below it less the number of products ranked above ($p = 1, 2, 3$ and 4).

Thus the values of s_p range from -3 to $+3$ in such a way that for each individual respondent

$$s_1 + s_2 + s_3 + s_4 = 0$$

The scores and ranks are related by the equation

$$s_p = 5 - 2r_p$$

but scores were considered more informative than ranks since their sign, positive or negative, indicated at once whether the product versions are preferred or disliked, respectively.

One of the most difficult decisions to make in designing an experiment of this kind is the number of individuals needed. Often the choice is made more on cost considerations than on statistical grounds. However, it is important to decide at the outset on the kind of product difference that one is trying to detect, then the sample size can be chosen to give an acceptably high probability of being able to detect that difference if such a difference does exist. It is pointless carrying out an experiment which is not sensitive enough to detect important differences but alternatively it is wasteful of resources to use large samples if the same conclusions could have been obtained with smaller samples. It is usually possible to obtain some idea of the sample size required to detect important differences even if several simplifying assumptions have to be made.

Determination of sample size

For this experiment a simulation study was carried out to determine the probability of correctly identifying the best product, using groups of four and using sample sizes ranging from $n=100$ to $n=500$. The product scores were simulated on a computer using four random normal deviates with zero means, to one of which was added an amount d, called the 'shift parameter'. This was repeated for the n individuals and the product with the highest aggregate score was selected as the best. The entire procedure was repeated 100 times and the proportion of occasions on which the 'best' product was correctly chosen was recorded. This was done for each sample size and for a range of shift parameters with values from 0 to 0.5. The power functions so produced are shown in Fig. 12.1, from which we may see that if one product is shifted relative to the others by an amount $d=0.18$, we need about 400 observations in order to have more than a 90 per cent chance of correctly identifying this product as the best.

Employing normal approximations, a shift of $d=0.18$ of one product relative to another corresponds roughly to 55 per cent of the population preferring that product. Although there are many simplifying assumptions underlying these arguments, the results suggest that, if possible, we should consider using about 400 to 500 individuals in the experiment.

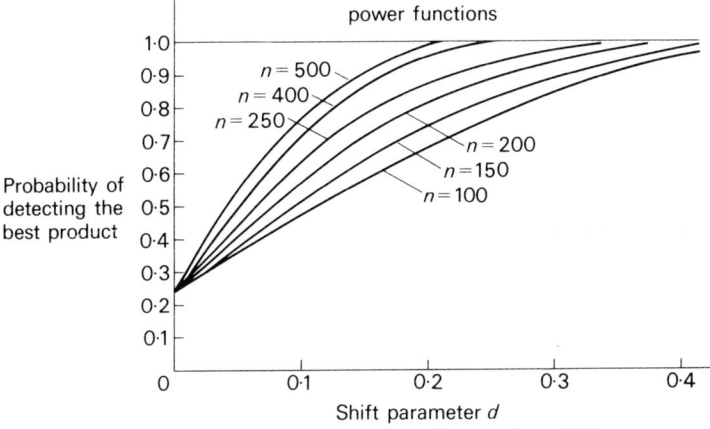

Fig. 12.1 Probability of detecting the best product against shift parameter

Other factors which could influence the results

In designing the final structure of the experiment it is important to consider any factors, in addition to those being examined in the experiment itself, which could have an effect on the results.

The first of these which springs to mind is the *order* of presentation of the four product versions to any particular individual. It is conceivable that a person's ranking may be affected by which pie he or she tasted first. It would be sensible therefore to arrange the experiment in such a way that all product versions were treated fairly in this respect. Suppose that the four pies being presented to an individual are represented by V_1, V_2, V_3, and V_4. There are 24 different ways of ordering these four product versions which may be produced by cyclic rotation of the six basic orderings:

$$V_1 V_2 V_3 V_4 \qquad V_1 V_3 V_4 V_2$$
$$V_1 V_2 V_4 V_3 \qquad V_1 V_4 V_2 V_3$$
$$V_1 V_3 V_2 V_4 \qquad V_1 V_4 V_3 V_2$$

The cyclic rotations of the first ordering are $V_1 V_2 V_3 V_4$, $V_2 V_3 V_4 V_1$, $V_3 V_4 V_1 V_2$, and $V_4 V_1 V_2 V_3$. Thus the effect of order of presentation may be taken into account if each set of four product versions is tasted by 24 individuals using all possible orderings.

The second external factor which could influence the results of the test concerns problems of quality control. Quality is strictly controlled on baking standards of production pies but for the test the bakery was being asked to produce a large number of pies to different recipes. The pies were to be specially made during the night for the test on the following day. It was desirable therefore that all product versions should be included in a single night's baking and that the entire test procedure should be repeated over a number of days so that day-to-day variations could be assessed as part of the experiment.

The main effects and interactions of the five factors

The design of the experiment is now beginning to take shape:

(i) each individual ranks four products
(ii) each set of four products is to be compared by 24 individuals using all possible orders of presentation
(iii) the basic design is repeated over a number of days.

We now need to consider how to select the sets of four product versions to be ranked by an individual. Remember that the original objective is to assess the importance of the five factors: *A* lemon, *B* pastry case, *C* dried fruit, *D* spices, *E* water.

In order to measure the effect of 'lemon', for example, each individual should compare two products with lemon at each level, that is, two of the products should contain lemon and two should not. Similarly two should have open cases while two should be covered, and so on for all five factors.

It is possible by a suitable choice of the sets of four products to arrange for these requirements to be satisfied. One solution using all 32 product versions in eight sets of four, is given below.

Individual	Set of four product versions			
1	(1)	ace	abd	bcde
2	a	ce	bd	abcde
3	b	abce	ad	cde
4	c	ae	abcd	bde
5	d	acde	ab	bce
6	e	ac	abde	bcd
7	bc	abe	acd	de
8	be	abc	ade	cd

Notice that for each individual two of the products contain *a*, two contain *b*, two *c*, two *d*, and two *e* as required. Therefore, it is possible with this arrangement to measure the main effects of each factor *within* each individual. Differences between individuals will not affect the comparisons between the high and low levels of each factor.

More information is available from this structure than just the main effects of the five factors. Notice that within each individual the letters *a* and *b*, for example, are in one case absent, and also occur as '*a*', '*b*', and '*ab*', so that factor *A* is at both high and low levels when *B* is at both high and low levels. This means that it is possible to measure the effect of *A* at the low level of *B* and the effect of *A* at the high level of *B* within an individual. If these two effects are different then there is evidence of an interaction between the factors *A* and *B*. Therefore with this design it is possible to investigate, say, whether people prefer lemon in open topped or closed topped pies.

Other interactions may be investigated with this design. Of the ten possible interactions between pairs of factors, eight may be examined with this structure. The two which are not available are the interactions between *C* and *E* and between *B* and *D*. This is because *c* and *e* either appear together twice in a set of four or they appear separately twice. The same thing applies to '*b*' and '*d*'. Such a design is called a 2^5 factorial design in eight blocks of four with *CE* and *BD confounded* with blocks.

This design has several nice features but has two major disadvantages in this situation:
(i) To include all orderings, 192 (i.e. 8 × 24) individuals would be required on each day of the trial. This was considered to be too many for the interviewers that were available.
(ii) All 32 product versions would have to be prepared. The bakery was worried that the quality of the pies would be difficult to maintain and some confusion in their preparation would be almost inevitable.

Because of these problems the design was modified. The basic structure was maintained but on any particular day only 16 of the product versions were used.

The final design employed was the following:

Individual	Set of four product versions			
1	(1)	acde	abce	bd
2	ab	bcde	ce	ad
3	cd	ae	abde	bc
4	abcd	be	de	ac

All main effects may still be estimated within individuals, but in this design only seven of the ten interactions between pairs of factors are examinable, the three which are confounded with individuals are AC, CE, and AE.

The number of individuals required to cover all possible orderings for one day (96) was now considered feasible. The design was replicated on five days to give the required sample size of $5 \times 96 = 480$ individuals.

The fieldwork

It is evident that a highly balanced design such as that used here, requires the greatest care in application to avoid errors which could seriously affect the subsequent analysis. The organisation of the fieldwork is an important part of any experiment or survey and as much care and attention should be applied in collecting the data as in designing the experiment or analysing the results. This organisation involves designing the response form or questionnaire training interviewers, and ensuring that the correct combinations of product versions are being compared.

A simple, yet very effective, procedure was employed to ensure that there was no mix-up over which combination of pies was being presented to an individual and that all combinations and orders of presentation were used during a day's experimentation. Firstly four envelopes were prepared to correspond to the four sets of combinations of pies to be compared. Each envelope contained 24 circular paper doilies, one for each of the 24 possible orderings of the four pies. For each individual the interviewer would first extract a doily from the envelope and place it on a circular container. The four specimens of pie indicated on the label on the envelope would be arranged round the doily to correspond to one of the six basic orderings. The container would then be rotated so that each specimen became first in the sequence of tasting (four variations, each one corresponding to a rotation of the container through 90°). The label of the envelope would then be marked to show that that particular ordering had been tested. The procedure would be repeated until all 24 doilies in the envelope had been used.

Analysis of the preference scores

The results of the experiment were returned in the form of completed questionnaires containing an appropriate code number to identify the respondent, the product versions being compared and the order of presentation used. The form also contained the rankings of the four products and spaces for the corresponding scores to be inserted. Over the five days of the experiment, each set of four products was compared by 120 (i.e. 5×24) individuals, so that the data could be regarded as consisting of four separate sets of 120 rankings (or scorings) as follows:

Product	120 individuals					Totals
(1)	3	−1	−3	...	−3	$S(1)$
acde	1	3	3	...	3	$Sacde$
abce	−3	1	−1	...	−1	$Sabce$
bd	−1	−3	1	...	1	Sbd

In the table the total scores for the four products are denoted by $S(1)$, $Sacde$, $Sabce$, and Sbd. Similarly, total scores for the other sets of four product versions were computed, and the four sets of totals can be shown symbolically as:

Block	Totals			
1	$S(1)$	$Sacde$	$Sabce$	Sbd
2	Sab	$Sbcde$	Sce	Sad
3	Scd	Sae	$Sabde$	Sbc
4	$Sabcd$	Sbe	Sde	Sac

The main effects and interactions of the five factors may be obtained from these total scores. For example the main effect of factor A is given by

$$\hat{A} = \frac{1}{8 \times 120}[-S(1) + Sacde + Sabce - Sbd + Sab - Sbcde - Sce + Sad$$
$$- Scd + Sae + Sabde - Sbc + Sabcd - Sbe - Sde + Sac].$$

Notice that the eight plus signs are associated with the totals involving 'a' and the eight minus signs with totals not involving 'a', also that there are two plus signs and two minus signs within each block of four. If respondents tend to rank pies with lemon higher than pies without lemon then $\hat{A}$ would be positive; if there is no difference between the results for the two levels of lemon, $\hat{A}$ would be closer to zero. Similar formulae may be used for the other main effects.

The interaction between factors A and B, for example, is measured by

$$\widehat{AB} = \frac{1}{8 \times 120}[S(1) - Sacde + Sabce - Sbd + Sab - Sbcde + Sce - Sad$$
$$+ Scd - Sae + Sabde - Sbc + Sabcd - Sbe + Sde - Sac].$$

Large values of $\widehat{AB}$ indicate that the effect of A is different at the different levels of B, while small values indicate that A and B are not interacting with each other.

In order to be able to say whether or not the computed values of the main effects and interactions are significantly large, it is necessary to know their variances. In most applications of factorial designs the responses at each treatment combination are independent and the analysis of variance may be used to examine the significance of the main effects and interactions. In this experiment, however, the analysis of variance cannot be used since the scores (and therefore the ranks) are not independent — the scores for any individual sum to zero.

On the assumption that there is no difference between products (which is equivalent to the hypothesis that the factors have no effect on the rankings — the hypothesis that we are trying to test), it is relatively simple to compute the means, variances and covariances of the ranks. If k products are being ranked the ranks consist of the numbers $1, 2, \ldots, k$. If r_p and r_q are the ranks associated with pth and qth products, the mean value of r_p is

$$E(r_p) = \frac{1}{k}\sum_{i=1}^{k} i = \frac{k(k+1)}{2k} = \frac{k+1}{2}.$$

The variance of r_p is

$$\text{Var}(r_p) = \frac{1}{k}\sum_{i=1}^{k} i^2 - \left(\frac{k+1}{2}\right)^2 = \frac{(k+1)(2k+1)}{6} - \frac{(k+1)^2}{4}$$

$$= \frac{(k+1)(k-1)}{12}$$

and the covariance between r_p and r_q is

$$\text{Cov}(r_p, r_q) = \frac{1}{k}\sum_{i \neq j}^{k}\sum^{k} ij - \left(\frac{k+1}{2}\right)^2$$

$$= -\frac{(k+1)}{12}.$$

Since ranks and scores are related by

$$s_p = (k+1) - 2r_p$$

the corresponding results for scores are

$$E(s_p) = 0, \quad \text{Var}(s_p) = (k^2 - 1)/3,$$

and
$$\text{Cov}(s_p, s_q) = -(k+1)/3,$$

The total scores $S(1)$ etc. are sums of 120 scores so that

$$E(S_p) = 0, \quad \text{Var}(S_p) = 120(k^2 - 1)/3,$$

and
$$\text{Cov}(S_p, S_q) \begin{cases} = -120(k+1)/3, & p \text{ and } q \text{ in the same block} \\ = 0 & p \text{ and } q \text{ in different blocks.} \end{cases}$$

The main effects and interactions are all of the form

$$\frac{1}{8 \times 120} \Sigma(\pm 1) S_p$$

where the sum contains eight $(+1)$s and eight (-1)s. The variance of each main effect and interaction is therefore given by

$$\left(\frac{1}{8 \times 120}\right)^2 \left[16 \times \frac{120(k^2-1)}{3} + 16 \times \frac{120(k+1)}{3}\right]$$

$$= \frac{k(k+1)}{3 \times 480}.$$

Since in our experiment we are ranking four products, $k = 4$, and the standard deviation of a main effect or interaction is

$$\sqrt{\frac{4 \times 5}{3 \times 480}} = 0.1178.$$

All main effects and interactions not confounded with individuals are of this form and have the same standard deviation. Their significance may be examined by comparing the computed values with their standard deviation 0.1178.

Table 12.2 Total scores for the 16 product versions

Block	Product version	Total score
1	(1)	−2
	acde	76
	abce	−39
	bd	−35
2	ab	−86
	bcde	−3
	ce	49
	ad	40
3	cd	94
	ae	56
	abde	−53
	bc	−97
4	abcd	−17
	be	−64
	de	86
	ac	−5

Table 12.3 Main effects and interactions

Factor/interaction		Effect
A	lemon	−0.058
B	pastry covering	−0.821
C	dried fruit	0.121
D	spices	0.392
E	water	0.225
AB		0.067
AD		−0.142
BC		0.050
BD		−0.021
BE		0.067
CD		0.113
DE		0.175

Results and conclusions

Table 12.2 shows the total scores for the 16 product versions. From the totals given, the estimated main effects of each factor and the seven interactions were computed and are shown in Table 12.3. Comparing these estimated effects with the standard deviation 0.1178, we see that the main effects of factors B and D are more than three times their standard deviation and are therefore highly significant. There is some evidence that factor E is also important since 0.225 is nearly twice the standard deviation.

It is therefore reasonable to conclude that
(i) open pastry coverings were preferred
(ii) spicy fillings were preferred
(iii) moist fillings were preferred.
The addition of dried fruit tended to increase the scores but the increase was not sufficiently large to make any firm recommendations. The presence or absence of lemon made hardly any difference to the scores.

Final recommendation

This analysis has shown that open-topped apple pies with spicy, moist fillings would be preferred by most people. The addition of dried fruit would tend to increase the acceptability of the product.

I have attempted in this brief outline of a recent practical problem to give some idea of the processes involved in carrying out a consumer preference test. The details of the mathematics need not concern us too greatly here, the important point is that it is always well worthwhile spending time and effort asking questions before the experiment begins. In this way a suitable design may be found which uses the data to full advantage. This is particularly important in experiments involving several factors, where the investigation of interactions between factors could be as important as the assessment of their main effects.

13 Modelling in hot water

J. G. Andrews

Energy has always been essential for our survival but now uncertainty about its continued supply is becoming an increasing cause for concern. The known resources of coal, oil, and nuclear fuel are likely to be exhausted within the next few generations and the present supplies are controlled largely by unstable political forces. This problem has stimulated a wide search for alternative sources of energy. Some of these are old warhorses which have been known about for a long time but not developed because conventional supplies of energy have been cheaper. These include wind power, wave power, and ambitious projects like damming the river Severn to make use of the colossal tidal range. Others, such as solar cells and geothermal power, have required technological developments before they could be exploited on a large scale.

Fig. 13.1 With increasing costs of fossil fuels many alternative natural energy sources are under investigation, all of them requiring a theoretical assessment of their viability in the manner of this chapter. Illustrated here is the Cockerell Raft which can extract power from waves. This method has a great attraction in a maritime nation like Britain, but there are practical difficulties. *Courtesy Energy Technology Support Unit, AERE Harwell.*

In this chapter we confine our interest to the exploitation of geothermal power. The total scale of the resource is immense, but it is usually too expensive to extract, except from certain favourable spots. However, if cheaper extraction methods are developed over the next few years, it is conceivable that a virtually unlimited amount of geothermal heat could be obtained for electricity production, as well as for domestic and commercial heating applications.

Geothermal power

Natural sources of hot water are in abundance in some parts of the world, for example Iceland, Italy, and New Zealand, but are almost non-existent elsewhere. In the UK there are just a few isolated spots such as the Roman baths in Bath and the watercress district of Hampshire. Hot springs and geysers, along with volcanoes and earthquakes, tend to occur in regions of rapid geological change. The last volcano in the UK erupted 60 million years ago and there has not been a really violent earthquake in recorded history. However, hot water at around 50–100°C can be trapped underground at depths of 2–3 km in porous rock formations called aquifers. This water is at the same temperature as the surrounding rock. Heat is produced throughout the Earth by the decay of radioactive isotopes and it is conducted through the mantle to the surface. The heat flux varies significantly over the Earth's surface due to variations in the thermal conductivity of rock. For geothermal exploitation we look for suitable porous rock formations in regions of large surface heat flux, because high flux implies rapid rise in temperature with depth and drilling costs are therefore minimised. Two such favourable areas in the UK are the Hampshire and Lincolnshire Basins.

How do we get the heat out of the ground? One solution is inspired by North Sea oil technology, in which the oil trapped in porous rock formations is driven out of the rock by pumping in high pressure water. We aim to drive out the existing hot water by drilling down to two different parts of the aquifer and pumping cold water at high pressure through the aquifer between the two boreholes (see Fig. 13.2). In this way the hot water already in the rock is driven out and replaced by cold water, which is heated in turn by the remaining hot rock. Eventually, the rock cools down and the water extracted becomes too cold to use. A new 'seam' would then have to be found since it takes thousands of years for the rock to regain its original temperature.

Choosing a suitable site to sink a borehole is a risky business. It is also very costly and it is therefore advisable to find out as much as possible about the likely geological conditions, the drilling and pumping requirements, and, most importantly, whether there is a local customer who could use the hot water. Possible applications of geothermal heat include power stations,

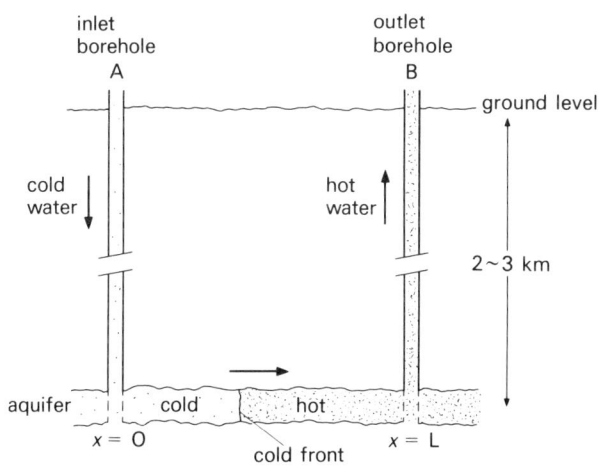

Fig. 13.2 Twin borehole system for heat extraction from aquifer

greenhouses, fish farms, swimming pools, and domestic hot water systems. Not surprisingly, geologists and engineers are needed to assess the risks and uses, and in order to calculate the heat output from a given aquifer they need a mathematical model. The problem is to use the information that can be gained about the nature of the rock to make predictions about the lifetime of the aquifer and how much power can be extracted.

Heat content of rock

Consider a block of hot dry rock. How much heat does it contain? According to calorimetry experiments, the heat content (measured in joules) of a given mass of material is linearly proportional to temperature, $T(°C)$, that is

$$\text{heat content per unit mass} = cT$$

where the coefficient, c, is called the specific heat. In this problem we must consider the heat content of a given volume, that is

$$\text{heat content per unit volume} = \rho cT \qquad (1)$$

where ρ (kg m^{-3}) is the density of the material. For example, if a cubic metre of sandstone ($\rho = 2.3 \times 10^3$ kg m^{-3}, $c = 966$ J/kg°C) is cooled through 50°C, the heat released is $h \simeq 1.1 \times 10^8$ J $= 1.1 \times 10^2$ MJ (1 MJ $\equiv 10^6$ J).

An average household in the UK uses an equivalent of 1.3 kW of thermal power, or an average of about 110 MJ of thermal energy per day. Hence, our cubic metre of sandstone cooled through 50°C has just enough heat to supply one household for one day. A typical sandstone aquifer (say, one which was once a primeval river bed) might have dimensions 20 m × 50 m × 10 000 m = 10^7 m^3.

Fluid flow

To assess the lifespan of an aquifer we must consider the water flow through the rock in more detail. Now, porous rocks such as chalk and sandstone can absorb water through a myriad of tiny inter-connected microscopic channels (see Fig. 13.3). The 'porosity' of the rock, φ, is defined as the fraction by volume occupied by these channels, called pores. Thus, a lump of rock of total volume, V, comprises a volume φV of pores and $(1-\varphi)V$ of actual rock material:

$$\underset{\text{total volume}}{V} = \underset{\text{volume of pores}}{\varphi V} + \underset{\text{volume of rock}}{(1-\varphi)V} \qquad (2)$$

If the rock is saturated with water, the entire volume of the pores, φV, will be occupied by water, assuming all pores are connected (i.e. no dead volume).

Now consider the motion of water through the porous rock. Since the orientation of pores is random, the detail of the flow at a microscopic level is very complicated. However, over a large enough area the random variations tend to cancel out and we need consider only the average flow per unit area. The first systematic experimental study of flow through porous media was performed by Darcy (1856). He found that the volume flow of water per second, Q, is directly proportional to the pressure gradient (see Fig. 13.4). Thus, for one-dimensional flow through a planar slab,

$$Q = qA = -kA\frac{dp}{dx} \qquad (3)$$

where k is a constant, called the permeability, and A is the cross-sectional area of the slab. The negative sign means that water flows in the direction of decreasing pressure. Hence, for a planar slab of rock of thickness L and cross-sectional area $1\,\text{m}^2$ with a pressure difference Δp applied across the slab, the volume of water flowing per second is

$$q = k\Delta p/L \quad (\text{m}^3\,\text{s}^{-1}). \qquad (4)$$

For example, sandstone, with $k = 10^{-8}\,\text{m}^3/\text{kg}$, $\Delta p = 10^6\,\text{N}/\text{m}^2$, $L = 10^3\,\text{m}$, gives $q = 10^{-5}\,\text{m}^3/\text{s}$. Thus, Darcy's law enables us to calculate the volume flow rate of water which can be pumped through rock in terms of the applied pressure drop and the permeability of the rock. To calculate the heat output of the system, we need to consider the heat transfer from the rock to the water.

Modelling in hot water 165

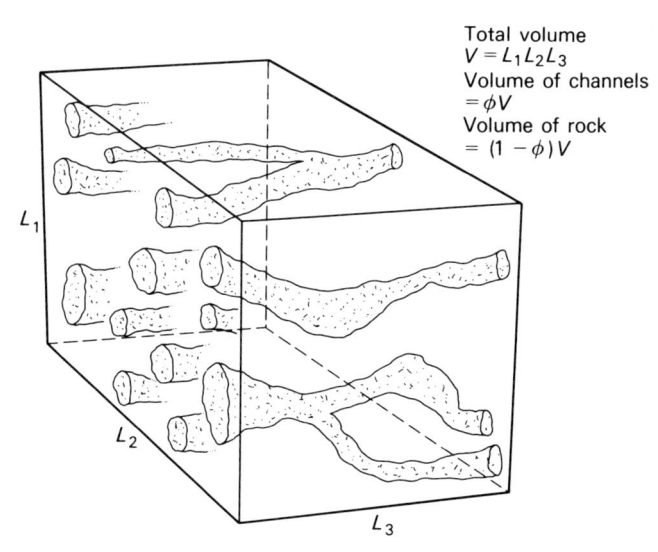

Total volume
$V = L_1 L_2 L_3$
Volume of channels
$= \phi V$
Volume of rock
$= (1 - \phi) V$

Fig. 13.3 Microscopic channels in porous rock

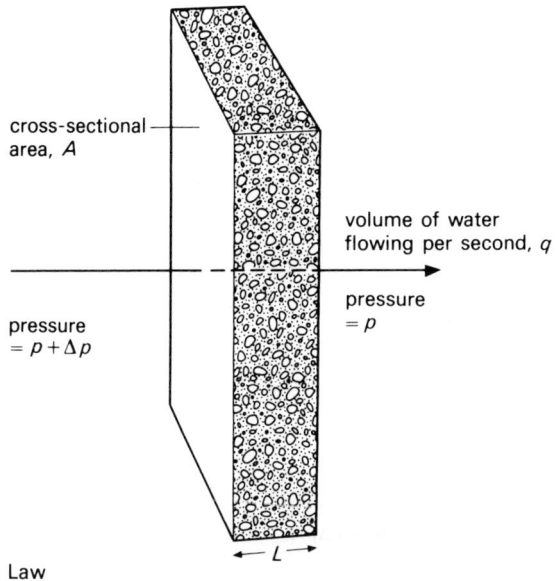

cross-sectional area, A

volume of water flowing per second, q

pressure $= p$

pressure $= p + \Delta p$

$\leftarrow L \rightarrow$

Darcy's Law

$$\begin{pmatrix} \text{Volume} \\ \text{flow rate} \\ \text{per second} \end{pmatrix} \propto \frac{\begin{pmatrix} \text{Cross-} \\ \text{sectional} \\ \text{area of slab} \end{pmatrix} \times \begin{pmatrix} \text{Pressure} \\ \text{difference} \\ \text{across slab} \end{pmatrix}}{(\text{thickness of slab})} \qquad q = \frac{-kA\,\Delta p}{L}$$

Fig. 13.4 Darcy's law for flow through a porous medium

Heat transfer

Returning to Fig. 13.2, we note that cold water enters the system through the inlet borehole, A, and leaves as hot water through the exit borehole, B. Let us assume that at the start of the pumping process the rock and the water already contained in the rock are at a uniform elevated temperature. As the first slug of cold water is injected at A, it will push the existing hot water towards B and will enter pores surrounded by hot rock. Heat is then transferred from the exposed hot rock to the incoming cold water, thereby heating the water and cooling the rock. Thus, at some point across the distance between the two boreholes, the water jumps up to the initial temperature of the rock but leaves the rock behind at the temperature of the incoming water. There will, therefore, be a sharp change in temperature, that is a 'cold front', moving slowly across the system from inlet to outlet. The system will be exhausted when the front reaches the outlet borehole. In order to calculate the lifespan of the aquifer, we must therefore calculate the speed of this cold front. For simplicity, we assume the front moves in one dimension only, i.e. the positive x-direction from $x=0$ to $x=L$ (see Fig. 13.5).

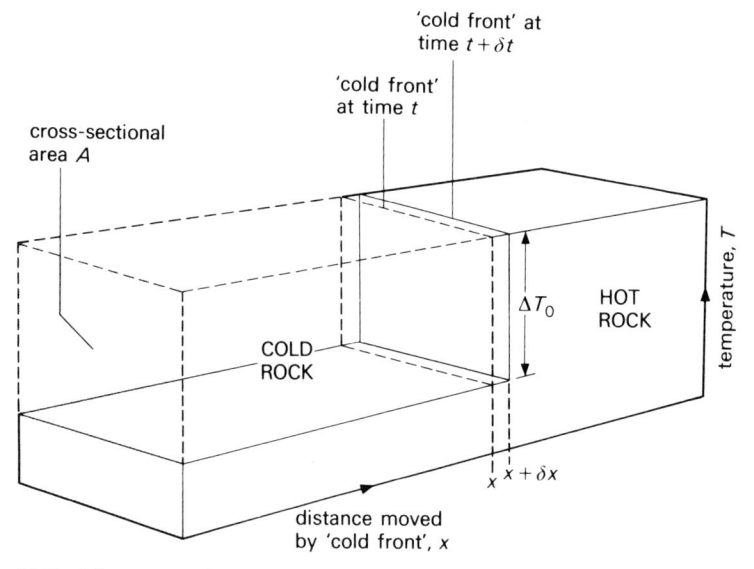

Fig. 13.5 Movement of a 'cold front' through an aquifer

Modelling in hot water

By energy conservation, the heat lost by the rock is absorbed by the water. Let the position of the front at time t be $x(t)$. In the next small time interval δt, suppose the front moves from x to $x+\delta x$. The total volume exposed is then $A\delta x$, where A is the area of the front. From equation (2), the volume of actual rock material contained in this element is

$$\delta V_r = (1-\varphi)A\delta x \tag{5}$$

where the subscript r refers to rock. Combining equations (1) and (5), the heat lost by the rock, δh_r, is given by

$$\delta h_r = \rho_r c_r \Delta T_0 \delta V_r$$
$$= \rho_r c_r \Delta T_0 (1-\varphi)A\delta x. \tag{6}$$

Now consider the water. Inside the front the temperature of the water jumps by an amount ΔT_0 and hence, for the water

$$\text{heat gained per unit volume} = \rho_w c_w \Delta T_0 \tag{7}$$

where the subscript w refers to water. The volume of water entering our small region in a time interval δt is

$$\delta V_w = Aq\delta t \tag{8}$$

and combining equations (7) and (8) we find that the heat gained by the water is

$$\delta h_w = \rho_w c_w \Delta T_0 Aq\delta t. \tag{9}$$

Applying energy conservation and equating the heat lost by the rock (equation (6)) to that gained by the water (equation (9)),

$$\rho_r c_r \Delta T_0 (1-\varphi)A\delta x = \rho_w c_w \Delta T_0 Aq\delta t.$$

If we now rearrange this equation and let $\delta t \to 0$, we obtain the speed of the front:

$$\frac{dx}{dt} = aq \tag{10}$$

where

$$a = \frac{\rho_w c_w}{(1-\varphi)\rho_r c_r} \tag{11}$$

is a constant, depending only on the properties of the rock and water. Thus the speed of the front is directly proportional to the volume flow rate of water per unit area.

Lifetime and power output

Integrating equation (10), taking a and q as constants, and putting $x=0$ at $t=0$, gives the position of the front at time t as

$$x = aqt. \qquad (12)$$

The lifetime of the system, t_B, i.e. the time at which the cold front breaks through to the outlet borehole B, is obtained by putting $x=L$ in this equation, giving

$$t_B = \frac{L}{aq}. \qquad (13)$$

The power output of the system is

$$P = dh_w/dt$$

which, from equation (9), is

$$P = \rho_w c_w \Delta T_0 A q. \qquad (14)$$

Thus equation (13) tells us that the lifetime varies inversely with flow rate, q, and equation (14) that the power varies directly with flow rate. Hence, for long life we require small q, but for large power q must be large! The problem is therefore one of finding the optimum operating regime, subject to the various constraints imposed by physical and economic considerations.

The conflict between long life and large power arises from the fact that the total energy initially present in the rock, E_r, is fixed. The energy content in the rock is

$$E_r = \left\{\begin{matrix} \text{fraction by} \\ \text{volume of rock} \end{matrix}\right\} \times \left\{\begin{matrix} \text{heat per unit} \\ \text{volume of rock} \end{matrix}\right\} \times \left\{\begin{matrix} \text{total volume} \\ \text{of rock} \end{matrix}\right\}$$

i.e.

$$E_r = (1-\varphi)\rho_r c_r \Delta T_0 A L. \qquad (15)$$

Hence, from equations (13) and (14),

$$Pt_B = \rho_w c_w \Delta T_0 A q \frac{L}{aq}$$

and on substitution for a from equation (11), we obtain

$$Pt_B = E_r = \text{constant}.$$

One economic constraint is that the lifetime would need to be in excess of ten years for useful commercial exploitation. Another constraint is that the flow rate of water through the aquifer has to be restricted, otherwise the

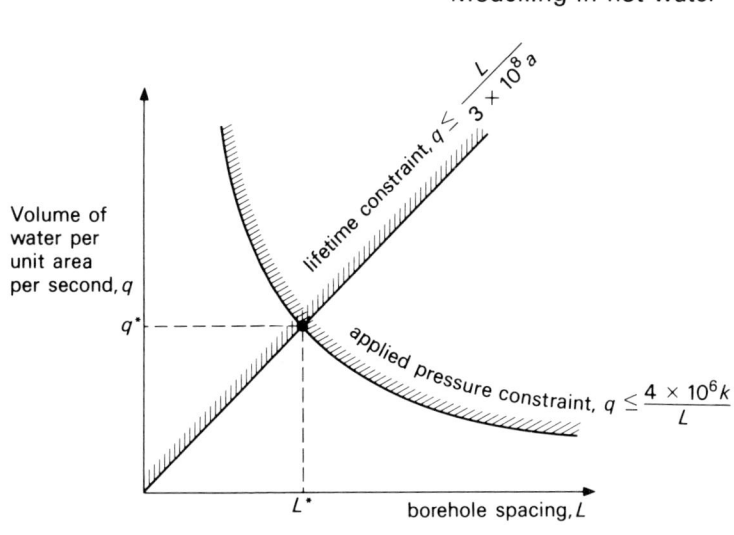

Fig. 13.6 Optimum spacing for maximum output (schematic)

outlet borehole can get blocked by silt and small fragments of rock dislodged by the flow. To avoid such occurrences, the 'over-pressure' at each borehole must be kept below about 20 atmospheres, i.e. 2×10^6 N m^{-2}, so that the pressure difference $\Delta p < 4 \times 10^6$ N m^{-2}. We are then left with the simple optimisation problem:

$$\text{maximise } P = \rho_w c_w \Delta T_0 A q$$

such that

$$t_B = \frac{L}{aq} \geq 10 \text{ years} \simeq 3 \times 10^8 \text{ s} \tag{16}$$

and

$$\Delta p = \frac{qL}{k} \leq 4 \times 10^6 \text{ N m}^{-2} \tag{17}$$

where ρ_w, c_w, ΔT_0, A, a, and k are given constants.

Rearranging equations (16) and (17) yields

$$q \leq \frac{L}{3 \times 10^8 a} \tag{18}$$

and

$$q \leq \frac{4 \times 10^6 k}{L}. \tag{19}$$

In Fig. 13.6 the limiting lines defined by these two last equations have been plotted. From the graph we can deduce that the optimum spacing, L^*, which gives the greatest flow (and hence the largest power output), is given by

$$\frac{L^*}{3 \times 10^8 \, a} = \frac{4 \times 10^6 \, k}{L^*}$$

or

$$L^* \simeq 10^7 \sqrt{12ak} \text{ m}.$$

Thus, for sandstone with $a = 2$ and $k = 10^{-8}$ m^3 s/kg, we find

$$L^* \simeq 5 \text{ km}$$

with a corresponding flow of

$$q^* = \frac{L^*}{3 \times 10^8 \, a} \simeq 8 \times 10^{-6} \text{ m/s}$$

and power output (putting $\Delta T_0 = 50°C$, $A = 10^3$ m^2)

$$P^* = \rho_w c_w \Delta T_0 A q^*$$
$$\simeq 10^3 \times (4.2 \times 10^3) \times 50 \times 10^3 \times (8 \times 10^{-6}) \text{ W}$$
$$= 1.7 \text{ MW}.$$

Over ten years, the average household in the UK uses 4×10^5 MJ of heat energy, equivalent to an average power of around 1.3 kW. Thus, our aquifer could supply heat to about 1300 households. Alternatively, for the same period it could heat about $1\frac{1}{2}$ acres of commercial glasshouse for out-of-season tomatoes, say, or be used for the generation of electricity (White, 1980).

Practical complications

Our simple model has enabled us to make rough estimates of the lifetime and power output from the aquifer. To make closer predictions we need to take account of the rock properties, fluid flow, and heat transfer processes in more detail. Some of the practical complications are listed below:
(a) aquifers are not homogeneous, their geological formation may vary considerably, particularly in different horizontal strata, leading to variations in permeability of two orders of magnitude
(b) the resistance to flow of water through porous rock depends on temperature, so that water in the cold region behind the 'cold front' will be harder to pump than the hot water ahead of the front
(c) as the aquifer is cooled behind the front, some heat will be conducted into the aquifer from the neighbouring impermeable rock

(d) in general, the fluid flow from the inlet borehole to the outlet borehole will not be one-dimensional — indeed the volume of 'swept' rock will always be larger than that we have considered, leading to larger heat outputs and lifetimes.

[A more detailed account of these effects can be found in Andrews, Richardson, and White (1981). A good geological survey of the heat flow field in mainland UK can be found in Richardson and Oxburgh (1979), and a discussion of the preferred applications of geothermal heat in Richardson and White (1980) and also White (1980).]

References

1 Andrews, J. G., Richardson, S. W. and White, A. A. L. (1981) 'Flushing geothermal heat from moderately permeable sediments', *J. Geophys. Research*, Vol. 86, No. B10, pp. 9439–9450
2 Darcy, H. (1856) 'Les fontaines publiques de la ville de Dijon', p. 590
3 Richardson, S. W. and Oxburgh, E. R. (1979) 'The heat flow field in mainland UK', *Nature*, Vol. 282, pp. 565–567
4 Richardson, S. W. and White, A. A. L. (1980) 'How to use geothermal energy', *Nature*, Vol. 286, pp. 103–104
5 White, A. A. L. (1980) 'Advantage of incorporating geothermal energy into power station cycles', *IEE Proc.*, Vol. 127, No. 5, pp. 330–335

14

B. J. R. Bailey

Probably guilty: the evidence against a parking meter offender

The use of probabilistic or statistical evidence in the courts of this country is somewhat rare; perhaps the most noted examples were those concerning the unfair application of the gaming laws in a casino. The case described in this chapter was more down to earth. It took place in the magistrates' court of a large town, and the background to it was as follows.

A company director was charged with jamming, on several occasions, three adjacent parking meters outside his office in, let us call it, Mint Street. By doing this he hoped to park all day without moving his car or feeding the meter. It was obvious that, at his trial, his defence would be that he had been extraordinarily unlucky in that the three meters he regularly used were faulty models which often jammed. Consequently, I was called as an expert witness by the prosecution to demonstrate that a defence of bad luck was stretching the belief of a reasonable person beyond its limits. A large amount of data was made available to me and to the court, and in order to understand it we must first appreciate the way in which it was collected.

Traffic wardens and mechanics

We are all familiar with the sight of a traffic warden walking the streets, affixing messages to car windscreens which state, in effect, that the law is not being kept as well as it might be. The warden does, however, have another role. Each day he or she carries a sheet of paper on which any parking meters that are inoperative or broken are noted down. On being returned to the office, this list is handed to a meter mechanic who then sets off to carry out the necessary repairs.

Now, there is a card corresponding to each meter where the date on which that meter was repaired is recorded along with a tick in one of six columns headed *Fault*, *Damage*, *Bad coin*, *Police*, *Other*, and *In order*. The mechanic, on his return to the office, makes an entry for each meter he has visited, choosing which column to tick according to the following lists.

Fault: coin jammed (accidentally), clock stopped, faulty clock, broken gate

carrier spring, dirty coin contact, push rod in need of adjustment, main spring broken, split coin frame, etc.
Damage: coin jammed (deliberately), damaged coin, foreign coin, foreign body (can ring, matchstick, putty, chewing gum), vandal damage, etc.
Bad coin: thin coin, etc.
Other: coin box jammed, coin box full, wet coins, etc.
The column headed *Police* seems never to be used.
In order: the mechanic finds the meter in working order on visiting it.

Our main concern in this case is with the first two columns. The essential difference between them is that *Fault* includes all those causes of breakdown considered to be accidental, and *Damage* those considered to be deliberate or wilful, and the mechanics believe they are capable of distinguishing between a coin jammed accidentally and a coin (or coins) jammed deliberately. Hence, since the form of jamming noted on the three suspect meters in Mint Street was considered to fall into the latter category, it was recorded under the heading *Damage*, and the prosecution's question to me was, 'Were the numbers of instances of *Damage* recorded for these three meters compatible with the numbers for the other meters in the street, or in the town?'

The distribution of Damage

In Mint Street there were 51 parking meters, but because three of them (in adjacent positions) were of special interest, it was considered wise to base inferences concerning the behaviour of meters in the street on the remaining 48. For these, the recorded frequencies of *Damage*, during the year 1 February 1979 to 31 January 1980 were as follows:

Number of recorded instances of Damage (x)	0	1	2	3	>3	*Total*
Observed number of meters	37	8	2	1	0	48

Although the street contained a finite number of meters, it is not unreasonable to regard them as a random sample from an infinite population, since, when they were placed in the street, they were taken from a large number of meters in the town's store, this large number itself being a sample from the manufacturer's much larger output for that year. We therefore assume that the above data constitute 48 independent observations of the random variable X defined as 'the number of recorded instances of *Damage* to a meter in Mint Street per year'.

Now, if it is true that in a short period of time, say a day, each meter in the street has the same probability of being deliberately damaged, independently

The evidence against a parking meter offender 175

of what happened in all previous time periods, we should expect X to have a Poisson distribution with some mean, μ, say. In which case, the probability that X takes a particular value x is given by

$$p(x) = P(X = x) = e^{-\mu}\mu^x/x!, \qquad x = 0, 1, 2, \ldots$$

We can estimate the unknown μ from the data by means of the maximum likelihood estimator. This is the estimator that assigns to μ the value that maximizes the probability of observing the sample we have, in fact, obtained. In this case the estimator, $\hat{\mu}$, turns out to be the sample mean $\bar{x} = 15/48 = 0.3125$. Substituting this value into the probability function, multiplying the function by 48, and evaluating it for $x = 0, 1$, and 2, we obtain the following set of expected frequencies:

x	0	1	2	≥ 3	Total
Expected number of meters	35.12	10.97	1.71	0.19	47.99

There is no evidence to suggest that these frequencies are incompatible with the observed frequencies given above (the Pearson χ^2 goodness-of-fit statistic has the value 4.42 even when based on all four cells). Consequently the Poisson distribution, with mean 0.3125, gives us a good working model for the distribution of the random variable X.

What then were the observed values of X for the three particular meters at the centre of this case? They were 9, 11, and 47, extraordinarily large values, so large, in fact, that in any ordinary analysis they would, without further calculation, be regarded as outliers, that is as observations not belonging to the same population as the rest of the data. Nevertheless, it is extremely difficult for the layman to appreciate just how unlikely such values are. Hence the court, in its wisdom, insisted on putting on record estimates of the probabilities of obtaining values at least as great as those observed. Using our estimated Poisson probability function, we find these to be

$$\widehat{P(X \geq 9)} = 5.91 \times 10^{-11}$$
$$\widehat{P(X \geq 11)} = 5.22 \times 10^{-14}$$
$$\widehat{P(X \geq 47)} = 5.16 \times 10^{-84}.$$

(The reader is invited to check the calculations.)

These probabilities are numbers so small as to defy comprehension, except by way of comparison with the probabilities of other nigh impossible events. For example, the probability of dealing a hand entirely of one suit at Bridge is 6.30×10^{-12}, and the chance of performing this feat seven times consecutively is 3.93×10^{-79}. Further, the probability that, of the 51 meters in the street, one manifests *Damage* at least nine times in a year, an adjacent one at least 11 times, and yet another, adjacent to the first two, at least 47 times, is even smaller than any number we have so far calculated, so small that for all practical purposes it is zero.

Confidence limits to μ

In the above analysis of the Poisson distribution, we estimated μ by a point estimate, that is by a single number derived from the data, and, I must admit, that was as far as I was willing to educate the court in the matter. However, this number, by itself, contains no information about its accuracy or possible variability; for instance, a value of $\hat{\mu}=0.3125$ based on 48 observations needs to be interpreted differently from a value of 0.3125 based on only 16 observations, or again based on 160 observations. One way of providing a more informative estimate of μ is by means of a confidence interval.

Before we derive one, we need to state a result about the Poisson distribution. If X, 'the number of recorded instances of *Damage* to a meter in Mint Street per year', has a Poisson distribution with mean μ, then $U = \sum_{i=1}^{n} X_i$, the total number of such incidents over n meters, has a Poisson distribution with mean $\mu' = n\mu$, so long as the meters behave independently in this respect. Making this assumption, let us now consider the following argument: for given values of μ' and the probability α (say 0.05 or 0.01), suppose c is the smallest integer such that

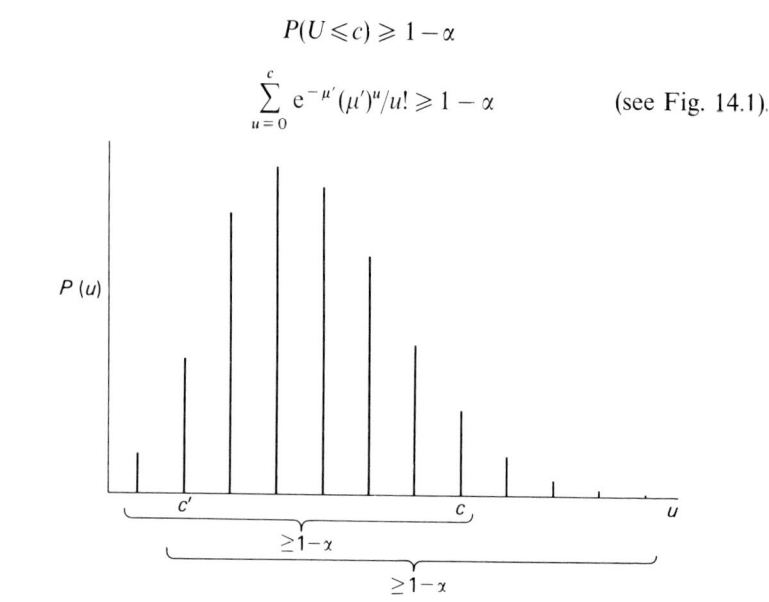

$$P(U \leqslant c) \geqslant 1 - \alpha$$

i.e.
$$\sum_{u=0}^{c} e^{-\mu'} (\mu')^u / u! \geqslant 1 - \alpha \qquad \text{(see Fig. 14.1)}.$$

Fig. 14.1

Now, if we actually observe $u=c$, the set of values of μ' satisfying this inequality, say $0 \leq \mu' \leq \mu^+$, is called a $100(1-\alpha)\%$ (one-sided) confidence interval for μ', μ^+ being the upper confidence limit. This, in turn, leads to a $100(1-\alpha)\%$ confidence interval for μ given by $0 \leq \mu \leq \mu^+/n$, so that the interval becomes shorter in length with increasing n. The point of this exercise is that if we were able to carry out these calculations for a large number of samples, drawn from the theoretically infinite population, a proportion (which is at least $1-\alpha$) of the confidence intervals so constructed would contain the true value of μ.

In a similar way, suppose c' is the largest integer such that

$$P(U \geq c') \geq 1 - \alpha \text{ (again see the figure).}$$

Then, if $u=c'$ is observed, there is a $100(1-\alpha)\%$ confidence interval of $\mu^- \leq \mu' < \infty$ for μ', μ^- being the lower confidence limit, or $\mu^-/n \leq \mu < \infty$ for μ. The values of μ^- and μ^+ have been calculated and can be read from special tables.

A little consideration reveals that $0 \leq \mu \leq \mu^+/n$ is a confidence interval for μ that ought to be preferred by the prosecution, who wish to present μ as being as small as possible, while $\mu^-/n \leq \mu < \infty$ ought to be preferred by the defence, who want to suggest that a large mean, and hence a large value of X, is not beyond the bounds of possibility. For the 48 parking meters of Mint Street, the resulting 95% and 99% one-sided confidence intervals for μ are

	Prosecution preferred	Defence preferred
$1-\alpha=0.95$	$0 \leq \mu \leq 0.481$	$0.193 \leq \mu < \infty$
$1-\alpha=0.99$	$0 \leq \mu \leq 0.557$	$0.156 \leq \mu < \infty$

A reasonable compromise, if such a thing were possible in an English court of law, would be for both sides to accept a two-sided central confidence interval, i.e. one that is derived from the two inequalities

$$P(U \leq c) \geq 1 - \alpha/2, \qquad P(U \geq c') \geq 1 - \alpha/2.$$

For our observed data, this procedure leads to

$$1-\alpha=0.95: \quad 0.175 \leq \mu \leq 0.515$$
$$1-\alpha=0.99: \quad 0.144 \leq \mu \leq 0.587$$

If we insert these limits to μ into the probability function of X, we can evaluate central confidence intervals for the tail probabilities of the distribution corresponding to the three suspect meters. Thus, for example, the 99% intervals are

$$6.25 \times 10^{-14} \leq P(X \geq 9) \leq 1.34 \times 10^{-8}$$
$$1.17 \times 10^{-17} \leq P(X \geq 11) \leq 4.15 \times 10^{-11}$$

$$7.91 \times 10^{-100} \leqslant P(X \geqslant 47) \leqslant 2.84 \times 10^{-71}.$$

Note that the point estimate of each probability has roughly the same order of magnitude as the geometric mean of the two confidence limits, and that the conclusions drawn about the three meters from these intervals are in no way different from those given earlier.

The distribution of Fault

When presented with the minute Poisson probabilities given two sections back, the defence did not accept defeat easily. 'Suppose', said the barrister, 'that the instances of alleged deliberate jamming had been classified under *Fault* and not under *Damage*. What difference would that have made to the apparent ill-functioning of the three special meters?'

Well, the recorded frequencies of *Fault* for the 48 control meters in Mint Street are as shown below, together with the expected frequencies if a Poisson distribution is 'fitted' to the data.

Number of recorded instances Fault (y)	Observed number of meters	Expected number of meters (Poisson)
0	13	4.46
1	10	10.60
2	8	12.59
3	6	9.97
4	2	5.92
5	2	2.81
6	3	1.11
7	2	0.38
8	1	0.11
9	0	0.03
10	0	0.01
11	0	0
12	1	0
> 12	0	0
Total	48	47.99

Clearly, the distribution of the random variable Y, 'the number of recorded instances of *Fault* in a meter in Mint Street per year', is decidedly unlike a Poisson, a fact that may be surmised from a comparison of the sample mean, 2.3750, with the much larger sample variance, 6.6927. (Remember that the mean and variance of a Poisson distribution are equal.) There are a number of possible reasons for this lack of fit. The random variable Y is really the sum of a number of component random variables arising from the list of causes under *Fault* on p. 173, and some of these may have peculiar distributions, or they may not be independent, or the meters, or their parts, may have been made on a number of different machines or from different samples of metal. It may, nevertheless, be true that the distribution of *Fault* is still Poisson for each meter but with the value of μ varying from one meter to another. In such circumstances it is not unusual to find that a negative binomial distribution fits the data and so gives a feasible model for the distribution of Y. The probability function of this distribution is

$$p(0) = P(Y=0) = \pi^m$$
$$p(y) = P(Y=y) = \frac{m(m+1)\dots(m+y-1)}{y!}\pi^m(1-\pi)^y,$$
$$\text{for } y = 1, 2, 3, \dots$$

the probabilities $p(y)$ being given by the terms in the expansion of $\pi^m[1-(1-\pi)]^{-m}$, a binomial expansion with a negative exponent. Moreover, the distribution depends on two parameters, π and m, unlike the Poisson with its single parameter μ, and it has mean $E(Y) = m(1-\pi)/\pi$ and variance $V(Y) = m(1-\pi)/\pi^2 > E(Y)$.

The maximum likelihood estimators of the parameters, based on the above 48 observations, are $\hat{\pi} = 0.3389$ and $\hat{m} = 1.2176$, and with these values substituted into the probability function, the expected frequencies now become

y	Expected number of meters (negative binomial)
0	12.85
1	10.35
2	7.58
3	5.38
4	3.75
5	2.59
6	1.77
7	1.21
8	0.82
9	0.56
10	0.38
11	0.25
12	0.17
>12	0.35
Total	48.01

The fit is good (Pearson's χ^2 equals 8.05 even when based on all 14 cells), hence the negative binomial provides us with a model of the distribution of Y by means of which we can estimate its probabilities, in particular the tail probabilities associated with the three suspect meters. For these, the observed values of Y were 12, 15, and 48, and the relevant estimates are

$$P(Y \geq 12) = 0.0108$$
$$P(Y \geq 15) = 0.00324$$
$$P(Y \geq 48) = 4.79 \times 10^{-9}.$$

The first two of these are no longer sufficiently small to lead a court to convict on the basis of their values alone, though in other applications they may well be considered small or 'significant'. The third is tiny, albeit of nothing like the order of magnitude found under the Poisson model, but certainly small enough to convince any reasonable person that the particular meter behaved, or was treated, in an extraordinary way during the year in question. Moreover, if we think of the 51 meters in the street distributed round a circle — say, up one side of the street and down the other — the joint probability of finding one of them with at least 12 instances of *Fault*, an adjacent one with at least 15, and yet another adjacent to the first two with at least 48, is less than 4.35×10^{-11}, which is far too small to allow one to believe the accused's hard luck story. He was found guilty and fined.

Unfortunately, it is not possible to provide confidence intervals for the probabilities under the negative binomial model.

Distribution-free results

In the preceding analyses, we were fortunate in that the random variables X and Y, the numbers of instances of *Damage* and *Fault* per year to a meter in Mint Street, could be closely fitted by well-known simple distributions, the Poisson in one case and the negative binomial in the other. But suppose this had not been possible, what inferences could we then have drawn? Here, we briefly describe a method of analysis that is distribution-free, i.e. that does not depend on the assumption that the random variable of interest has a particular distribution. It will be seen, though, that it does not provide estimates of tail probabilities anything like as small as those given earlier.

The method depends on Chebyshev's inequality. This states that, if a random variable U has mean μ and variance σ^2, then, for any positive value of k,

$$P(|U - \mu| \geq k\sigma) \leq 1/k^2$$

Applying this to the random variable X, with the sample mean and variance substituted for μ and σ^2, we obtain the estimated inequalities

$$P(X \geqslant 9) \leqslant 0.0056$$
$$P(X \geqslant 11) \leqslant 0.0037$$
$$P(X \geqslant 47) \leqslant 0.00019.$$

Taken separately, these are not particularly small, but the joint probability of finding three adjacent meters in the street with at least 9, 11, and 47 recorded instances of *Damage* is less than 7.9×10^{-7}, probably just small enough to lead to a conviction.

The application of Chebyshev's result to Y yields the following inequalities:

$$P(Y \geqslant 12) \leqslant 0.072$$
$$P(Y \geqslant 15) \leqslant 0.042$$
$$P(Y \geqslant 48) \leqslant 0.0032.$$

with the corresponding joint probability being less than 0.0020, which would give the defence a rather strong case for claiming that the defendant had been unlucky in his choice of parking meters, but not unlucky beyond belief.

The town as a whole

Since the number of parking meters in Mint Street was not too small (51), we were able to make worthwhile inferences about their behaviour, and the three suspect meters in particular, without looking beyond the limits of the street. But what happens if we consider the meters in the town at large? The following tables give the observed numbers of instances of *Damage* and *Fault* recorded for a sample of 50 meters drawn systematically (every twentieth card) from the filing cabinet in the traffic wardens' office.

Table 14.1 Distribution of *Damage* in a sample from the whole town

Number of recorded instances of Damage (x)	0	1	2	$\geqslant 3$	Total
Observed number of meters	36	5	9	0	50

Table 14.2 Distribution of *Fault* in a sample from the whole town

Number of recorded instances of Fault (y)	0	1	2	3	4	5	6	7	8	9	10	11	>12	Total
Observed number of meters	8	9	6	5	6	6	4	1	2	1	0	1	1	50

In view of the large number of occurrences of $x=2$, it should not be surprising that the distribution of the random variable X cannot be approximated by a Poisson distribution as was the case in Mint Street. But perhaps we should not expect a single Poisson distribution to fit the data in the first place, since there are bound to be some meters in gloomy back streets favoured by the local vandals who are not so keen to be caught tampering with the meters in the well lit high street. In other words, the distribution of X is likely to be a mixture of distributions, some Poisson, some perhaps not, that correspond to different streets or different areas of the town. A sample of size 50 is not large enough to permit any safe conclusions about the component parts of this mixture. Armed only with this data and not with the sample from Mint Street, I would have pointed the court's attention to the fact that $x \geq 3$ just did not occur in the sample, and estimated the relevant probabilities using Chebyshev's inequality, as outlined in the previous section.

The distribution of Y, on the other hand, can be modelled by a negative binomial distribution as before, although with a slightly larger mean and variance. This *Fault* data could therefore be used to provide estimates of tail probabilities for the three suspect meters in Mint Street, although these meters would then have to be viewed as three meters in the town at large. The probabilities would all be somewhat larger than those found earlier, but the overall conclusions would be unchanged.

David Bennetts

15 Thunderstorms

Everyone is aware of the main characteristics of a thunderstorm — thunder, lightning, heavy rain, hail, and strong winds. The combined effect is spectacular but usually such storms pass over quickly, leaving only the wet ground to mark their passage. Occasionally a particularly severe storm develops, producing local flooding, causing structural damage to buildings, and sometimes resulting in loss of life. One such storm occurred at Hampstead in London on 14 August 1975, giving 170 mm of rain in $2\frac{1}{2}$ hours. Fortunately storms of this type are rare in the United Kingdom, but in the central plains of Europe and America they are comparatively common and often produce large hailstones which cause extensive damage to crops. One of the most severe storms on record occurred on 31 July 1976 over the Big Thompson Canyon, Colorado, when a thunderstorm complex produced a devastating flash flood which killed 139 people and cost approximately £20 million in property damage. In consequence there is a powerful motivation to understand the factors which influence the severity of this wide spectrum of storms.

Fig. 15.1 An aerial photograph (taken at 12 000 feet) showing the characteristic flat top of a cumulonimbus cloud with the 'anvil' leading to the right. Such clouds are often associated with thunderstorms.
Photograph by permission of the Meterological Office

The problem

All atmospheric motion is ultimately caused by solar heating but there are many ways in which this energy becomes available. One of the more direct is through air being warmed by contact with the ground. Some surfaces, for example hill slopes facing the sun, are better than others at absorbing solar radiation and this leads to local increases in the air temperature. In these regions the air can become buoyant and rise as a thermal. However, as it rises, the ambient pressure decreases and the air expands, cooling adiabatically, as the energy for expansion is drawn from within.

Water vapour is an important but variable component of the atmosphere, contributing typically one per cent of the total mass. As air cools, its capacity to retain water in the vapour form decreases, until at a certain height, referred to as the condensation level or cloud base, it becomes saturated, and cloud forms by condensation onto the small particles that are always present in the air. The condensation process releases latent heat which warms the air and maintains the buoyancy of the thermal.

At the beginning of the condensation process the individual cloud droplets within the thermal are small, typically 1 or 2 μm in diameter. They grow rapidly, initially by condensation, but as they become larger, by mutual collisions and coalescence. In deep clouds some droplets begin to freeze at temperatures of about $-10°C$, whilst at about $-40°C$ (typically at a height of 7 km) almost all cloud particles are ice. The drops of water and ice crystals if present, eventually become so heavy that they fall through the buoyant updraught and grow even larger by 'sweeping up' smaller droplets. They emerge from the base of the cloud as raindrops and hailstones which then fall to the ground. Below cloud base the air is unsaturated and often above the freezing point. In consequence the hail begins to melt and the rain partially evaporates, both processes leading to a cooling of the air as the latent heats of melting and condensation are extracted. The cold air sinks and forms a downdraught which spreads out on encountering the ground to produce a gust front at its boundary with the ambient air. This creates the localised, strong, cold winds that are frequently associated with thunderstorms.

Thunder and lightning, although spectacular, are in fact of minor importance to the storm evolution, and severe storms can occur without their presence. The severity of a storm is essentially determined by the strength and duration of its up- and downdraughts, for which the above descriptive model gives a qualitative explanation. However, the atmospheric physicist invariably wishes to quantify the effects, for unless the amount of rain and the strength of the winds can be related to the initial environmental conditions, it will not be possible to give advanced warning of such storms.

The experimentalist approach to such a problem would be to observe changes in the evolution of the storm resulting from slight changes in the initial conditions. The important aspects might then be isolated and quantified. Unfortunately, in the atmosphere this approach is not viable. The researcher has no control over the phenomena that he or she is studying, but can only observe what the atmosphere provides. Furthermore, there are several practical difficulties. First, storms are widely scattered in both space and time. It is difficult, therefore, to be in the right place at the right time to make the measurements. Secondly, the storms are both large, typically 25 kilometres in diameter, and evolve quickly. A storm may last from three to six hours, but conditions within it vary much more rapidly, typically over 10 to 15 minutes. The difficulty, therefore, is to obtain the necessary spatial resolution sufficiently often to resolve the changing conditions. Thirdly, there is the problem of physically obtaining the measurements. Some information can be obtained remotely, for example by radar, but many of the measurements can only be made from an aircraft and there are very few of these which are both equipped with the necessary instrumentation and able to withstand the stresses imposed by flying within such storms.

These difficulties, which are present to a greater or lesser degree in all meteorological investigations, have necessitated an alternative approach, based on the construction of mathematical models. The models are designed to reproduce the more important aspects of any problem, and have the advantage that their initial conditions can be carefully and systematically controlled. However, the penalty for this simplification is that there is no guarantee that the model's behaviour is the same as that of the atmosphere. The remainder of the chapter will be concerned with these two aspects, namely, the development of the model and the evaluation of its ability to simulate the important features of thunderstorms.

Formulation of the equations

Consider a parcel of warm, moist air within the rising thermal. Let the environmental air have a temperature T_0 ($\simeq 300$ K) and the air within the parcel a temperature T_1 with $T_1 - T_0 = T'$, a small quantity of typically 1 or 2°C. Provided the ambient pressure is the same as that within the parcel, the fundamental gas equation implies

$$\rho_1 T_1 = \rho_0 T_0$$

and hence

$$\rho_0 = \rho_1 \left(1 + \frac{T'}{T_0}\right)$$

where ρ_0 and ρ_1 are the densities of the environment and parcel respectively, and include the contribution of the water vapour.

The forces acting on the parcel are, then, the buoyancy which acts upwards, and is proportional to the density difference $(\rho_0 - \rho_1)$ and the weight of the condensed cloud water, $\rho_1 g l$ (where g is the acceleration due to gravity and l the fractional mass of water substance within the parcel). The vertical acceleration (dw/dt) is then given by the expression

$$\frac{dw}{dt} = g\frac{T'}{T_0} - gl \tag{1}$$

where w is the vertical velocity.

However T' and l vary with both position and time. For example consider T', the temperature difference between the thermal and the environment $(T_1 - T_0)$. As the parcel rises with velocity w, its temperature T_1 changes due to adiabatic expansion, $w\gamma$, and the release of latent heat $kLdC/dt$, where γ represents the adiabatic lapse rate (about $-9°C$ per kilometre), dC/dt is the rate at which water vapour condenses, L is the latent heat of condensation, and k is a 'constant' which includes the specific heat of air and varies only slowly with height, z. (We are using a 3-D cartesian co-ordinate system with z as the vertical co-ordinate.)

In the absence of turbulent mixing between the parcel and the surrounding air

$$\frac{dT_1}{dt} = w\gamma + kL\frac{dC}{dt}.$$

But, as the parcel rises, the local environment changes and consequently, using $w = dz/dt$

$$\frac{dT'}{dt} = \frac{d}{dt}(T_1 - T_0) = w\left(\gamma - \frac{dT_0}{dz}\right) + kL\frac{dC}{dt}. \tag{2}$$

In a dry atmosphere, where the last term in equation (2) is zero, there is instability if, and only if

$$\gamma > \frac{dT_0}{dz} \tag{3}$$

when the atmosphere is said to be superadiabatic. However, this rarely occurs over any great depth, and in practice, instability (usually referred to as convection) is possible only when

$$kL\frac{dC}{dt} > w\left(\frac{dT_0}{dz} - \gamma\right).$$

Since

$$\frac{dC}{dt} = \frac{dC}{dz}\frac{dz}{dt} = w\frac{dC}{dz}$$

this can be rewritten as

$$\left(\gamma + kL\frac{dC}{dz}\right) > \frac{dT_0}{dz}$$

where the left hand side of the inequality expresses the rate of change of temperature of a moist parcel of air, with height. In the absence of mixing, its value is determined by the initial conditions within the parcel, dC/dz, depending only on the temperature T_1 at $z=z_0$, the condensation height.

The expression $\gamma + kLdC/dz$ is called the moist adiabatic lapse rate (γ_w, typically $-4°C$ per kilometre) and (cf. equation (3)) a moist atmosphere is unstable when

$$\gamma_w > \frac{dT_0}{dz}. \tag{4}$$

The above equations deal with changes of temperature for a particular parcel. In mathematical terms this is indicated by use of the 'total' derivative dT'/dt which gives the change with time of the parcel, following that parcel. It is, however, awkward to follow parcels, and for mathematical analysis it is easier to work with local changes, that is, changes at a fixed point. The local rate of change of T' with time is indicated by the partial derivative $\partial T'/\partial t$ (that is, the rate of change of T' with respect to time t, when we consider all the other variables to be constant).

When local changes are to be estimated, additional terms appear in some of the equations. These additional terms express changes due to advection, which are the result of new air replacing the old air at a given place because of horizontal or vertical motions. The change T' at a point is therefore expressed as

$$\underset{\text{'Total' change}}{\frac{DT'}{Dt}} = \underset{\substack{\text{local change} \\ \text{in time}}}{\frac{\partial T'}{\partial t}} + \underset{\substack{\text{change due to} \\ \text{horizontal motions}}}{u\frac{\partial T'}{\partial x} + v\frac{\partial T'}{\partial y}} + \underset{\substack{\text{change due to} \\ \text{vertical motion}}}{w\frac{\partial T'}{\partial z}}$$

and so, relative to a fixed point of reference, equation (2) is written

$$\frac{DT'}{Dt} = w\left(\gamma_w - \frac{\partial T_0}{\partial z}\right). \tag{5}$$

Equation (5) is called a non-linear partial differential equation. It is non-linear because it contains product terms, such as

$$w\frac{\partial T'}{\partial z}\left(=\frac{dz}{dt}\frac{\partial T'}{\partial z}\right).$$

Such equations can be derived for all the dynamic and thermodynamic variables, which consist of the three velocity components (u, v, w) relative to a rectangular set of axes (x, y, z), the temperature of the air and the water vapour content. If these variables are represented by Φ, then the solution to the corresponding five equations can be written

$$\Phi = \Phi(C, l).$$

In other words the dynamic and thermodynamic variables and equations form a consistent set which respond to the microphysical quantities cloud water, cloud ice, rain and hail only through the latent heat released and the weight of the cloud substance suspended.

The significance of this result will be discussed later. For the moment it will be assumed that C and l are known and that the problem reduces to the solution of five simultaneous partial differential equations. The complexity of these equations is such that no general analytic solution can be found and therefore they must be evaluated numerically. So how are the equations transformed for numerical solution on a computer? The first step is to move from a continuous to a 'finite' form.

Finite difference approximations

Consider a quantity Q (Fig. 15.2) which is a continuous function of a variable x. At the point i the gradient

$$\frac{dQ_i}{dx} \simeq \frac{Q_{i+1} - Q_{i-1}}{x_{i+1} - x_{i-1}}$$

where the right hand side is called the finite difference approximation. The accuracy of the finite difference approximation depends on the length of the interval $\Delta x (= x_{i+1} - x_{i-1})$ and the gradient of the curve. For example at the point j the approximation is poor for the chosen interval Δx.

To illustrate how Δx might be chosen for a practical problem, consider Fig. 15.3, which shows the magnitude of the wind measured by an aircraft as it traversed the top of a large cumulonimbus cloud. Three representations of the data are given in Fig. 15.3(a), (b), and (c) corresponding to mean winds over 1, 10 and 100 second intervals respectively. Since the aircraft was flying at approximately 100 metres per second, these represent means over 100 metres, one kilometre, and ten kilometres.

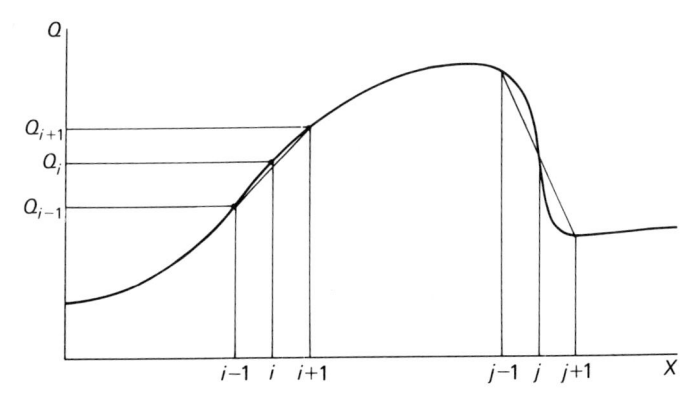

Fig. 15.2 Q is a continuous function of x. At the point i the gradient dQ_i/dx can be represented by $(Q_i - Q_{i-1})/(x_{i+1} - x_{i-1})$, which is called the finite difference representation. The accuracy of the approximation depends on the gradient of P and the interval $x_{i+1} - x_{i-1}$. At the point j the approximation is poor.

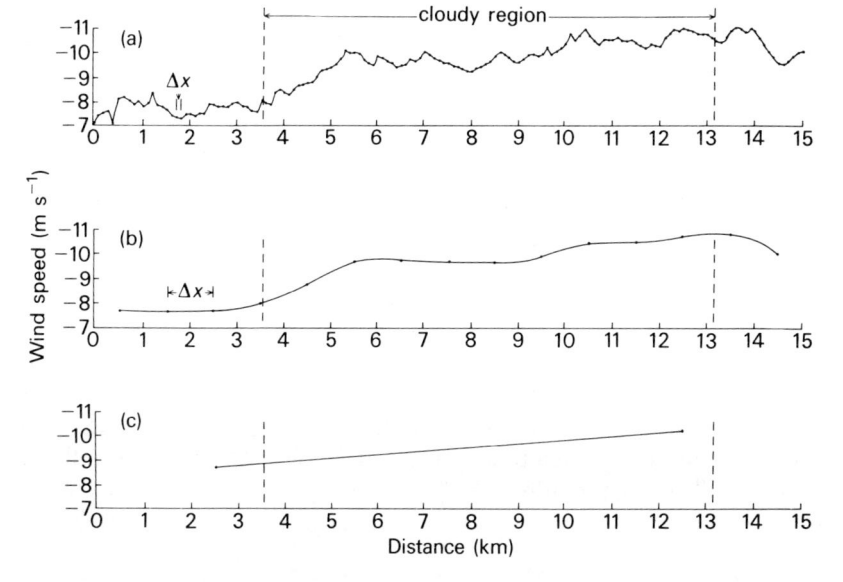

Fig. 15.3 The wind velocity as measured from an aircraft flying through the upper part of a cumulonimbus cloud. Figures (a), (b), and (c) are plots of the magnitude of the wind, as a function of distance, for wind values meaned over 100 m, 1 km, and 10 km, respectively. For further details see text.

Each figure resolves features of these characteristic scales and clearly the choice of Δx depends on a judgement about the importance of these scales. The aim is to study cumulonimbus clouds, and, in the first instance, the scale is chosen to reflect the motions relevant to the convective processes. For example, the fine structure on the 100 metre scale, due to turbulent motions, is clearly of lesser magnitude than the variation over the width of the cloud. On the other hand, the ten kilometre scale is too coarse to resolve any of the cloud's internal motion. A good choice is the one kilometre scale with $\Delta x = 1$ km. Note that the data is adequately resolved by the finite difference representation (cf Fig. 15.2) at the same interval as it is specified, a feature that minimises the storage requirements which are discussed below. Such a favourable choice does not occur on the 100 metre scale, with $\Delta x = 100$ m, indicating that the turbulence is not fully resolved even on that scale. A similar analysis can be applied to the vertical direction and a suitable value for Δz is found to be 0.5 kilometres, the slightly higher resolution being required because of the steeper gradients in that direction.

The cloud may therefore be represented as a series of discrete quantities at uniformly spaced grid points separated horizontally by one kilometre and vertically by 0.5 kilometres, the value at each grid point being representative of a parcel of air having dimensions 1 km × 1 km by 0.5 km in the vertical. The whole cloud can be represented by 25 × 25 × 25 points, at each point the value of nine variables being required, i.e. $\sim 1.4 \times 10^5$ quantities, or in computational terms, a storage requirement of $\sim 560\,000$ bytes of information, a requirement within the capacity of modern computers.

The problem now is to proceed from this one spatial representation at a given time, to a solution of the finite difference equations for all time. Consider equation (5) which may be written

$$\frac{T'_{n+1} - T'_n}{\Delta t} = w_n \left(\gamma_w - \frac{\partial T_0}{\partial z} \right)_n - u_n \frac{\partial T'_n}{\partial x} - v_n \frac{\partial T'_n}{\partial y} - w_n \frac{\partial T'_n}{\partial z} \qquad (6)$$

where $\partial T'/\partial t$ has been represented in finite difference form, and the suffices n and $n+1$ refer to the given time t_0 and a new time $t_1 = t_0 + \Delta t$, respectively. This formally gives a solution for T'_{n+1} (T' at t_1) in terms of variables whose values are known at time t_0. The process is referred to as the integration of the equations.

Unfortunately, the solution resulting from the numerical integration of the equations is not unique. Of course, the same is true of the continuous equations, but there the unique solution (S) can be chosen from the infinite number available (S^n) by seeking the one that fits the boundary conditions.

For example if
$$S'' = at + be^t$$
and the boundary (initial) conditions are
$$S = 0, \quad \frac{dS}{dt} = 1 \text{ at } t = 0$$
then $a = 1$, $b = 0$ and $S = t$.

With numerical integration it is again possible to apply the condition at $t = 0$. However, suppose that there is a small error in the solution and instead of $a = 1$, $b = 0$ the solution starts at $a = 1$, $b = 10^{-6}$, then the numerical solution differs from the analytic solution by $10^{-6} e^t$, and after approximately 16.5 seconds the 'error' exceeds the value of the true solution. Although this is an over-simplification of the problem, it serves to illustrate how small numerical errors can grow and render the integration valueless. Consequently the choice of Δt is much more difficult than the choice of Δx and requires a knowledge of the behaviour of the solutions. By a careful choice of both the form of the temporal finite difference approximation and of Δt, unwanted growing modes can be eliminated. In the present problem a suitable value of Δt is 15 seconds.

Physical quantities

The physical processes that lead to the production of cloud water (l_c), cloud ice (l_i), rain (l_r), and hail (l_h) take place on the scale of individual drops and for a full description of their effects, a knowledge of the complete history of each drop and particle is required. This is clearly impossible. However, it has been shown that to a first approximation the dynamic and thermodynamic variables depend only on the release of latent heat (C) and the mass of suspended water substance ($l = l_c + l_i + l_r + l_h$), and both these quantities, on the chosen scale of analysis, are independent of the precise nature of the droplet interactions.

The problem is, therefore, to describe the behaviour of the population of cloud particles whilst being unable to resolve the fundamental processes that control their evolution. This is accomplished by a mathematical technique called parametrisation.

Consider one of the processes that contribute to the formation of rain, the 'sweeping up' of small cloud droplets by larger drops during their fall through the cloud. The simplest parametric representation of Δl, the mass of cloud water swept up, is

$$\Delta l = \beta_1 l_c l_r \qquad (7)$$

where the parameter β_1 is chosen to represent all the physical effects neglected, for example, the size and spatial distribution, the terminal fall speed, the collection efficiency, etc. The equation as presented represents the simple fact that the more cloud and rain present, the greater the number of collisions that will occur and hence the larger the value of Δl. However, theoretical and observational studies show that the size and spatial distribution as well as the mean fall speed of a population of drops is related to the total mass of rain falling. If this is taken into account equation (7) becomes

$$\Delta l = \beta_2 l_c l_r^{7/8}. \qquad (8)$$

A parametrisation scheme is therefore not unique but can take one of several different forms. The final choice depends on many considerations, but the most important is that it should only require variables resolved explicitly by the model and not be too sensitive to unresolved variables. For example, the fact that equations (7) and (8) are similar, indicates that Δl is sensitive to the product $l_c l_r$ but is insensitive to the precise microphysical characteristics, which are proportional to $l_r^{-1/8}$, a quantity close to unity in deep convective cloud where the value of l_r ranges typically from 0.5 to 2 (g kg^{-1}). Hence equation (7) is a good choice, as it is simple and has a parametric constant which is relatively insensitive to the microphysically changing conditions.

However, in, for example, the modelling of drizzle falling from stratocumulus layer cloud, this parametrisation would not be suitable, as here the range of l_r is typically 0.01 to 0.1 (gkg^{-1}) and hence the added complexity of equation (8) would be required. Unfortunately the choice is rarely as clear cut as in this example.

A solution

The original problem was to develop a mathematical model to help in the study of severe convective storms. This has involved the following steps:
(i) the derivation of the equations
(ii) the derivation of the finite different approximations
(iii) the choice of a scale
(iv) the choice of a parametrisation scheme.

These steps have been presented sequentially for clarity, but in practice they are highly interactive.

Each of the steps involves a degree of approximation, and the question that must be asked is 'Is the solution to the final set of equations a solution to the original problem?' We must decide whether the numerical model behaves in the same manner as the descriptive model.

Figs. 15.4(a) and (b) show a simulated cloud at two stages in its development. The integration was started by introducing a small heat bubble

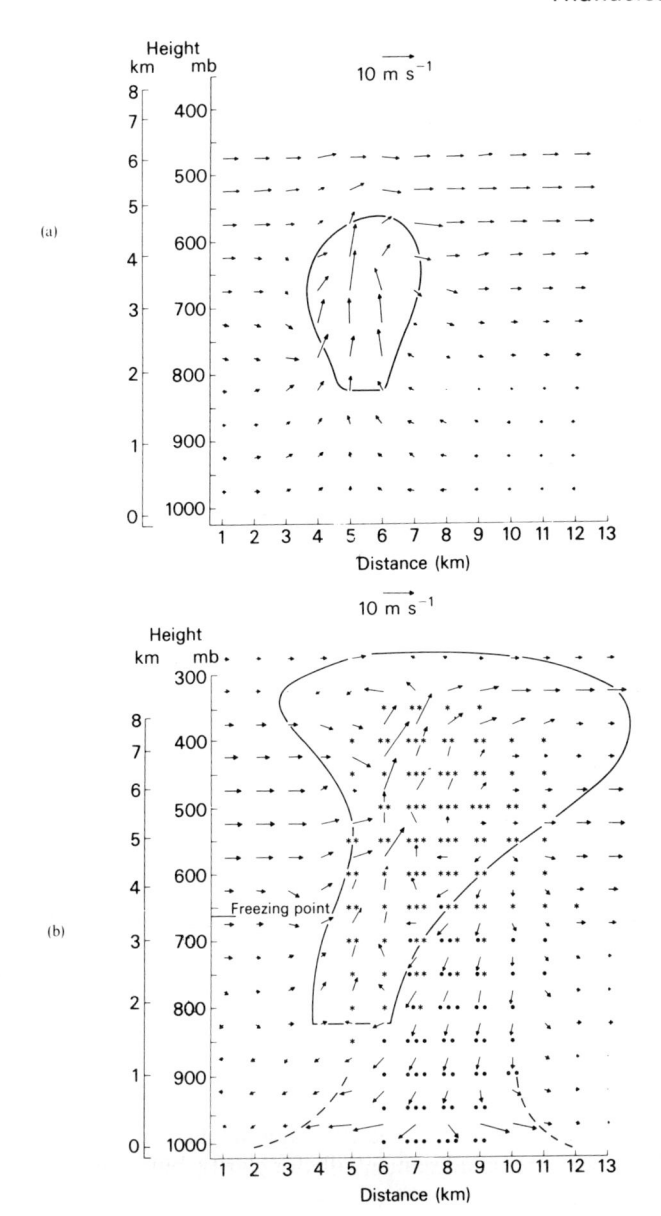

Fig. 15.4 Vertical cross section through the simulated cloud: (a) at 28 minutes showing the low level inflow and updraught, and (b) at 56 minutes when the downdraught and gust front had formed. The length and direction of the arrows indicate the instantaneous local wind vector, and the arrows at a distance from the cloud give a measure of the ambient wind shear. • represents rain and ∗ hail, the number of symbols indicating intensity. ---- outlines the gust front.

at the lowest levels of the model to mimic the effects of solar heating on, for example, the side of a hill. The bubble rose, slowly at first, but then with increasing velocity as additional unstable low level air was drawn into the cloud, the bubble only acting as the 'trigger' to start the convective process. In Fig. 15.4(a) the low level inflow and the strong updraught can clearly be seen. The wind shear caused the updraught to tilt at an angle to the vertical and the rain fell away from the updraught core allowing it to grow freely, unrestrained by the weight of the rain and hail (equation (1)). This is in contrast to the behaviour of a cloud grown with no ambient shear, when the rain and hail would fall through the updraught.

Figure 15.4(b) shows a later time in the development of the cloud when the downdraught had formed. The gust front is clearly marked by the directional change in the instantaneous wind vectors near the surface, and the melting of hail and evaporation of rain can be inferred from the changing distribution of these variables. At the top of the diagram the cloud can be seen spreading out to form the well-known anvil shape due to the upper level winds: a feature that is frequently observed in large storms.

Superficially, the numerical and descriptive models are similar. In addition the numerical model quantifies all the variables as functions of x, y, z, and t. Nevertheless, if some of the parametric constants are altered, there are changes to the solution, although its general behaviour might remain similar. Consequently, if two clouds resulting from slightly different initial conditions are compared, the differences cannot with confidence be attributed to those changes, but may instead result from differences arising from the parametrisation, or possibly from the approximations in the finite difference scheme. So, although a solution has been found, it is as yet of limited value.

One way of increasing confidence in a solution is to compare simulated and observed clouds. On a given convective day as much information as possible is gathered about the environment in general, and about a few specific clouds in detail. Using satellite photographs, precipitation radar, and research aircraft it is possible to determine some characteristics of:
(i) the instantaneous rate and total rainfall from the cloud
(ii) the height, size, and rate of growth of the cloud
(iii) winds, temperature, humidity, and microphysical properties at specific points and specific times throughout the cloud's lifetime.

Although only a few specific measurements can be obtained, rather than a complete set of data, this is no longer a serious disadvantage. The numerical solution is known completely, so the observations can be compared with the relevant part of the simulated cloud.

The value of the parametric constants within the model can then be adjusted so that the simulated and observed clouds agree as closely as possible. The procedure can be repeated for different clouds on different days. If for these subsequent clouds the parameters required complete reevaluation, then the parametrisation scheme, or the scale and corresponding finite difference approximation, were poorly chosen. On the other hand, if the process of 'tuning' tends to a limit and subsequent clouds are well simulated with only minor changes, then the model can be said to produce a solution that closely simulates reality.

Discussion

Recently, the Meteorological Office has been conducting an investigation into cumulonimbus convection. Part of this project involved a study of cloud clusters, for few large convective storms occur completely in isolation. The observations were made with precipitation radars. It was noticed that occasionally one cloud developed much more vigorously, and produced up to fourteen times the total rainfall and had ten times the rainfall rate of the surrounding cells. Such an increase occurred when two clouds came into close proximity. However, the converse was not true, for only in a few per cent of the cases when two clouds interacted was such a dramatic increase observed. Indeed in many cases the rainfall was reduced.

Since these events occurred within cloud clusters, they were invariably obscured by the surrounding clouds and were difficult to identify visually. Study by aircraft was therefore not possible. Furthermore, because most previous studies had concentrated on single clouds, it was difficult to predict how two clouds would grow when in close proximity. Accordingly they were simulated in the numerical model and their spacing and relative sizes varied, at first using environmental conditions appropriate to a day on which such events were observed, and then contrasting the results with those from other days when they were not. Eventually clouds were simulated which behaved in a similar manner to those observed. The integration which simulated the large increase in rainfall was then studied in detail.

This simulation is illustrated in Fig. 15.5. Fig. 15.5(a) shows an early stage when the two clouds were close, but as yet were having little influence on each other. As they grew stronger and increased in size their wind fields interacted and developed a clockwise rotation relative to the clouds that enhanced the cloud on the left and suppressed that on the right, moving the centres of the clouds so that one lay above the other (Fig. 15.5(b)). Rain from the larger cloud could then fall through the smaller cloud and, by the process described in equation (7), the quantity of water swept up (Δl) was greatly increased due to the high value of l_r falling from the large cloud, and the high value of l_c within the smaller.

Supplementary integrations showed that if the two clouds had a different relative size and separation to that shown, the clockwise rotation did not develop and the clouds did not 'merge', possibly explaining the scarcity of observations of mergers.

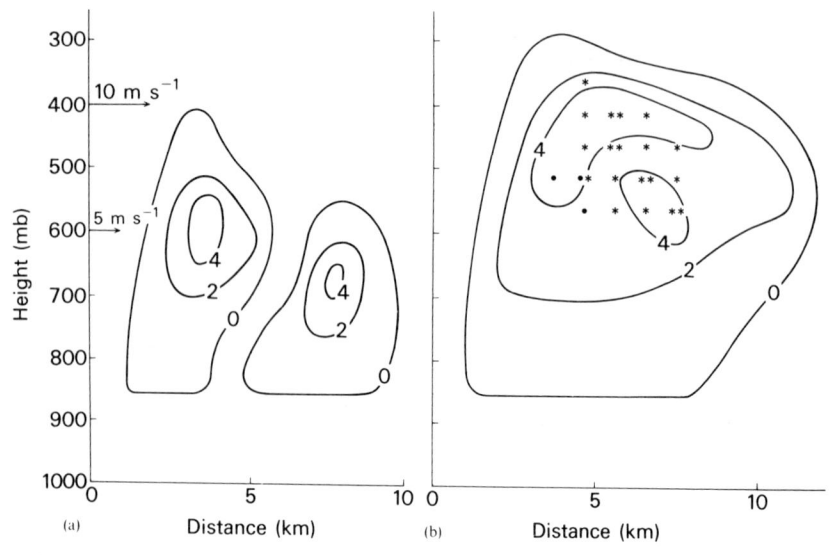

Fig. 15.5 Simulation of a merger. (a) shows an early stage in the development when the two clouds were separate and (b) a later stage when the left-hand cloud had been enhanced and the right-hand cloud moved so that its active centre was below that of the larger cloud. The contours are of cloud substance (water and ice), and • and * indicate rain and hail. For further details see text.

There is no claim that every detail of the simulated clouds is the same as that observed, for few precise details are available, only that the general behaviour is the same. The numerical model gives a general understanding of the process of merging, and allows the important features, for example the relative sizes of the clouds and their initial separation in relation to the ambient shear, to be identified. This points to ways of testing the first predictions.

Conclusions

This paper has demonstrated how, from an original descriptive model of a thunderstorm, a mathematical model can be developed. Of necessity there are many approximations within the model and many ways of making those approximations. However, if care is taken, the model can have a 'solution' which is sufficiently close to reality to be of considerable help in understanding the structure of the storms. Results from the model can be used both to understand how different types of severe storm can occur and to indicate further areas of research which may help improve our knowledge of the convective processes.

I would like to thank Dr P. Ryder and Dr A. J. Thorpe for their helpful advice during the preparation of this article.

Do it yourself

The following are suggested problems you may wish to try for yourself. Some are real, some hypothetical (!), and a few are exercises based on the text.

1   Your rich uncle has died and left you a lot of money. You decide to spend £10 000 000 on saving life, using existing knowledge and methods. Naturally, you want to save as many lives as possible for your money. How would you spend it? Would you give it to road engineers, to doctors, to safety officers in industry, to the Coal Board, to the nuclear industry, or to whom?

On second thoughts you decide that, as well as saving life, you would like to get public recognition for what you have done — you would like to be hailed as the man or woman who saved the lives of so many coal miners or aircraft passengers or whatever. Will this change the way in which you spend your money? Should it?

You decide that you would like to spend a further sum of several million pounds on research into new ways of saving life. Obviously you would not spend it on, say, better ways of curing snake-bite or rabies because so few people die in this way. You want to spend it on new ways of curing diseases or preventing accidents that kill a lot of people. How would you spend your money?

To simplify the problem let us assume that the money will be spent in the UK — or in your own country if you live elsewhere. You may also like to know that in 1980 the cost of saving each life by preventive measures was assessed as follows:

	£
Lung X-rays for addicted smokers	1 200
Cervical cancer screening	4 200
Breast cancer screening	12 000
Provision of intensive care units	15 000
Artificial kidneys	28 500
Removal of road hazard	up to 200 000
Chemical industry	1 000 000
Pharmaceutical industry	10 000 000
Reinforcement of high rise flats (following the collapse of Ronan Point in 1968)	30 000 000

2   Quicksale Stores Ltd are concerned because a particular product, which was bought in large quantities in the expectation of a fast turnover, has proved difficult to sell. Build a model which will indicate whether the retailer should cut his losses by selling at a much reduced price, or invest in a new image advertising campaign.

3   The arrival of ships at a particular port in a 24 hour period was found to be Poisson distributed. If the mean number of arrivals is 90 ships per day, find the proportion of days when the number of arrivals will exceed 110 ships per day.

4   Assuming that a ship decelerates uniformly in such a way that it can be brought to rest from a speed of 14 km/h in a distance of 1 km, find the time interval which would be required between ships passing through the Suez Canal if the speeds of the ships were increased by 50%. Remember that the time gap between ships must be sufficient to allow for a ship stopping instantaneously, e.g. by embedding in the banks of the Canal. (A small safety factor time must also be added.) What effect would these changes have on capacity?

5   A well-known local figure of uncertain athletic ability has agreed to run for charity in the 'people's marathon' to be held round the town. He is sponsored
    (a) to complete the course
    (b) to complete various stages in given times.
    Suggest a model which relates his tactics in aiming to complete the run to the various levels of sponsorship.

6   How might the model developed in Chapter 6 be modified to include hurdling races?

7   A pelican crossing operates by push-button demand. When the button is pushed the lights to road traffic change through amber to red, and after a time interval back via flashing amber to green. Pedestrians have priority on flashing amber; traffic must stop on amber and red. The key to successful operation lies in the relative time intervals for each phase of the cycle, and in allowing a minimum green time to permit the flow of road traffic. Develop an effective cycle for a particular pelican crossing in your area.

8   A new housing development is being constructed by a main-line railway. The builders are aware of the possible adverse effect of the noise levels on sales but have commissioned you as an engineering consultant to prepare a case which shows that the annoyance level is acceptable, in order to convince prospective purchasers. How would you set about this brief?

9   Devise a scale of premiums for a company specialising in motor insurances in the Channel Islands. Could such a company survive without diversifying into other business? [There is a large element of car hire by holidaymakers.]

10 Use the model described in Chapter 11 to calculate the monthly repayment for a £15 000 mortgage to be repaid by conventional means (i.e. reducing capital over the term) in 20 years.
11 A pensioner takes advantage of the facility offered to buy a £1 TV licence stamp every week and completes the investment six weeks before the licence is due for renewal. How much would she have saved if she had invested the same amount weekly in a Savings Bank? (Assume a return of 10% on investment.)
12 The preference test in Chapter 12 had five factors each of which were represented at two levels. Design a test in which one of the factors (e.g. water level) was held at one level only. In what way does this differ from having only four factors?

The following three questions relate to Chapter 13.
13 Consider a single borehole of circular cross-section (radius $r = r_0$) used for storing hot water in a thin aquifer of infinite lateral extent and initially saturated with cold water. By mass conservation, the speed of water, v, at some radius r is given by

$$2\pi r h \rho_w v = \text{constant}$$

where h is the thickness of the aquifer. Adapt the model in the text to calculate how the position of the cold front varies with time as it moves radially outwards from the borehole.
14 Develop a one-dimensional model for oil extraction from porous rock by the water drive method (**N.B.** $k_{oil} \neq k_{water}$).
15 Construct an aquifer using a thin bed of warm fine sand in a long tilted tray. Place thermometers in the sand and measure the variation in water temperature with position and time after cold water is inserted at the elevated end. Compare theory and experiment and discuss reasons for any discrepancy between the two.
16 A private steam railway in central Hampshire runs at present over a single-track line between two stations but when in full operation will run through four stations with passing facility at the two intermediate stations (see diagram).

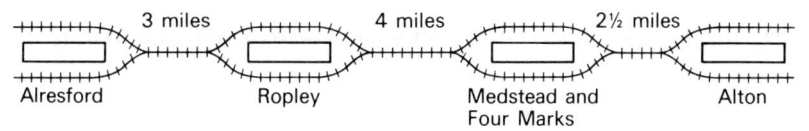

| Alresford | 3 miles | Ropley | 4 miles | Medstead and Four Marks | 2½ miles | Alton |

The aim will be to run as many trains as feasible on the days when the railway is open to the public, but the company only have sufficient rolling stock to form three trains. Devise an operating timetable, given that the distance between stations is as shown, and a certain amount of time is needed to service the trains at each end. (It is also known that British Rail runs an hourly service to London from Alton.)

17 A small port handling grain cargo has just one berth able to receive the cargo boats which use the port. On average two ships arrive every three days, and each ship is in dock for one day. This results in some ships having to wait for the berth and the port management are considering the construction of a second berth for such traffic. (It would be possible to charge higher dues in that case, for the benefit of reduced waiting time.) Could you, as a mathematician, offer advice to the management on whether to proceed? What data would you need to collect?

Index

analogue computer, 74
arithmetic, nursing 16f
average, 8f, 69f, 96, 128f

Binomial coefficients, 119
 distribution, 129, negative 179
 theorem, 73, 129
block designs, 153f

calculators, pocket, 27, 104
centrifugal force, 72f
changes, small 36, 71, 167
Chebyshev's inequality, 180
chi-squared distribution, 121–2, 175, 180
combinations, 119f, 129f, 149
computer simulation, 3, 37, 90–1, 151, 193–6
confidence limits, 176
constraints, 55f
correlation coefficient, 68
covariance, 157

decimals, 18
dendrogram 116–8, 123
design of experiments, 148f
differential equations, 50, 71f, 164f, 186f
differentiation, partial 187f

eigenvectors, 123–4
energy, 69f, 96, 167f
equations, linear simultaneous 89f, 133
exponential, 71f, 86, 143

finite difference approximations, 188f
flow diagram, 44
formulae, algebraic, 23f, 30f
fractions, 18

geometric progressions, 138f
geometry of roundabouts, 86f
graphs, 3, 24f, 30f, 46f, 53f, 66f, 83f, 95f, 115f
 distance–time 53f
 logarithmic scales 32, 67–8, 96f

hyperbola, 31

inequalities, 45, 55f, 83, 169, 176f, 186
integration, 70f, 98f, 190f
interest, 135f
interpolation, 145

limits, 87, 143
linear equations, simultaneous 89f, 133
linear programming, 56f
logarithm, 32, 65f, 96f

matrices, 115–6, 122–5

Newton–Raphson formula, 146
nomograms, 3, 21–2, 105
null hypothesis, 121

optimisation, 34, 38, 51f, 76f, 115f, 169

percentages, 30f 135
permutations, 152
Poisson distribution, 175f
power, 69f, 168f
probability, 10f, 34, 43f, 119f, 129f, 151, 175f
 conditional, 44
 cumulative, 34
 distributions, binomial 129
  chi-squared 121–2, 175, 180
  negative binomial, 179
  Poisson, 175f
programming, linear, 56f
 mathematical, 38

queues, 82f

regression lines, 65, 85

scattergram, 125
SI units, 19f
systems of algebraic equations, 89, 133f

tree, minimum spanning, 115

variance, 49, 156f